ESSAYS ON REVOLUTIONARY CULTURE AND STALINISM

ESSAYS ON REVOLUTIONARY CULTURE AND STALINISM

Selected Papers from the Third World Congress for Soviet and East European Studies

Edited by

John W. Strong

Slavica Publishers, Inc.

Slavica publishes a wide variety of scholarly books and textbooks on the languages, peoples, literatures, cultures, history, etc. of the USSR and Eastern Europe. For a complete catalog of books and journals from Slavica, with prices and ordering information, write to:

Slavica Publishers, Inc.
PO Box 14388
Columbus, Ohio 43214

ISBN: 0-89357-210-1.

Contents

Foreword

The articles selected for publication in this volume were chosen from among those presented at the Third World Congress for Soviet and East European Studies held in Washington, D.C., from 30 October to 4 November 1985. The Congress, which was sponsored by the International Committee for Soviet and East European Studies and the American Association for the Advancement of Slavic Studies, attracted over 3,000 scholars from forty-one countries. This figure represents a two-fold increase over the number of delegates who attended either the First Congress in Banff, Canada, in 1974 or the Second Congress in Garmisch-Partenkirchen in 1980 and reflects the revival of Slavic studies throughout the world.

More than 600 papers were formally presented or distributed at the Washington Congress. From among the substantial number submitted for possible publication in this series, the Editorial Committee has selected 160 to appear in fifteen volumes. Five volumes are being published in the social sciences; three by Cambridge University Press and two by Lynne Rienner Publishers. Five volumes devoted to history and literature are being published by Slavica Publishers while the remaining five in education, law, library science, linguistics and Slovene studies are appearing as part of established series or as special issues of scholarly journals. The titles of all these publications will be found at the end of this volume.

As general editor for the Third Congress I should like to express my sincere appreciation to Donald W. Treadgold, the program chairman, and Dorothy Atkinson, executive director of the AAASS, who were responsible for the efficient organization of the Washington Congress; to Oskar Anweiler and Alexander Dallin, the past and current presidents of the International Committee, for encouraging the publication of these proceedings; and to Roger Kanet, the general editor for the first two congresses, whose advice has been invaluable to his successor. Thanks also are owing to the Congress participants who submitted their papers for consideration, to the Editorial Committee that selected those to be published, and to the editors of the various volumes.

R. C. Elwood
General Editor

Selected Papers from the III World Congress for Soviet and East European Studies

Washington, D.C.

30 October - 4 November 1985

Sponsored by
International Committee
for Soviet and East European Studies
and
American Association
for the Advancement of Slavic Studies

General Editor
R. C. Elwood
Carleton University

Editorial Committee Members

Oskar Anweiler, Ruhr-Universität Bochum
Christopher Barnes, St. Andrews University
Thomas J. Blakeley, Boston College
Deming Brown, University of Michigan
Marianna Tax Choldin, University of Illinois at Urbana-Champaign
J. Douglas Clayton, University of Ottawa
N. F. Dreisziger, Royal Military College of Canada
Dennis J. Dunn, Southwest Texas State University
N. J. Dunstan, University of Birmingham
F. J. M. Feldbrugge, Rijksuniversiteit te Leiden
John P. Hardt, Library of Congress
Roger E. Kanet, University of Illinois at Urbana-Champaign
Mark N. Katz, Kennan Institute
Stanislav J. Kirschbaum, York University
David Lane, University of Birmingham
Carl H. McMillan, Carleton University
Arnold McMillin, University of London
Richard Peace, Bristol University
Peter J. Potichnyj, McMaster University
Tom M. S. Priestly, University of Alberta
Don Karl Rowney, Bowling Green State University
Fred Singleton, University of Bradford
Benjamin A. Stolz, University of Michigan
John W. Strong, Carleton University
Beatrice Beach Szekely, White Plains, N.Y.
William Mills Todd III, Stanford University
John Westwood, University of Birmingham

Introduction

John W. Strong

During the past ten years there has been an ongoing, interesting debate about Stalin's character, his real historical influence, the true nature of Stalinism and its impact on Soviet political, economic and social development. These problems have been debated in Western journals and at countless conferences and symposia. The ideas expressed in these debates have often been described as revisionist history versus traditional history. However, this description is both unhelpful and misleading. The debates have occurred because of new ideas emerging from more in-depth research and more careful analysis of the source materials. New ideas in their turn naturally generate controversy and challenge.

In recent years, many of the questions concerning Stalin and Stalinism are beginning to be faced and argued among groups and individuals in the Soviet Union. This new dimension to the Stalin debates is usually attributed to Gorbachev's attempts either to reform, to reconstruct or at least drastically to alter the inherited Stalinist system. It has also been occasioned by the efforts of Soviet scholars, journalists and politicians to place Stalin in a more realistic historical context. These efforts in the USSR are not easy and can be fraught with danger.

Many of the leading Western experts participating in the new research and writing about Stalin are represented in this volume with essays on some of their latest findings. The volume begins with two essays on revolutionary culture and two essays on Soviet attempts to spread this influence abroad. Richard Stites presents a fascinating account of the use of public spectacles in consolidating Soviet rule in the years immediately following the Bolshevik takeover. Gabriele Gorzka describes the use of worker clubs in giving Soviet workers an organization through which to identify more closely with the new regime and new social order. Felix Patrikeeff discusses Russian and Soviet attempts to exert economic and political influence in the volatile regions of Manchuria and North China during the thiry-eight-year period from 1895 to 1933. Ben-Cion Pinchuk analyzes both the pros and cons of the Sovietization impact on Jewish communities in Eastern Europe during the time of the "strange alliance" from 1939 to 1941.

The volume continues with six essays by Michal Reiman, Pierre Broué, Graeme Gill, Neils Rosenfeldt, Michael Gelb, William Chase and Arch Getty devoted to specialized studies on Stalin and the Stalinist system. The volume concludes with an interesting essay by Roberta Manning on rural administration which seeks to show that the effects of Stalin's collectivization of agriculture perhaps were not necessarily as draconian and evil as most people have come to believe.

These eleven essays were selected from papers presented to the Third World Congress of the International Committee for Soviet and East European Studies held in Washington, D.C., from 30 October to 4 November 1985. The editor believes that this collection demonstrates the value of such international gatherings of experts to share and debate their research and findings on topics of mutual interest. This current volume is a truly international undertaking, with scholars from seven countries represented: Australia, Denmark, France, Germany, Great Britain, Israel and the United States. It is hoped that the reader will find these essays both informative and interesting.

Carleton University

Festival and Revolution: The Role of Public Spectacle in Russia, 1917-1918

Richard Stites

It may be wise at the outset to enumerate the major points I wish to make in this essay. The first is that although the study of ritual may not tell us anything new about political programs or specific historical events, it does allow us a new angle of vision on human expression and can illuminate the emotional levels and the mythic layers of people who organize or display festive activities connected to a major upheaval such as the Russian Revolution. In this context, the Provisional Government comes off as a singularly unemotional organism, in spite of the sentimental and feverish rhetoric of some of its leaders (A. F. Kerenskii in particular). The Bolsheviks, by contrast, though wordy in the extreme, combined their ocean of verbiage with a forest of symbols for maximum expressive effect, and the feelings they expressed were emphatically "popular" with all that the word entails. The sheer facility with which the Bolshevik festival designers and symbolmakers, Lenin among them, plugged into popular aspirations and revolutionary myths ought to give pause to those who still maintain that the Bolsheviks were essentially alien conspirators or German agents. The second major point concerns the speed at which state ritual overcame and coopted popular festival. Within a few months of the fall of the monarchy, the joyous spontaneity of urban masses was superseded by stiff and well-planned celebrations of army, nation, church, and state by the Provisional Government. Within a year of the October Revolution, the carnival elements of earlier celebrations were dimmed by politicization, uniform symbols, and an even more formidable celebration of state power in the new Bolshevik national center of Moscow.

The Russian Revolution drew on a rich tradition of ritual culture, of forms, traditions, and motifs rooted in the past. Of greatest antiquity were the survivals of pagan festivals — song and dance, lewd carnivals, and bear ceremonies, ritual burnings of stylized devils and the like. Also of great antiquity were the Orthodox Church festivals and processions which combined hierarchical order, music, stationary worship, a luxorious array of vestments and ornament, and the popular traditions of feasting and frolic connected with holy days. The military review, established in the eighteenth century, differed strikingly from these. It was power, rationally and geometrically deployed. Its collectivism was impersonal and palpably hierarchical and deferential; its splendor was panegyric art. Its practical purpose was, theoretically, kinetic and psychological preparation (the root of the word *parade*) for combat; its symbolic purpose — often overshadowing the former — was the display of strength, organization, and efficiency in a realm where these things were in short supply. The ceremonial parade, embellished with horse, rolling cannon, fancy caparisons, bright uniforms, flags and gonfalons, and glistening bayonets — all moving to a lively martial air — was designed to produce euphoria, loyalty, readiness, and a sense of menace to the enemies of the state. Finally, there was the court culture of the Romanov dynasty, extraordinarily rich in symbols, regalia, and pageantry — an elaborate visual ornament to the sacred and charismatic persona of the emperor-tsar.[1]

All of these celebratory forms were open and legal. Revolutionary ritual was by definition illegal. Workers and radicals possessed neither the means nor the freedom to deploy their ranks regularly or display an elaborate set of symbols. Their ritual took shape in two environments: secret meetings and illegal or semi-legal demonstrations. In the former, beginning in the late 1890s, the focus was May Day, the socialist international holiday recently imported from Western Europe, and the routine utterly simple: radical songs, a show of red (another import), and speeches. Demonstrations of protest, such as strike marches or funeral processions for fallen comrades, began to multiply after 1905. Since the atmosphere was tense and the space constricted, the marchers were militant tresspassers into alien zones, sometimes menaced by police. Their feelings of outrage, anger, indignation, or funerary sadness had to be compressed into taut slogans borne aloft on red banners (often shaped like church gonfalons), molded into shouts, or translated into songs. The principal songs of revolution in that period, many of them imported, were either prison laments, funeral dirges (especially the enormously popular "You Fell Victims"), critiques of the autocracy, or visions of a dawning world of freedom. The demonstration thus resembled a parade in form, in its graphic message of solidarity, and in the "tangible impression of its own power," to use the words of Henrik de Man. In its emotional shape and show of pathos, it also resembled the religious procession. The march of Father Gapon on Bloody Sunday was a spectacular, but also typical, example of this syncretism in mood and form.[2] When the tsar fell in 1917, all these forms took on new meaning.

What more natural occasion for an emotional people to celebrate than the quick and relatively bloodless overthrow of a despotic government? For three generations thousands of people had longed for, fought for, and died for the abolition of the autocracy. Suddenly, after a week of rebellion and street fighting in the capital, with minor skirmishes elsewhere, Tsar Nicholas II had abdicated, removing himself and the heir apparent from the historic line of Russian princes that stretched back for a millenium. On the following day, his brother Michael followed suit and refused the crown. Russians were stunned at the news, some were overjoyed, some were appalled, but no one was indifferent. In the urban festivities that occurred in the weeks after the fall of the monarchy, two themes emerge from their forms, rituals, symbols, political content, and social makeup: joyful deliverance and mournful thanksgiving. Deliverance was expressed in the carnivalic and the festive side of the celebrations: euphoric days of tsarlessness, a high feeling of *volia* or release. This was symbolized by the liberation of prisoners, acts of burning and iconoclasm, the huge spontaneous crowds, the minimality and speed of the planning (if any), and the atmosphere of fun, play, tolerance, good will, and the transcendant solidarity of a free people. The other mood was thanksgiving to those who had worked to bring this about: the iconic prisoners, now paraded and exalted, and the "martyrs" of the revolution who had fallen in the street fighting. Its tone was solemn, dignified, majestic; and its main expression was the civic-religious public burial ceremonies.

The mass street demonstrations that precipitated the fall of the monarchy contained elements of future festivals: placards and red flags, throngs in a holiday mood, speeches and flash meetings at the statues of Romanov monarchs, and songs. An eyewitness from the Volynian Regiment recalled that military bands of assorted size were playing the "Workers' Marseillaise" during, and as a part of street actions, in the revolution itself. Crowds incessantly sang it, the "Varshavianka," and "Boldly, Comrades." Red banners were everywhere, and the police tore them hatefully. On Nevskii Prospekt, a young woman emerged from the crowd and handed a bouquet of red roses to the Cossacks, symbolizing the crowd's hope that the government's soldiers were on their side.[3]

Like the French revolutionary *journées*, the "Days of the Russian Revolution" (so-called in some locales) in Saratov (3 March), Odessa (7 March), Ekaterinoslav (10 March), Moscow (10 March), Kharkov and Kiev (16 March), were big turnouts of popular celebration, hastily organized by the local Soviet, municipal, or Provisional Government authority—sometimes together.[4] Tsarlessness was shared by all classes of the population, standing or marching together in an eclectic confluence of Russia's ritual traditions: the military parade, the church procession, the workers' demonstration — often inextricably mixed and unnoticed. Ecclesiastic hymns alternated with the "Workers' Marseillaise" while red banners mingled with Orthodox gonfalons and crosses. This accorded with the broadness and generosity of the rhetoric in celebratory speeches, and with the social mix of the crowds and organizers, particularly with the novel and thrilling spectacle of revolutionary workers' formations marching side by side with military units.

Neither the intrusion of official solemnity not the class tensions that might have underlain these events seemed to dampen the element of fun and laughter in them. Pageantry, gaiety, and good humor were on full display. Ethnic and local costumes enlivened the scene as at village festivals, full-throated multitudes broke into song again and again. Spontaneous acts broke the rhythms of parade and procession. In Odessa, former political prisoners were pulled out of the crowd, exalted, and drawn on carts and carriages for public homage. At the courthouse in Ekaterinoslav crowds cried out "down with the eagle. Tomorrow it won't be there to claw the tormented flesh of a long-suffering people." In Kharkov speakers urged outlawing the word *barin* (lord and master). The color red was apparent everywhere; when flags were in short supply, people brought dresses or waved red robes from their windows. It was an unrestrained public exhibition of cheer and good feelings, an all-Russian solidarity of joy.

Common euphoria and collective emotion were also in evidence in the solemn funeral services arranged in the early days for those killed in the fighting. The first such burial of martyrs took place in Moscow on 4 March, a ceremonial funeral of three students of the Military Cyclist Academy killed in the street fighting in February. The cortège, with workers bearing red banners and slogans, a hundred military men, automobiles, cycles, ladies with bouquets of red tulips, and huge crowds, was the earliest example of the combination of a military funeral and a workers' demonstration. In Helsinki, site of a major Russian naval base, 20,000 workers turned out for the last rites of two sailors on 17 March and, on the following day, in Oranienbaum near the capital the pattern of military formations, red banners, workers, revolutionary songs, and mixed slogans reappeared. It was the success, the dignity, the overall unanimity, and the solemnity of the revolutionary funeral that led the new government in the capital to mount on 23 March its first major public celebration of the revolution as a funeral — the Burial of the Martyrs.

The ceremonial interment of the 184 people killed in the February Revolution was held twenty-one days after the abdication and was the perfect vehicle for a physical and iconic exaltation of "Free Russia." The organizers from the Petrograd Soviet and the Provisional Government chose the Field of Mars as the burial site and arranged it as a massive demonstration of columns marching in from the working-class districts through the center of town (as they had done during the February days), about a million people moving constantly for twelve hours in great order and solemnity. The craze for order and security was matched by the elegant precision of the marchers. Though traditional forms of religious burial techniques were employed, no member of the clergy was permitted to officiate or participate — a drastic break with all past practices of public ceremonial. Columns of workers and soldiers marching together bore the coffins to the graves to the strains of the purely revolutionary hymn "You Fell Victims." Solidarity in freedom was in full display in the mixed participants of all classes, the unconflicting slogans, and the themes of release and gratitude to the martyrs. Conservative commentators were happy with the mood of renewal and the absence of deep class conflict. But strongly revolutionary signs were everywhere: the workers songs, the draping of the city in red, and the geography of workers occupying the opulent center of town. It was the first secular outdoor ceremony in Russian history; the first, the largest and indeed the only non-oppositional and all-class ceremony in the lifetime of the Provisional Government; and the only one without a central charismatic figure as focus.[5]

The tableau of domestic peace and social harmony provided by the March celebrations and obsequies crumbled within a few weeks. Society divided bitterly over the linked issues of war and social change. The Provisional Government, the moderate Soviet leaders, and the forces of order continued the war against Germany and delayed the reforms. The Bolsheviks and other oppositional parties and social elements — peasants, soldiers, sailors, workers — demanded a deeper revolution and immediate peace at the front. The red flags that had helped to adorn the revolutionary days of good will and unanimity in March now became the symbols of opposition once again as demonstrators took to the street in the manner of bygone days. The Provisional Government possessed no symbolic culture of its own to set against the seas of red that swirled around the streets of the capital. The tricolor flag of Peter the Great was pronounced politically neutral and retained. "God Save the Tsar" was outlawed and the government adopted the "Workers' Marseillaise" whose melody was a solid French bourgeois republican hymn. It was hated by conservatives, however, because of its association with radical workers. No monuments were erected. City fathers in Ekaterinoslav voted to rename a square after Michael Rodzianko, a prominent conservative, and put his bust in it. The government itself had an offer from American businessmen to help finance a monument to the Russian revolutionary movement, to be "visible from one end of Russia to another." Nothing came of these or similar schemes.[6]

Most astonishing, in retrospect, was the Provisional Government's approach to remaking the national seal and emblem. These were essential for conducting business in chancery and mint, but the Romanov eagle had obviously become too repugnant for continued use. The Juridical Council of the government made the dubious judgment that the two-headed eagle, in and of itself, did not connote monarchy. It commissioned the well-known artist Ivan Bilibin to design a new emblem for seal, money, and stamps with the double-headed eagle now astride the Tauride Palace (home of the government), but with wings folded down, domesticated, devoid of monarchical ornaments. The two-headed eagle, with its tearing claws and beak, had become virtually a metaphor for tsarist reaction, barbarous cruelty, and aggressive imperialism by the time of the revolution. Thus armed with a Petrine flag, a still very Byzantine eagle, and a hymn that evoked both solidarity with the Entente and the excitement of street demonstrations, the Provisional Government, when it wished to show a symbolic face, could only show one that was either traditional or highly ambivalent.[7]

This was vividly illustrated in the Provisional Government's last attempt to mount a public outdoor ceremony: the 15 July funeral of the seven Cossacks killed in the July Days. The depth of political change since 23 March was enormous: division over the war was sharper than ever, masses in town, country, and garrison were visibly more radicalized, and Lenin had returned to Russia to help mobilize the Bolshevik Party in militant actions.   One of these was the July Days, an armed demonstration that flowed into a failed attempt to replace the Provisional Government by Soviet power. Among the casualties were seven Cossacks who had defended the government. The government, after suppressing the uprising, decided to make the interment of these Cossacks a political statement. They were buried with full military regalia. The service was embellished by all the resources of the Orthodox Church in Petrograd: St. Isaac's Cathedral for the Requiem mass, massed choirs from the major churches, high prelates of the capital, and the full repertoire of icons, crosses, censers, and vestments — a striking contrast to the secular funeral of 23 March. The military-patriotic motif was undiluted: no workers' formations, no "Workers' Marseillaise," no revolutionary or anti-war banners. The all-day ceremony terminated at the sacred Alexander Nevskii cemetery, where the symbols, speeches, and wreaths continued to celebrate the spirit of traditional, Orthodox, patriotic Russia.[8]

In the rhetoric of the ceremonies, speakers called for "loyalty to the revolution." In the symbolic context of the moment, it sounded like a hollow reification of an abstract concept. In fact, the ceremony was displaying a powerful impulse of counter-revolutionary revulsion and an upsurge of the spirit of order, discipline, stability, state power, and frontline patriotism. We know from the memoirs of Paul Miliukov and other members, former members, and supporters of the Provisional Government that this was precisely their private mood; a mood that was given muted utterance at the Moscow State Conference later that summer. In the funeral of the Cossacks, we have it on full and open display. It is to my mind the sharpest and clearest "document" that we possess on the actual aspirations of the Provisional Government leaders in mid-summer of 1917. Since it possessed no "modern" symbols to express its themes and goals, that government automatically drew on the symbols and rituals that were rich in the imagery of patriotism and social order: the army and the church.[9] Thus within a few months after the fall of the monarchy, two rival cultures had emerged. As before the revolution there was the public official style, faintly modified in graphic and ceremonial form from that of the old regime, whatever words its leaders might voice in obeisance to a revolutionary sensibility. And there was the oppositional ritual style — revived, thrown into the streets once again, but possessing infinitely more self-confidence and power.

There were no "days of revolution" after the Bolshevik seizure of power in October 1917. By this I mean there was nothing resembling the festivities that broke out in March of that year after the fall of the monarchy. There was, to put it another way, no joyful celebration of Kerenskii-lessness. The reason was only partly seasonal. The Bolsheviks proved one year later that it was not only possible, but also esthetically satisfying to organize a festival in a snowclad city. The frosts of October-November 1917 did not encourage spontaneous demonstrations, but the main problem was the political frame. The first side of this frame was popular lack of clarity about what this seizure meant and how deep the change would be from the "other" revolutionary regime. The second was the continuation of political war in the capital, including demonstrations of anti-Bolsheviks. The third was the prolonged fighting in Moscow and other cities before Soviet power was visibly established across the heartland of Old Russia, thus adding uncertainty about the longevity of the new government. And the fourth was the emergency nature of this government which was determined to maintain and restore order, defend itself, and make peace. The absence from history of "October days," though certainly well enough known, is upon reflection a striking historical fact. Among other things, it explains why the mythologized "storming" of the Winter Palace has always remained a truncated narrative lacking the orgiastic release that drama would require; and also why the Bolsheviks subsumed and collapsed the drama of the February Revolution into their own.

Although the Bolsheviks were instantaneously and concretely aware of the cultural power of symbols in the new revolutionary order, it took them about a year to put together a new symbolic and ritual system. The main ingredients were the first festival on 1 May 1918; the adoption of a new anthem, arms, and flag, completed in the summer; and the Red Calender promulgated on 5 December. In regard to the earliest festivals of revolution, the Bolsheviks were bound by an ambilvalence, faintly apparent at first. They wished to keep alive the élan and the mystique of October as a liberating event of profound historical importance, their Foundation Tale in fact; and at the same time they wanted to deflect revolutionary energies to state-building, war-fighting, and the maintenance of order. A. V. Lunacharskii, the new People's Commissar of Culture, bestrode this tense dualism. Although his retrospective theory on this did not emerge until 1920, Lunacharskii from the outset hoped to keep the flame of revolution alive through symbols and festivals that would celebrate his vision of collective immortality and a new socialist region. Lunacharskii lacked the status and power of a Jacques-Louis David, the pageant-master of the French Revolution, who had possessed political weight, an artistic reputation of his own, and a ready-made culture to draw from (classical Greece and Rome). Lunacharskii, though resposible for the festival style, was poised between Lenin's conventional taste in art and his preferences for solemn and orderly styles on the one hand, and by the avant-garde festival artists on the other who favored the shock effect, irreverence, and laughter of traditional carnival over stiff and heavy ritual.

May Day 1918 in Petrograd gave the Bolsheviks their first chance to celebrate the seizure of power; it was the first purely joyful city-wide celebration of either revolution, in that the Provisional Government's March outdoor ceremonies had been funereal. It differed from the March "days" of 1917 in that it came six months after the event observed and was carefully organized. On the other hand, despite some working class unrest in the city, May 1918 was still a time of relatively good feelings in the revolution. The Civil War was just beginning and the large-scale violence, the universalization of social and political hatred, the assassination of Bolshevik leaders, the Red Terror, and the extreme rigors of War Communism all lay ahead. May Day was also the onset of spring following the first bleak winter with its mass egress from the city and its material deprivation. The explosion of color and movement on 1

May was bound to seem, then and in retrospect, more spontaneous and joyous than those that came later. It seems clear from contemporary descriptions that some of the spontaneous good will of the March Revolution had survived the crushing events of Year I of the Revolution. Since it preceded the standardization of signs and monuments, the May Day festivities allowed a freer milieue of décor and visual improvisation.[10]

The May Day Parade or "demonstration" in Petrograd was the main element in the celebrations. Unlike that of 23 March 1917 and unlike those to come in Moscow, there was no central target or objective. It began at Smolny, the Bolshevik headquarters in the October Revolution, marched to the Palace Square, and thence to Mars Field. Speakers roved the city in open cars, regaling the public with words. The décor was extremely original, having been given over to the talented artists who remained in Petrograd after the movement of the capital to Moscow. Petrov-Vodkin executed a famous Panel to Labor in beautiful pastels, while ultra-leftists did wall frescos in screeching colors, praised by Lunacharskii for their visibility, but criticized by later Soviet historians of art and ritual. The military, though prominent, had their horses and weapons adorned with red ribbons and green sprigs, combining revolutionary and pagan motifs. Most affecting were the celebrations after the march: garlanded ships on the Neva River playing music to the masses on shore, bonfires, searchlights, torchlight parades, fireworks, and dancing on the banks of the rivers and canals. Noise, frolic, and good cheer seem to have dominated the daytime hours of this holiday.

The solemn, quasi-religious part of May Day was the natural pendant to rolicking celebration, and no more in conflict with it than was Easter service or wedding mass to the feasting that went with it. The Bolshevik solemnities took the form of indoor concerts of mixed genres. The most moving of them was a performance of the Mozart Requiem for the martyrs of the October Revolution, held in the Capella of the Winter Palace; an exceptionally ornate and elegant setting, framing the entire event with the utmost dignity and beauty. Lunacharskii struck a religious note. "I made some general remarks," he reported, "about the Requiem, about Mozart, and about the way we now look at death, at the judgment on the human personality and its victory in the historical triumph of the idea of humanity." During the performance of the Requiem, a small boy fell to his knees and remained kneeling for half an hour, thinking he was in church. The audience was mute and bowed and filed out reverently at the end. It was one of the first opportunities for Lunacharskii to display publicly his old aspiration to combine religion and revolution.[11]

The Moscow May Day was a rough and makeshift holiday in a city recently redesignated the new capital. One of the reasons for Petrograd's

striking superiority was the fact that most of the major artists and
Lunacharskii himself stayed on in the old capital. Artists were unleashed
to deploy their talents in fantastic graphic decor, imparting to squares,
bridges, and broad avenues a religious and carnival quality; Petrograd
became a cartoon, a Pleasure Island, a Castle in Spain, and a Land of
Cockaygne under their hands. It was adorned with flags, pennons, ample
yardage of bunting in fabulous colors, and an almost primitive blaze of
imagery controlled by sophisticated design. Carnival emerged in a mock
burial of the Autocracy (not of the Provisional Government), circus
performers, traditional Russian booth-shows (*balagan*), fairyland theater
sets in the streets, and laughing and shouting décor. The vision of a free
and happy world pervaded the holiday, retrieving that euphoria of a year
ago and transcending it with more extravagant and deliberate acts of
collective rejoicing. Despite the official sponsoring and the intrusion of
political and military themes, this day was party time and not only the
Communist Party's time. Later a camp of insignia would choke off the
flamboyant art, Lenin's frowns would darken the carnival fun, and
political statues would cast their shadows over the circus routines. This
transformation did not occur all at once but it came all the same.
Lunacharskii, who witnessed the dampening of revolutionary carnival,
was bitter-sweet in 1926 when he nostalgically recalled this day as the
happiest national holiday he had ever experienced.

The anniversary celebration in November 1918 of the October
Revolution contrasted sharply with May Day in Petrograd. The political
frame was of course far more grim. Certain changes in the Bolshevik
ritual style, independent of the crisis, began to assert themselves visibly:
standardized symbols, greater planning and control, a sacred center as
the target for all movement, a charismatic living symbol (Lenin), a
reinforcing iconography of monuments to the heros of the past.
Together, these elements helped to create the myth of revolutionary
pre-history, and a religious aura that was both less conscious in its
articulation than the "immortality" cult of Lunacharskii and at the same
time heavier and more durable. At its center was Lenin's "monumental
plan of propaganda." It has been called "utopian" both in the trivial
sense of the word (impractical) and because of its original inspiration,
Tomasso Campanella's *City of the Sun*. Its true relation to the utopian
tradition of Russia may be seen in its underlying vision and the uses to
which it was put then and later.

Campanella seems an unlikely spark to Lenin's architectural
imagination. "Prometheus in a Naples dungeon," as the Manuels have
called him, he was a fanatical seventeenth-century Catholic, heretic,

religio-political rebel of great complexity, whose ultimate vision was a Papal world-state. His 1602 utopian *City of the Sun* was an ideal city state which turned religion into science and the urban landscape into a museum and outdoor school. Both of these ideas appealed mightily to the schoolmaster in Lenin. Campanella's model city had seven concentric walls, adorned on both sides with the rules and laws of the major sciences, alternating with statues of dead heroes in the realm of knowledge, religion, and war. Gorkii had brought this book to the attention of Lenin and Lunacharskii before the revolution, during the Capri years. Two Russian translations appeared in 1918.[12]

Lenin was determined to build on Campanella. He told Lunacharskii in the winter of 1917-18 that he wanted Petrograd decorated before May Day with plaques and blocks of stone, inscribed with passages containing the essential principles of Marxism as well as busts, statues, or bas-reliefs of great figures in the history of socialism, revolution and culture. These would replace the hateful tsarist statues that were to be taken down. Lenin wanted, in a still illiterate society, a city that talked: engraved solemnities on the walls, and unveiling speeches for the new statues placed at strategic places throughout the city as constant reminders for the pupils of his gigantic new revolutionary school.[13]

Between 1918 and 1921 about fifty or sixty such monuments were erected, mostly in Moscow, as well as dozens of inscriptions. The list of figures to be honored went through much discussion and revision; Lenin removed people (such as Vladimir Solov'ev) who did not seem to fit his notion of a historical hero and added (in the case of Heine) those who did. The list included about twenty each of Russian and European radical thinkers and activists, and a smaller number of Russian and European art and cultural figures. The latter group was eclectic and arbitrary, clearly the fruit of bargaining. The revolutionary figures, however, were subjected to political judgment. The following list will give an immediate sense of the themes and the balance in this, the first public lesson in the pre-history of the Russian Revolution given by the Bolsheviks:[14]

RUSSIANS		EUROPEANS	
Bolotnikov	Chernyshevskii	Spartacus	Owen
Razin	Dobroliubov	Gracchus	St. Simon
Novikov	Karakozov	Brutus	Marx
Radishchev	Lavrov	Voltaire	Engels
Ryleev	Mikhailovskii	Rousseau	Lassalle
Pestel	Perovskaia	Danton	Jaurès
Herzen	Zheliabov	Marat	Luxemburg
Belinskii	Khalturin	Robespierre	Liebknecht
Bakunin	Kaliaev	Babeuf	Garibaldi
Shevchenko	Plekhanov	Fourier	Blanqui
	Baumann		

This display of history-by-monument was a reasonable rendition of the accepted intelligentsia tradition of the Russian revolutionary movement: Radishchev, the Decembrists, the thinkers of the 1840s and the 1860s, and the Populists, including even an assassin from a rival party — Sergei Kaliaev. Missing from the Populists were the still living N. A. Morozov, P. A. Kropotkin, Vera Zasulich, Catherine Breshkovskaia, M. A. Natanson, and N. V. Chaikovskii — all neutral or anti-Bolshevik. G. V. Plekhanov (a former Populist) was the only Russian Marxist, and also a bitter enemy of the October Revolution. His inclusion is thus all the more significant. N. E. Baumann was the star martyr of the labor movement; he was joined by V. Volodarskii and M. S. Uritskii after their murder in the summer of 1918. A fairly high number of regicides, would-be regicides, and assassins were honored by monuments (K. F. Ryleev, P. I. Pestel, D. V. Karakozov, S. N. Khalturin, A. I. Zheliabov, S. L. Perovskaia, and Kaliaev — all hanged by the autocracy), a signal perhaps that the recent execution of the tsar and his family was an act imbedded in the revolutionary tradition. The inclusion of the traditional rebels Ivan Bolotnikov and Stenka Razin joined the Cossack-peasant rebellions of early modern times to the intelligentsia-radical revolt of the nineteenth century in a schema of continuous popular revolution. This scenario was enriched by including an almost equal number of European rebels and socialists. The founding fathers of Marxism were given special place, but so were rebels of antiquity and of 1789, the "utopian" forerunners of Marx and Engels, and a selection of "internationalist" Marxists such as Jean Jaurès, Rosa Luxemburg, and Karl Liebknecht (the latter two after their martyrdom in 1919).

The experiment was not an artistic success. Some revolutionaries looked askance at the whole idea. Alexander Bogdanov had disallowed monuments to people, dead or alive, in his communist utopia on Mars, *Red Star*. Avante-gardists such as Vladimir Tatlin and Nikolai Punin thought heroic statuary undignified and unsuitable to a revolutionary state. The practical difficulties were prodigious. Materials, talent, and labor were in short supply and this caused the delays that so enraged Lenin. The project yielded only temporary busts and figures, poorly executed in plaster and cement. Some were never even unveiled, others crumbled under the elements or were withdrawn as substandard. At least two — Robespierre and Volodarskii — were dynamited by unknown persons. By 1920-21 the unveilings ceased and the experiment was abandoned, incidentally causing Soviet sculpture to decline through the twenties until revived in quite another style under Stalin.[15]

Lenin was not much perturbed by the rapid erosion of the statuary. He knew they were temporary, but he badly wanted them up, and fast. He became very angry and shrill in his complaints about the slow pace to Lunacharskii and the sculptor N. D. Vinogradov, one of sixty-five working on the project. His angriest moment came at a time of crushing political crisis: the Socialist Revolutionary rebellion in Moscow and the rising of the Czech Legion in Siberia, a major episode in the onset of Civil War. How is one to explain this passion for made-to-order monuments of stone? It was I believe Lenin's overpowering desire to legitimize the revolution historically and to communicate rapidly with the urban masses. The teacher in him was straining for expression and the tone of his political pedagogy was emphatically solemn and pious. He wanted busts and statues that were "appropriate and accessible to the people" and was thus angered by the cute, the humorous, and the esthetically trendy productions of some Cubists and abstractionists, particularly the later figure of Bakunin in a Cubo-Futurist style by B. D. Korolev. Nor did he want the sinuous and heroized monumentality that was found on posters and that would mark the Stalinist style in the 1930s. He wanted to show life-like figures of men and women of his own intelligentsia tradition who had talked and acted and written. Lenin may have known that many people who, before having seen him, envisaged him physically as a muscular giant of revolution, were then puzzled by his "bourgeois" stature and then enthralled at last by the power of his thought and speech.[16]

Lenin's monumental propaganda scheme should be read only partly as graphic heroization and the birth of cultic idols. His central compulsion — it was exactly that — was to get out the *word*. The monuments, he said, should be "professors' podiums of the street from which fresh words and rousing thoughts and notions must soar straight to the people." His Campanellan city was to possess the artifacts of a museum, the teachers of a school, and the reverant milieu of a church. School-children in particular were to be taken round the city and told of the exploits and the life meaning of the statues' subjects, relating these stories to the present revolution. In a gloss on this, Lunacharskii added that every Sunday should be devoted to an unveiling and an evening celebration of the subject's life. The stone slabs and plaques with text seemed as important to Lenin as the personal monuments. He selected some texts himself and the authorities held a contest to generate more. Lenin's relative indifference to outer form was strikingly illustrated when he was asked what to do with the Romanov Tricentennial obelisk outside the Kremlin (erected in 1913). His response was to keep the obelisk, erase the tsarist inscription, and replace it with the names More, Campanella, Winstanley, Fourier, and Chernyshevskii.[17]

The 7 November celebrations of 1918 in the new capital illustrate the intrusion of the Lenin style of ritual into earlier, more spontaneous expressions. I must emphasize that this intrusion created a juncture of the two and not the obliteration of the latter. The planners, who were professional revolutionaries turned bureaucrats, were asked by the Moscow Committee of the party to stress the "inner," "intellectual" side (meaning political) over the "external" in the coming festivities. Richard Wortman has shown that tsarist political art and ritual almost always projected its image and mystique graphically, in contrast to the intelligentsia who dealt in words and ideas. The Bolsheviks were not ready to adopt an exclusively "subrational" mode of communication. Speech filled the air at almost every point in the three days of celebration. Set texts and explanatory lessons surrounded the unveiling of the revolutionary statues and monuments in a way that would have been unthinkable (and perhaps useless) in tsarist days. However, the art of carnival was not rejected, only toned down. Garlands, placards, and red bunting abounded, the red being even more effective against the cold whitened city of early winter than it had been in May when it had to compete with colorful flowers and dress. Hunters' Row in the center of town was decked out by avant-garde artists to look like a "wonderful red city," colorful and festive in the extreme and a delight to the eye of witnesses. The early extravagances of the artistic left were muted and mass produced discs emblazoned with the new hammer and sickle proliferated around the city. A typical Leninist touch was the order by the planning committee to preserve all the decorative artifacts after the ceremonies as the basic collection of a new Museum of the October

Revolution.[18]

The standardization of revolutionary symbols took place in the interval between May Day and 7 November 1918. These symbols, fashioned and adopted in a remarkably short time, were novel and fully expressive of Bolshevik social and political values. The red star of the new Soviet armed forces may have been inspired by Bogdanov's 1908 science fiction utopia, *Red Star*. In it the color red of European socialism was joined to a sign of ancient cosmic meaning, a portent of impending liberation or redemption (communism in the ascendant), and—via a popular gloss published along with it—a symbol of the Good in its struggle with Evil. The hammer and sickle emerged out of a contest held by the new regime. It celebrated the union of workers and peasants, city and country, and (in variant poster renditions) of men and women in revolution and in the building of a new society. The original winning entry contained a sword looming up from below. Against much resistance, Lenin had this sword removed and a final version of the hammer and sickle motif made its way to the new flag and became the symbol of the Soviet state. The "Workers' Marseillaise", with its lingering ambivalence, was rejected in favor of the "Internationale." The Kremlin bells were reset to play the new Soviet anthem at regular intervals. The striking thing about all this was the utter seriousness if not solemnity with which the Bolsheviks went about rejecting the old and the ambivalent, and in choosing new symbols that were clearly radical, politically resonant, and easily mass produced. The dazzle and the individuality of the avant garde décor was soon overshadowed and choked in the forest of standardized Bolshevik signs.[19]

The official ceremonies on Red Square and the march past the Kremlin were the main spectacles of the anniversary day, and Lenin was the visible focus of it all. When he walked, always heading a column of government colleagues, the deference to him was palpable. His first act was the unveiling of a statue to Marx and Engels in Revolution Square beside the Bolshoi Theater. His brief speech established, for those who did not yet know it, these two Germans as the ideological and spiritual forefathers of the Russian Revolution. Awaiting his return at the Senate Tower of the Kremlin were assembled delegates of various kinds, military units, foreign communists, an orchestra, a huge chorus from Proletcult studios and, according to one account, great excitement and exultation in the crowd. The second act was the solemn unveiling of a big memorial plaque by Sergei Konenkov, symbolic of Liberty and commemorating the fallen martyrs of the revolution. The revolutionary funeral hymn "You Fell Victims," by now rich in associative memories, was played. Then, amid triumphant cheers, Lenin mounted the tribune to honor "those who fell in the struggle for peace and the brotherhood of all people." His speech was filled with national pride, international solidarity, emotion, hope, and messianism. As the march past began, the poet Sergei Esenin declaimed:

> Sleep, dear brothers, sleep.
> Past you march the people's hosts
> Toward a universal dawn.

The march itself, rolling on for hours before the eyes of Lenin, was a parade, a procession, and a demonstration. On display were the corporate elements of revolutionary society in gild costumes with models of their work tools and products, Committees of the Poor, unions, Futurist floats that "dazzled the eye."[20] Proletcult shows, an allegorical tableau from Red Presnia district, the martyred neighborhood of the 1905 Revolution, showing a chained peasant and worker about to be liberated, units of schoolchildren, military horse soldiers, cannons, national music ensembles, ethnic minorities in full costume—all filed past the Kremlin and then returned to assembly points for the unveiling of statues in the main squares.

The ancillary festivities were extremely elaborate. Twenty-one theaters were taken over for the various performances between 6 and 8 November, and blocks of tickets were assigned to officials, workers, and children of the poor. Musicians were virtually drafted to perform all over town: in concert halls, Proletcult clubs, theaters and union headquarters, even in the premises of the CHEKA. Among the items performed were the Brutus monologue (again invoking the theme of a just regicide), and the verses of Emile Verhaeren (a favorite of Lunacharskii) and of Aleksei Gastev (a hero of the Proletcult). Lenin made token appearances and short speeches at many of these events. The main performance of the three-day festival was Beethoven's *Fidelio* (renamed *Liberation*), characteristic of the traditionalism that dominated the operatic stage throughout the Civil War. The finale was given a Bolshevik addendum. A member of the cast stepped forth and addressed the audience:

> Forward! One fortress had fallen, but there are others—fortresses of inertia, ignorance, falsehood. Shatter the frontiers of nations and bring the cart of liberty and Brotherhood to all peoples. Rejoice—the past no longer exists. A new life has dawned. Let us go forth and liberate the entire world.[21]

An interesting symbolic novelty of the 7 November celebration was the mass burning of emblems and effigies. At eleven designated points around Moscow, straw figures of the Entente leaders—Wilson, Clemenceau, and Lloyd George—and those of Russian class foes (kulaks, landowners, barons, and generals) were made to burn for forty minutes, after which fireworks were set off and the new Soviet emblems were raised aloft. There had been a debate on this, some of the planners suggesting that it was politically dangerous to display such hostility in public to the European statesmen. The defiant gesture was made nevertheless, and repeated in many forms in coming years. This ritual was cleverly used. By replicating the exorcistic traditions of Russian Shrovetide (*Maslenitsa*) wherein straw demons were burned, the festival managers were presenting, in a political language, a gesture deeply familiar to the vast majority of their audience. By ritualizing iconclasm, they might have hoped to deflect the real iconoclasm and vandalism of the masses. It was a simple and effective method of symbolically cleansing the scene of repugnant figures and affirming the supremacy of the new.[22]

The Moscow ceremonies and celebrations accomplished what Petrograd was never able to do: to make itself the sacred center of the Russian Revolution as well as the capital, and to identify Lenin clearly as the central charismatic figure of that revolution. Recently the victim of an attempted assassination, Lenin had recovered to find himself already the object of adulation and rejoicing over his survival. From that moment, as Nina Tumarkin has so eloquently related, dates the cult of Lenin. The 7 November anniverary celebration was an important landmark in the emergence of the cult. The Kremlin was the point of convergence of all the processions—the point, in Christian ritual, where man, the earth, the universe, and God meet; and it resembles the central point of the city from which, in some utopias, radiated all streets, all roads, all energy, all power. Russian power seemed to have returned at last to its home in the heartland whence it had been removed for two centuries by Peter the Great. Lenin, though a partly Westernized intelligent who had lived abroad many years, though now surrounded by Letts, Georgians, Jews, and Poles (as well as Russians), nevertheless seemed to project a Russian *persona*. What Trotskii later called "the national in Lenin" and what others have seen as the peasant in Lenin harmonized well with the Kremlin Towers, the mood of national regeneration, and the Russianness of the moment. The very cultural geography of the city and the traditional holdovers in the syncretic ritual forms seemed to reinforce the national dimensions of the celebrations, and thus to give legitimation to the regime that occupied the territory of the Kremlin and arranged the festivities.[23]

The November celebrations did not represent an immediate descent from carnival to ritual. The former was still in evidence, though judging from the written sources, some of the fun and laughter must have been drowned out by the endless speeches. "Non-symbolic verbal ballast," writes Christel Lane, "deadens rather than sensitizes emotional responses of ritual participants." The utopia of release and reversal which carnival plays at was overlaid by Lenin's utopia of order, historical reverance, and political pedagogy. Krupskaia claimed later that this was the happiest day of Lenin's life, an interesting contrast to Lunacharskii's nostalgia over the previous May Day. Lenin in 1918 was probably unaware of the emerging resonance of Moscow as the Russian center of the revolution, the ecclesiastical and spiritual associations of the Kremlin area, and the growing perception of himself as the personification of the new order. Thus 7 November was a complex blend of carnival, monument, rhetoric, and sacrality which together offered a picture of continuity and change, of mystery and majesty. The irony was that Lunacharskii, who consciously invoked religious idioms and motifs in Petrograd, could not do for that eminently secular-looking city what Lenin and the festival planners did for Moscow without even trying.[24]

Georgetown University

Notes

[1] A major study of dynastic-monarchical ritual and imagery is in progress by Richard Wortman. I thank him for sharing his knowledge and insights with me.

[2] For an introduction, see Hendrik de Man, *The Psychology of Socialism*, 2nd ed. London: Allen and Unwin, 1928; P. G. Shiriaeva, "Iz istorii stanovleniia revoliutsionnykh proletariskikh traditsii," *Sovetskaia etnografiia*, no. 3 (May-June 1970), pp. 17-27; S. Dreiden, *Muzyka-revoliutsii*. Moscow, 1970.

[3] T. Hasegawa, *The February Revolution: Petrograd, 1917*. Seattle: University of Washington Press, 1981, pp. 248-253, 283-292, 309; T. Kirpichnikov, "Vozstanie 1.-Gv. Volynskago Polka v fevrale 1917 g.," *Byloe*, nos. 5-6/27-28 (November-December 1917), pp. 5-16.

[4] *Rech*, the files of March 1917, for the general pattern in many locales; Donald Raleigh, *Revolution on the Volga*. Ithaca: Cornell University Press, 1985, p. 85; *Rabochaia gazeta*, 14, 18, 22 March 1917; *Birzhevye vedomosti*, 4 March 1917, p. 3; *Den* 22 March 1917, p. 2; *Dlia narodnago uchitelia*, no. 7 (April 1917), pp. 2-5 (eyewitness accounts by schoolchildren); Allan Wildman, *The End of the Russian Imperial Army*, Princeton: Princeton University Press, 1981, p. 224.

[5] I list here only a sampling of contemporary sources: *Izvestiia* of the Petrograd Soviet, 21-24 March 1917; *Rech*, 25 March 1917; *Rabochaia gazeta*, 10-11, 16, 25 March 1917; *Den*, 25 March 1917; *Delo naroda*, 25 March 1917; *Pravda*, 23 March 1917.

[6] E. M. C. Barraclough and W. G. Crompton, *Flags of the World*. London: Warne, 1978, pp. 142-147; Dreiden, *Muzyka*, p. 144, argues that the Provisional Government

tried to capitalize on the mass popularity of the "Workers' Marseillaise," a doubtful proposition. Monuments: *Rech*, 7 March 1917, p. 5, and *Rabochaia gazeta*, 17 March 1917.

[7]G. F. Kiselev and V. A. Liubisheva, "V. I. Lenin i rozhdenie gosudarstvennoi pechati i gerba RSFSR," *Istoriia SSSR*, no. 5 (September-October 1966), p. 21; M. Iu. Liashchenko, *Rasskazy o Sovetskom gerbe*. Moscow, 1963, pp. 29-30, a popular, illustrated children's book.

[8]Alexander Rabinowitch, *The Bolsheviks Come to Power*. New York: Norton, 1977, pp. 39-43.

[9]For a superb study of its values, see William Rosenburg, *Liberals in the Russian Revolution*. Princeton: Princeton University Press, 1974. See also P. N. Miliukov, *The Russian Revolution*, tr. T. and R. Stites. Gulf Breeze, Florida: Academic International, 1978.

[10]My account is drawn from A. V. Lunacharskii, "Pervoe Maia 1918 goda," (1918) in *Vospominaniia i vpechatleniia*. Moscow, 1968, pp. 208-212; *idem*, "Pervyi pervomaiskii prazdnik posle pobedy," *Krasnaia niva*, no. 18, (12 May 1926), p. 8; E. A. Speranskaia, ed., *Agitatsionno-massovoe iskusstvo pervyikh let Oktiabria*. Moscow, 1971, pp. 32-33, 96-97; A. I. Mazaev, *Prazdnik kak sotsialno-khudozhestvennoe iavlenie*. Moscow, 1978, pp. 245-53; G. I. Ilina, *Kulturnoe stroitel'stvo v Petrograde – Oktiabr 1917-1920 gg.* Leningrad, 1982, pp. 215-217.

[11]Lunacharskii, *Vospominaniia*, pp. 210-211.

[12]Tomasso Campanella, *La Città del Sole* (1602), ed. D. Donno. Berkeley: University of California Press, 1981; F. and F. Manuel, *Utopian Thought in the Western World*. Oxford: Blackwell, 1979, pp. 261-288; N. A. Nilsson, ed., *Art, Society, Revolution: Russia, 1917-1921*. Stockholm: Almqvist and Wiksell, 1979, p. 42.

[13]I. S. Smirnov, *Lenin i Sovetsaia kultura*. Moscow, 1960, pp. 347-372; John Bowlt, "Russian Sculpture and Lenin's Plan of Monumental Propaganda," in H. A. Millon and L. Nochlin, eds., *Art and Architecture in the Service of Politics*. Cambridge, Mass.: MIT Press, 1978, pp. 182-193; *Istoriko-revoliutsionnye pamiatniki SSSR*. Moscow, 1972, pp. 4-6; A. Mikhailov, "Programma monumentalnoi propagandy," *Iskusstvo*, no. 4 (1968), pp. 31-34; and no. 5 (1968), pp. 39-42 (illust.).

[14]In addition to the works in the previous note, see *Iz istorii stroitel'stva Sovetskoi kultury: Moskva, 1917-1918 gg.: dokumenty i vospominaniia*. Moscow, 1964, pp. 38-44; Mikhail Guerman (German), ed., *Art and the October Revolution*. New York: Abrams, 1979, pp. 6, 7, 12-13, 277-278, 284-285, 299 (illust.) for both capitals. For Leningrad, see Ilina, *Kulturnoe*, pp. 203-226; for Saratov, Speranskaia, *Agit.-mass. iskusstvo*, pp. 141-143.

[15]Alexander Bogdanov, *Red Star: The First Bolshevik Utopia*. Bloomington: Indiana University Press, 1984, pp. 74-81. Bogdanov was very influential in the Proletcult movement at this point and his novel was reissued and widely read in 1918. For comment on the failure of the monuments from various perspectives, see Bowlt, in *Art and Architecture*, pp. 189, 192; Nilsson, *Art*, pp. 44, 48; L. Shervud, "Vospominaniia o monumentalnoi propagande v Leningrade," *Iskusstvo*, no. 1 (January-February, 1939), pp. 50-53; *Oktiabr v iskusstve i literature, 1917-27*. Leningrad, 1928, p. 64.

[16]Mikhailov, *Iskusstvo*, pp. 31-33; B. V. Pavlovskii, *V. I. Lenin i izobrazitelnoe*

iskustvo. Leningrad, 1974, pp. 52-53; for one example (of many) of what people imagined Lenin looked like before seeing him, see L. Stupochenko, "V Brestskie dni," *Proletarskaia revoliutsiia*, no. 16 (1923), p. 102.

[17]Ilina, *Kulturnoe*, p. 209; *Istoriko-rev. pamyatniki*, pp. 15, 16, 120-121 (illust.); A. V. Lunacharskii, *Ob izobrazitelnom iskusstve*, 2 vols. Moscow, 1967, vol. II, pp. 29-30.

[18]My account is drawn from *Izvestiia*, 3-9 November 1918, which is the fullest treatment; Mikhailov, *Iskusstvo*, pp. 39-41; A. Strigalev, "Proizvedeniia agitatsionnogo iskusstva 20-kh godov," *Iskusstvo*, no. 5 (1968), p. 44; Masaev, *Prazdnik*, pp. 262-270; Pavlovskii, *Lenin*, pp. 14-15; Guerman, *Art*, p. 282. My thanks to Professor Wortman for access to his unpublished work.

[19]For a more detailed analysis, see Richard Stites, "Adorning the Revolution: The Primary Symbols of Bolshevism, 1917-1918," in *Sbornik* of the Study Group on the Russian Revolution, no. 10 (1984), pp. 39-42.

[20]*Izvestiia*, 9 November 1918, p. 5.

[21]*Ibid*. For musical performances of the time, see *Krasnaia Moskva*, 1920, pp. 543-548, and *Muzykalnaia zhizn Moskvy v pervye gody posle Oktiabria*. Moscow, 1972, pp. 104-105.

[22]*Izvestiia*, 5 November 1918, p. 6. For Bolshevik fear of mass iconoclasm, see Richard Stites, "Iconoclastic Currents in the Russian Revolution," in A. Gleason *et al.*, eds., *Bolshevik Culture*. Bloominton: Indiana University Press, 1985, pp. 1-24.

[23]For the long duel between the capitals, see: Richard Wortman, "Moscow and Petersburg: the Problem of Political Center in Tsarist Russia, 1881-1914," in Sean Wilentz, ed., *Rites of Power: Symbolism, Ritual and Politics since the Middle Ages*. Philadelphia: University of Pennsylvania Press, 1985, pp. 244-271; Sidney Monas, "St. Petersburg and Moscow as Cultural Symbols," in T. Stavrou, ed., *Art and Culture in Nineteenth-Century Russia*. Bloominton: Indiana University Press, 1983, pp. 26-39. For the notion of an "animating centre of society," see Clifford Geertz, "Centers, Kings, and Charisma," in J. Ben David *et al.*, *Culture and its Creators*. Chicago: University of Chicago Press, 1977, pp. 150-153; for the emerging cult, see Nina Tumarkin, *Lenin Lives! The Lenin Cult in Soviet Russia*. Cambridge, Mass.: Harvard University Press, 1983, pp. 66-68.

[24]Christel Lane, *Rites of Rulers*. Cambridge: Cambridge University Press, 1981, pp. 203; N. K. Krupskaia, *Reminiscences of Lenin*. Moscow, 1959, p. 489. D. Fedotoff White, in *The Growth of the Red Army*. Princeton: Princeton University Press, 1944, p. 124, reminds us that having Moscow as their capital in the Civil War, in contrast to such "new fangled 'capitals'" as Omsk, Ekaterinodar, and Archangel, gave the Bolsheviks great prestige.

Proletarian Culture in Practice:
Worker's Clubs, 1917-1921

Gabriele Gorzka

Foundation of workers' clubs after the October Revolution

The development of workers' clubs after 1917 was accompanied by the claim, emphasized in various ways by different cultural organizations, that they related the socialist revolutionary process introduced by the October Revolution to the superstructure of society by establishing a specific proletarian class culture. This claim was discussed at the first conferences of cultural and political organizations in 1917 and was incorporated into programs for forming specific types of proletarian culture.

The demand for the creation of socialist workers' clubs arose from the aim of realizing proletarian self-determination beyond the sphere of production and of developing "purely proletarian" social and linguistic forms of expression. At the First All-City Conference of Cultural Organizations in February 1918 in Moscow a special resolution was passed on workers' clubs which contained the maxims:

> The workers' club must become a center for the worker's whole cultural life, by serving as a place of relaxation, sensible entertainment and education. It must train the workers, who are still far removed from every kind of organization, to common activity; must develop in them the feeling of solidarity; must kindle their understanding for the necessity of a fight for a better future — for socialism. As the club also tries to include the backward elements of the proletariat, it must be independent in the character of its work, but of course clearly socialist... The principles of active construction and participation of the proletarian masses themselves must be the basis of the building up of the club....[1]

In 1918 there were numerous reports in the Soviet press about the opening of factory clubs. In Petrograd, according to statements of the *Petrograd Pravda* (7 January 1919), prior to the end of 1918 there were 120 workers' clubs registered. In Moscow there existed at this time 82 clubs with another 20 to be opened shortly. Not only did a network of clubs arise in the industrial centers, but also in the provinces.[2]

Within the framework of the revolution of 1917 there was no comprehensive state cultural program which would have made provisions for the systematic, planned construction of a club infrastructure on a regional or supra-regional level. The decision about the establishment of clubs was largely made by the separate factories, or by the regional organs of the workers' power, i.e., the soviets of workers', soldiers', and peasants' deputies. In their administrative functions, the factory committees appointed cultural commissions which were responsible for fostering the cultural interests of the employees. Apart from the procuring of literature and the establishment of libraries and sports facilities, their tasks included the organization, financing, and equipping of the factory clubs.[3] The large number of clubs which were founded by factory committees at the request of workers' meetings is shown by the fact that, of the metal workers' clubs which existed in 1925 in the urban district of Moscow, all the clubs which were founded before 1920 owed their existence to the initiative of factory committees or active workers.[4]

Apart from the spontaneous foundation of workers' clubs by workers of individual factories or by regional initiatives of workers' self-administrative organs, various social organizations were concerned in the founding of clubs. Among these were Proletkul't, the Russian Communist Party (Bolsheviks), and the trade unions.

Proletkul't may be characterized as a cultural-political organization established by representatives of the revolutionary intelligentsia. Its underlying theory was the conception of revolution formulated by A. A. Bogdanov. In this theory the necessity of an upheaval of the social superstructure in the train of a socialist revolution is set down and possibilities and steps for a practical realization of these thoughts are shown. According to this conception, proletarian culture must be understood as a self-determination process of appropriation and critical conquest of the bourgeois cultural inheritance by the proletariat.[5]

Measured by its cultural-political demands and the structure of its organization,[6] Proletkul't defined itself administratively and program-matically as a politically independent authority for the organization of the cultural interests of the proletariat. This selfassessment corresponded with its concrete program of having substantial and structural influence on existing forms of proletarian cultural activity. The demand to join together the clubs spontaneously founded by workers, factory committees, soviets or trade unions in a uniform proletarian organization was supported by the fact that Proletkul't in 1918 (in contrast to the trade unions) had sufficient financial means at its disposal. In the first six months of 1918 Proletkul't received "9,285,700 rubles, a considerable sum of money at that time. As a comparison: the entire section for education outside of schools of the NARKOMPROS received 32,501,990 rubles, and universities had 16,705,700 rubles at their disposal."[7] The financing of clubs made up one-third of the total expenditures of Proletkul't in 1918. In the second half of 1918, 3,246,632 rubles were used for clubs and 2,573,650 rubles for libraries by Proletkul't out of a budget of just under 10 million rubles.[8]

Later the club departments of regional Proletkul't sections reported corresponding fusions, that is the tying in of artistic studios of Proletkul't to existing clubs. In 1918 a total of 284 clubs were financed by Proletkul't. For Petrograd alone, 77 applications were submitted in 1918 and the spring of 1919 by clubs which were applying to be taken into the Proletkul't organization.[9] Even when the management of a club officially stayed in the hands of the original founders, the financing, co-ordination of programs and thematic planning were run by Proletkul't. For example, the Moscow Council of Trade Unions applied to the financial department of the Central Committee of Proletkul't on 14 August 1918: "For the equipping and maintenance of 15 Trade Union clubs, a single sum of 23,000 rubles and 2,550 rubles monthly per club—for all 15 clubs, 383,250 rubles."[10]

Proletkul't was able to adopt a leading role in the building up and thematic planning of cultural establishments by regional and national standards on the basis of local initiatives, a firm organizational structure, and a clear programmatic conception. For the clubs founded before the October Revolution, and those founded by single factory committees in 1917, it offered an organizational as well as financial framework. Beyond this, Proletkul't attempted to transfer A. A. Bogdanov's theory of a proletarian cultural revolution into practical programs and offered these programs, with the help of publications, delegates, or club instructors, to activists on the factory level.

The Sixth Congress of the RSDRP(b), from 8-16 August 1917, stressed the necessity of political agitation within the broad mass of workers and especially emphasized the importance of factory clubs.[11] In accordance with these ideas, two different types of party political club activities were subsequently developed:

-Continuing in the tradition of Social Democratic agitation circles, the Bolsheviks founded their own party clubs which were only open to party members and served primarily to train agitators for political enlightenment among the population.[12]
-Parallel to the party-bound organization of purely party

political cultural institutions, the Bolsheviks tried to facilitate the development of political consciousness in the broad masses of the population by organized instructional work. For this purpose, in December 1918 the decree "On the mobilizing of the literate [*gramotnykh*] and the organization of the propaganda of socialistic construction" was passed. In view of such methodical party propaganda, workers' clubs became increasingly attractive for the party as meeting places for various circles of the working people where even those not very interested in politics could be agitated.

After Lenin also emphasized in 1918 the important role of the clubs for the political enlightenment of the masses,[13] the organization and supplying of these clubs gained importance within the specially formed agitation departments of local party committees. These were to propagandize in the factories for the introduction of clubs and to make their influence felt in the already existing institutions: "Importance is to be laid on a regular supply of newspapers, brochures, and literature; libraries must be installed in every organization, reading room, and club. Cultural work must be carried out in the clubs; a [party] cultural commission is to be organized in every club and in every club lectures are to be held."[14]

Systematic work with clubs by the trade unions ensued only a few years after the October Revolution and was less the result of an internal analysis by the trade unions about questions of the consciousness of the workers and insight into the necessity of furthering proletarian cultural interests, than it was a result of the newly defined role of the trade unions in a socialist society. Just after the October Revolution there was a controversy over the position of the trade unions concerning their involvement in culturally enlightening activities. In the first official announcements (as, for example, in the resolutions of the First All-Russian Congress of the Trade Unions), cultural-political considerations played only a secondary role. First priority was given to the question of the freedom of action of the trade unions in the field of production. Topics discussed at the conference included workers' control, relationship between the trade unions and the factory committees, economic construction, unemployment, and demobilization.[15] The setting up of programs in the cultural field was limited to the trade unions — represented by their All-Russian Central Council — "being represented in the organizations and institutions which deal with the cultural enlightenment of the proletariat."[16] To this end the construction of a Cultural Department within the All-Russian Council was decided upon, which, however, did not take up its duties until 1919.

In the official decisions of the trade unions in 1918 neither a distinct cultural-political concept became clear nor were central programs in the field of cultural agitation created. A potential for action, however, was developed at the factory level. In the course of 1918, cultural departments were instituted by individual trade unions on a regional level and trade union clubs were established. In Petrograd at the end of 1918 60 trade union clubs were registered (15 of these in the second urban district, 13 in the Nevskii district, and 24 in the Petrograd district). It was reported at the first meeting of the cultural commissions of the Metal Workers' Union on 21 May 1918 that out of 24 large factories represented, 14 had cultural commissions of their own.[17]

In every-day practice, it soon became obvious that the individual trade unions had overestimated their organizational strength and financial means. In time, individual trade unions were forced to give up the management of clubs they had founded. In April 1919 a new way of structuring the club organization was discussed by the Moscow Metal Workers' Union. The Union agreed "to enter into preliminary discussions with the appropriate institutions about the taking over of our clubs. The central organs [of the trade union] consider it unavoidable to dissolve the clubs of the trade union and their departments. In districts where no clubs exist negotiations should be held with other institutions about new establishments.... The organization of clubs, studios, and libraries should be taken over by the Moscow Proletkul't whereby influence should be exerted on the general functioning of the Proletkul't by personal representatives."[18] The situation in Petrograd was analogous. Looking back in 1920, the Petrograd City Conference of Workers' Clubs stated that "trade unions, as is generally known, tended in former times to construct clubs of their own — and not only trade unions, but also individual factory committees — but nowadays no such ambitions are evident."[19]

A comparison between the number of clubs established directly by the workers of individual factories and those set up by social organizations or state authorities, and between decentralized and centralized establishment of clubs can be shown by the following statistics. In Petrograd, of 110 clubs which were registered in April 1920, 63 (57%) were founded by non-factory initiatives, while 47 (43%) came into being through decisions inside of the factories; 40 per cent (44) were established by central, supra-regional organizations (RKP[b], trade unions, youth and cultural organizations), 60 per cent (66) as a result of decentralized, local decisions.[20]

Quantitative and structural development of clubs during War Communism

In spite of the extremely unfavorable economic and social conditions in a time marked by civil war, fuel crisis, famines, and the breakdown of the urban infrastructure, the process of expansion in the building of clubs continued in 1919. The regional and central press announced regularly new foundings of clubs, circles, studios, and other cultural institutions, and reported in detail about the various programs offered. In a survey of newspaper reports from June to December 1919 (which listed theatrical performances, exhibitions, educational programs by the new "proletarian universities," courses, and conferences of cultural organizations, as well as numerous openings of new clubs), the magazine *Proletarskaia Kul'tura* came to the conclusion that "one can say with great conviction that, in spite of the terrible events on the front, which did not allow one to concentrate solely on the work of enlightenment, a healthy instinct told the working class that no construction is conceivable without education of the masses.... The proletariat understood that one may not put the question this way: first the return of peace, then education, first victory, then the socialist construction, but that one must say: all possible efforts for victory, but at the same time a stable construction of cultural training and education."[21]

According to information from the Central Statistical Office, in 1920 there existed 4,483 clubs in 52 provinces.[22] The speed in founding clubs can be measured from the fact that of 110 workers' clubs registered in Petrograd in April 1920, 80% (88) were set up after the October Revolution. In the first quarter of 1920 alone, 31 clubs were opened, while in the period between October 1917 and January 1920 57 were set up. (See Table 1 on the next page)

This continuous process of growth from 1917 to 1920 was primarily the result of local and regional initiative. Although a part of the founding of clubs was coupled with the construction of Proletkul't sections, because of the large number of new foundations, communication and co-operation under the conditions of civil war were not very intensive between the local institutions and the responsible urban or district Proletkul't sections. Accordingly, complaints like the following were to be found in the central press organ of Proletkul't: "The political situation and especially the hard civil war takes from us all possibility for working and cuts us off from many districts, so that we do not know how the comrades there manage to realize their ideas of cultural work in practice."[23] Individual correspondence at these levels shows that the co-operation was more and more confined to the more or less regular dispatch of lecturers, theater groups and study material.[24] In this respect, things looked more favorable in the urban centers. Here there were much closer links between the individual clubs and the Proletkul't sections, because of their physical proximity. The club departments of Proletkul't recorded a variety of reconstruction activities: the spectrum ranged from repairs and supplying of inventory stock to the training of lecturers and the composing of methodological materials.[25]

Table 1: Workers' clubs on 1 April 1920 in Petrograd

District	Number of clubs	Before Feb. 1917	Feb.-Oct. 1917	Oct. 1917 Jan. 1920	1920	Number of Members
Vasile-ostrovskii	10	–	1	8	1	9,022
Vyborgskii	11	–	–	5	6	4,268
1. Gorodskoi	15	–	4	5	6	13,729
2. Gorodskoi	17	–	1	10	6	20,918
Moskovsko-Zastavskii	11	–	3	5	3	4,899
Narvsko-Petergovskii	8	–	3	5	–	4,146
Nevskii	11	1	4	4	2	6,381
Petrogradskii	16	1	4	8	3	10,717
Porochovskii	2	–	–	–	2	262
Smol'ninskii	9	–	–	7	2	7,257
Total	110	2	20	57	31	81,599

Source: *Materialy po statistike.* Petrograd 1920, p. 100.

The financing of the workers' clubs was not uniformly regulated, and was primarily dependent on the individual organizations. That is, while the clubs founded by the Bolsheviks were financed directly by the party, the few clubs which had stayed under the control of trade unions got financial support from their union. In 1919 and 1920, however, Proletkul't had the responsibility for the organization of adult education and cultural programs, and as a result, the financial security of the majority of the clubs lay in its hands. Although Proletkul't spent one-third of its budget on club activities, it found itself confronted with increasing difficulties in the face of the great expansion of its network and of the need to give individual clubs the desired material support.

Considering the increase in the number of clubs, especially in far-off areas, it is not surprising that complaints started appearing in the press in 1919 and 1920 about inadequate financial support by the Proletkul't central organization.[26] Accordingly, the financing by factory committees or by direct personal participation of the members became more and more important. In Petrograd, for example, 56 per cent (62) of the workers' clubs in April 1920 were financed completely by internal factory subsidies or members' contributions (see table 2). The information for Petrograd also shows how negligent the trade unions were in financing their clubs. While NARKOMPROS/Proletkul't took over the costs for 30 per cent and the party approximately for 10 per cent of the clubs, only 4.5 per cent of the factory clubs were financed by trade unions.

Table 2: Workers' clubs on 1 April 1920 in Petrograd

District	Number of clubs	Financed by NARKOMPROS /Proletkul't	RKP(b)	Trade unions	own subsidies
Vasile-ostrovskii	10	5	1	1	3
Vyborgskii	11	2	1	–	8
1. Gorodskoi	15	6	2	1	6
2. Gorodskoi	17	3	1	3	10
Moskovsko-Zastavskii	11	3	1	–	7
Narvsko-Petergovskii	8	2	1	–	5
Nevskii	11	2	2	–	7
Petrogradskii	16	6	–	–	10
Porochovskii	2	1	–	–	1
Smol'ninskii	9	3	1	–	5
Total	110	33	10	5	62

Source: *Materialy po statistike*. Petrograd 1920, p. 100.

Problems of financing impeded the commitment not only of trade unions in the cultural sector, but Proletkul't, which was subsidized by the public resources of NARKOMPROS, also had to fight against increasing difficulties in providing financially for the increasingly integrated grid of Proletkul't sections, factory clubs, and studios and supplying them with suitable skilled personnel and materials. The state subsidies which had shrunk in the course of the Civil War, the problem of supplies which arose from the widespread breakdown of transport communications, and the thinning out of the staff of teachers owing to the service at the front, all led to Proletkul't's revising its organization and rationalizing its operations. The total number of Proletkul't sections was reduced from 147 in 1918 to 86 (1919), and then to 37 (1921). A report of its Central Committee states that, "from 1919 onwards the Central Committee of Proletkul't has been reducing of its own accord the network of Proletkul't as a result of financial problems and communication difficulties, the lack of colleagues as well as the necessity of carrying out work only in certain districts."[27]

The process of concentration had immediate effects on the workers' clubs. Because of the diminishing number of Proletkul't sections, an alteration was planned in the organization of the existing clubs. In place of small clubs, which were intended for the employees of one factory, larger control units evolved; i.e., regional clubs which were to provide programs for a whole urban district. This implied a turning away from the principle of being tied to a certain branch of production. Instead of specific clubs for single branches of industry, the founding of new clubs or merging of already existing clubs was planned on the basis of purely regional factors.[28]

The aforementioned problems are not sufficient to explain the planned measures for centralization, when one considers the fact that even in 1919 a continual expansion of clubs and similar institutions was evident. In the years before, the development of clubs had been successful in spite of extremely difficult economic and social conditions. Apart from financial and organizational problems, getting more effective control over the club establishments and the contents of their programs became more and more important. The wish for centralization may be seen as an attempt by the central institutions of Proletkul't to gain a better view of the activities of the local clubs and to gain more influence over their program. The central press organs of Proletkul't adopted an increasingly critical attitude toward the decentralized cultural work in the factories. Club programs which concentrated on bourgeois behavior (card-playing, alcohol, dancing, etc.) were especially criticized for being destructive and in contrast to the development of proletarian forms of culture.[29] The measures developed in 1919 for a more systematic and organized contact between regional and national institutions may be seen as examples of a strategy of centralization and formalization of contacts. Among these measures were requirements to hand in information on current work, to render accounts every three months, and to compile minutes of meetings and lists of participants.[30]

The idea of strictly organized, centrally directed large clubs was, however, not to be realized. The establishment of district clubs outside the factories met with protest by many of the factory clubs. Although the club department of Proletkul't in Moscow was able to show the amalgamation of a few factory clubs, on the whole they had to admit the failure of the campaign:

> One of the first steps of the club department was the aim of introducing district clubs, but this idea...led to conflicts. A club which provides for a whole district must be situated in the center of this district; that is, it must be at the same distance from all the factories and works of this district. If the club is too far away, it is very difficult for workers to get there when they have to deal with inadequate transport. A second reason for the miscarriage of the planning of the district clubs was that it was impossible to heat the club buildings in winter because of the fuel crisis and therefore no work was possible.... This is why one had to dismiss the idea of district clubs and go over to the idea of setting up factory and smaller-scale clubs.[31]

Apart from these economic and administrative reasons, the failure of the concept of central clubs can be blamed on factors of social psychology. Especially notable is the marked "local patriotism" of the urban factory workers: "In some districts the number of clubs far exceeds the demand, but the workers always speak against an amalgamation of their clubs; they prefer their own club, even if it is not well equipped, to a good, large club."[32] There seemed to be a strong feeling of identification by the members of a factory with "their" club, which was founded in many cases on their own initiative, was equipped by their own actions, and so more or less was looked upon as a "second home." The refusal of individual clubs to integrate themselves into a system of central clubs, and the simultaneous reduction of Proletkul't sections, led to the fact that no uniform cultural program could be established. Although plans for organization and substantial concepts were developed by Proletkul't, the realization of these plans was still confined to individual efforts.

Club program and internal organization

Generally speaking the various functions of a club may be divided into three fields — educational and artistic circles, single performances, communication and information—which clearly vary in their aim, design and approach.

So-called circles were arranged according to the size of the clubs, their existing equipment, availability of instructors, and the special interests of club members.   In these circles a set group met regularly under the direction of an expert.   The circles dealt with the central themes of politics, science, art, social affairs, and sport; and in each of these fields embraced a broad spectrum ranging from the teaching of abstract basic knowledge to the discussing of everyday matters of interest.   For example, in the field of politics one could find circles about political economy or bourgeois ideology side-by-side with debates on regional political problems of the day.   In the field of social affairs the spectrum went from groups working on "the role of women in socialism" to meetings where concrete advice was given on such problems as hygiene, bringing up children, marriage guidance, and alcoholism.

According to the statute of May 1919, there existed an obligatory program of courses for all clubs looked after by Proletkul't which encompassed the following subjects:

> -The origin of the world, development of life, evolution of plants, animals and mankind;
> -political economy and cultural history;
> -history of socialism;
> -the workers' movement (political, trade union, co-operative and Proletkul't movements);
> -constitution of the Soviet Republic and socialist world revolution;
> -history and program of the Bolshevik Party;
> -history of literature (Russian and Western European — typical features of periods and trends).
> All courses are to be held from the point of view of a proletarian culture in the spirit of revolutionary Marxism.[33]

In the art circles and studios participants were to have the possibility of discovering for themselves under expert guidance practical artistic forms and of developing new artistic ways in the fields of drama, pictorial art, music, or literature.   It was characteristic of the work in these circles that further education in all fields was envisaged.   This did not mean a mere acquiring of basic knowledge, but the opening of new fields which up to then had been shut off from workers because of their economic and social situation.   This included a first visit to a theater or museum, learning to read and write, as well as practicing one's own artistic abilities or training in rhetorical skills in order to facilitate one's own confidence in articulating opinions and interests.   In the confrontation of participants with new fields of knowledge or experience, the form of this creative process was decisive.   According to the concept of A. A. Bogdanov, the collective consciousness which is characteristic of the working class should be carried over from the process of production, where it is generated, into the sphere of spare time. This was to be accomplished by the inclusion of the individual in a learning or experimenting group or by means of club events which disclose experiences and ways of thinking common to all participants.[34]

Apart from the continuous circles which were dependent on the active participation of a regular circle of members, individual events were arranged in all clubs for a wider public which was not yet engaged in club activities. Club festivities on social holidays were very popular (May First, New Year, or the anniversaries of the October Revolution), when all circles presented the results of their work, organized exhibitions, produced diagrams and similar pictorial material, put on theater plays, arranged concerts or choir evenings, etc. It was considered important for all members, as far as possible, to be included in the preparation and realization of such events in order to underline the feeling of a "social unit." Apart from this there were more or less regularly arranged theater, concert, or cinema evenings, as well as discussions and lectures, to which many clubs were eager to invite distinguished theater companies or well-known speakers. Here, in contrast to the circles, no active participation in the program was expected from the audience. Such individual events served to propagandize regular club work among a wider public in order to gain potential new members. While the regular work in the circles was free of charge for club members, the individual events provided a possibility to improve the finances of the clubs. In times when there was a shortage of state and factory allowances, the tendency to increase these activities became stronger. The consequences of such rearrangements could be seen especially during the time of the New Economic Policy when the principle of self-financing was put into practice in the cultural field.

In all factory clubs there were, according to their financial means, more or less well-equipped lounges, which were always open for general relaxation. Here one could get into conversation over a cup of tea, study the magazines and daily newspapers laid out in the reading room, play cards or chess, or listen to music. In many clubs consulting hours were set up when experts were available to give information about legal, labor, or social questions. Along with these organized forms of information and communication, during War Communism specific functions were allotted to the clubs which corresponded with the daily needs of the members and were introduced spontaneously into the daily life of the club. These functions included providing food supplies through the club canteen — an activity which greatly influenced the popularity of the clubs and their corresponding high rate of membership. With ironical exaggeration, the Club Commission of Proletkul't came to this assessment in its investigation of Moscow clubs in 1919: "One must ascertain that the anxiety about the founding and supply of the club canteen plays a prominent role in club life. In many cases factory clubs were apparently organized with the sole intention of acquiring food supplies from the Department of Social Nourishment."[35]

In the restless times of civil war, in the face of frequent breakdowns in transport and postal communications, the club was further considered as an "Information Market." Here, political as well as private messages about the fate of relatives or reports by soldiers about the situation at the front were made available. Parcels were sent via the club, job vacancies were passed on, and private exchanges were carried out such as buying and selling of food, household effects, and valuable possessions. If one considers the extremely cramped living conditions of the urban working class and the difficulties in the fuel supply in the years from 1918 to 1920, it is understandable that those clubs whose heating system still functioned represented a home away from home for many workers. This is expressed in a workers' report:

> At 11 o'clock in the evening the club begins to get empty. The comrades go home. I sit in the corner thinking. Some-how I don't want to go home − it is so pleasant and cosy in the club; you feel yourself so free here, the people are all so familiar. Comrade Z. sits down at the piano and beneath his hands such wonderful, coaxing sounds, sometimes solemn, sometimes sad.... And a memory comes over me.... But then I come back to reality and my thoughts are directed against their will from the delightful world of these sounds to home, to the dirty, damp, wretched hut with parents who are always depressed and complain of their fate and curse their lives.[36]

If we look at the internal organization of the factory clubs we find that the influence of the central cultural organs on the forming of individual clubs remained limited because of financial and personnel shortages as well as infrastructural problems. It is true that from 1919 onwards there were increased efforts on the part of Proletkul't to develop guidelines for the organization of clubs by circulating model statutes and methodological and programmatic periodicals as well as by supplying instructors. These actions, however, remained unsystematic and locally restricted. As the centrally introduced controlling mechanisms did not yet function as planned, the clubs were able to exercise considerable freedom in the planning of their programs, which they took advantage of in different ways. As far as their functioning was dependent on the initiatives and wishes of the respective club members, the general picture of workers' clubs was rather piebald. In this way not only different types of clubs existed side-by-side (from amalgamated large clubs to tiny factory clubs), but it often happened that some clubs prospered while in the very next neighborhood others were forced to close down.[37]

Internal decisions were normally made on democratic principles by the plenary session of the club members. The members' general meeting made decisions on the daily running of the club as well as on matters of principle concerning programmatic points. It elected the management of the club, passed plans for financing and made decisions about the exclusion of members. The club management was always elected for six months and consisted of representatives of the cultural commission of the factory in question, the members' general meeting, and possibly the local Proletkul't. The numerical size of the club management could also be fixed by the members' general meeting. Corresponding commissions were set up by the club management to carry out practical tasks; the management also set down the duties of members and made decisions on questions of organization such as fixing of opening times.

Diagram 1: Internal club structure

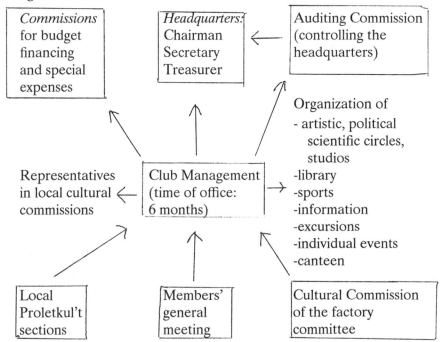

Daily problems in the clubs

Although club development in 1919 still showed a continuous enlargement on a national basis, there were nevertheless reports in the press about club problems and dissolution tendencies. Apart from the financial questions, which led to the closure or to the structural reorganization of several clubs, there was also a more noticeable fluctuation in membership. As an explanation of this tendency one can offer factors which are internally as well as externally related to the clubs. The general economic, political and cultural framework was not decisive in this regard, as this was the authority to which the clubs had to account for their concrete work. Let us look at two internal problems which made day-to-day club life difficult: (a) insufficient equipment and (b) insufficient number and quality of staff.

In the first years after the October Revolution one of the fundamental difficulties in the founding of a club was to find adequate accommodation. The clubs had to organize themselves according to the prevailing regional supply of confiscated property. Usually, the quarters which were allotted to them were cramped or in bad shape, and could only be used for club purposes with the maximum of improvisation (for example, private villas, churches, etc.). Although it was generally possible to find a club building, there were many more problems in the field of renovation. Even if the necessary sums of money for rebuilding had been granted, repairs and large-scale construction work on houses which had deteriorated through the indirect results of war or had been damaged by theft or vandalism was hardly possible. There was almost no way to get hold of the necessary building materials. The same difficulties were encountered here as in communal living during War Communism.[38] If the carrying out of the normal club programs was hampered by the shortage of buildings, the situation was made worse by the extreme shortage of fuel, which forced many clubs to close temporarily.

A further problem in the daily life of the clubs had to do with the available staff. It proved to be very difficult to find enough qualified lecturers, librarians and instructors. There are frequent complaints in the daily press referring to the turnover in lecturers. The reason for this was that a great number of club workers were called to the front during the civil war or were taken away for work in the state administration, in the workers' controlling organs, in the Bolshevik Party, or in the trade unions. Club activists who, as a rule, belonged to the small circle of better educated and more politically aware workers, were claimed for "more urgent" work in the field of political and economic reorganization. When there was a change of job or residential area, club membership usually came to an end. Available instructors often lacked experience or found it difficult to prepare themselves for the proletarian members of the circles in a methodological and didactic way. Many of the members of these clubs lacked even elementary knowledge. Great insight was necessary in order to break down the barriers against education and art which existed among the workers in spite of their general cultural interest. In practice, however, it often happened that scientists were invited who lectured about their own special fields and who demanded far too much from the audience and deterred them from attending further lectures.

On the other hand, complaints were heard about the terribly low standard of the club activities. Many instructors had taken only very short courses in preparation for their work in the clubs and hardly had more knowledge than their students. The inadequate equipment for work in the circles, for example, teaching materials, tools, and utensils, also made things very difficult. There was a lack of books, paper, writing and drawing material as well as theater properties, musical instruments, toys, and sports equipment. N. K. Krupskaia saw the reasons for the failure, or often the superficial program of many clubs, in these equipment and personnel problems: "The lack of means, room, musical instruments, the lack of instructors impeded the work incredibly; the lectures were of a random nature, the work of the preceding days was not carried on."[39]

Structure of membership

Reference is frequently made to the low level of education of club members. With regard to the effect of club programs, number of visitors, and individual interests of the members, one must therefore ask about the social structure of the clubs. For the analysis of the club membership structure let us take the example of the First Socialist Club in Kostroma (230 miles north-east of Moscow, situated on the Volga, a town with a textile industry and 74,000 inhabitants in 1926). This club offers the most detailed information for the period between 1918 to 1920.[40] On 1 April 1919 this club has 1,421 members, who could be tabulated as follows:

Table 3: Structure of club members in Kostroma, 1919

Age	Factory worker		Artisan		Office worker		Intelligen-tsia		Apprentices	
	m.	f.	m.	f.	m.	f.	m.	f.	m.	f.
up to 20	97	122	31	20	63	35	2	6	56	41
20-30	240	188	89	20	146	33	30	13	7	2
30-40	46	31	12	1	20	–	11	2	–	–
over 40	25	7	8	–	4	–	2	1	–	–
total	408	348	140	41	233	68	45	22	73	43
	together		together		together		together		together	
	756		181		301		67		116	

Source: M. A. Rastopchina, *Kul'tura nasha.* Kostroma, 1919, p. 28.

The information about the club members in Kostroma shows that, considering the division between the sexes, the proportion of men in all social classes is higher than that of women (899 to 522). It is, however, notable that among members under 20 years of age there are more female than male factory workers listed. There are presumably economic or political reasons for this (e.g., the large number of women in the textile industry, conscription of men into the army and similar factors), as in general the women did not play as large a role as men in public activities. Women were strongly underrepresented in factory committees, trade unions, soviets and party organs, and only achieved a rather larger representation ·on the workers' committees in the fields of production where they made up the majority of the employees.[41] With regard to age, the majority of club members in Kostroma were under 30 (in the group of factory workers only about 5 per cent were older than 40). With reference to their position in the process of production, the group of factory workers is predominant with almost 53 per cent of the club members, followed by office workers (21%), and artisans (just under 13%).

The proportion of the intelligentsia, to which belong the higher employees, engineers, technicians, scientists and teachers, is very small, with less than 5 per cent of the members. One must, however, bear in mind that such quantitative statements say little about the possibility of representatives of this group influencing the program of the club. Complaints can often be found in the press that "non-workers" had taken over the initiative in a club, planned the program according to their own tastes, and pushed the workers out of the club or into the role of passive observers.[42]

One of the main reasons for the apparent insecurity of the workers and for their effacing themselves before the more self-confident club members, seems to be their lower standard of education. In order to determine the level of education of club members during War Communism, one must look at the figures for the Kostroma club and then compare them with information on the level of education of the Russian workers on a national scale.

Table 4: Standard of education of club members in Kostroma

Not able to read or write	10
Hardly able to read or write	3
Elementary education	1,072
Secondary education	310
Higher Education	26
Total	1,421

Source: M. A. Rastopchina, *Kul'tura nasha.* Kostroma, 1919, p. 29.

Among the 1,421 members of the club in Kostroma there are only 10 who were illiterate, 1,072 members (75%) had had an elementary education, and 310 (22%) "secondary" education. In order to evaluate these figures correctly one has to take into account that the term "elementary" education only encompasses the ability to read and write as well as to do basic arithmetic, while "secondary" education means having attended primary school for three years. This shows that more than two-thirds of the club members possessed only the most basic skills of written communication, and more than 90 per cent had attended school for no more than three years. Although a very low standard of education is shown by these figures, they still support the assumption that the great majority of club members in Kostroma belonged to the group of skilled workers, if compared with the average standard of education of industrial workers. The results of an enquiry in 1918 show that in the Russian textile industry the percentage of literate workers was 55.4. One must, however, realize that the proportion of women in the textile industry is traditionally high and that there was a marked difference in the educational standard of men and women. On the national average of workers in flax processing, which was prevalent in Kostroma, 78.2 per cent of the men, but only 40.2 per cent of the women were literate.[43] In reference to all branches of production, 63.9 per cent of the industrial workers in Russia in 1918 were able to read and write, the proportion of men (79.1%) was far higher than that of women (44.1%) and became less with increasing age.[44]

The low standard of education of workers in Russia at this time can be illustrated by the standard of the Putilov workers in Petrograd. Although the literacy quota of the workers in Petrograd was above the average for the whole country (for men 88.2% as opposed to 79.1%, and for women 65.0% as opposed to 43.2%),[45] and although the employees in the metal-processing industry show the highest rate of literacy after the workers in the printing industry (for men a national average of 86.7%, in Petrograd 89.4%), a survey by S. G. Strumilin showed that the average time of school attendance was 2.6 years. This survey of fitters in the Putilov Works in Petrograd dealt with 767 people and can be considered representative for skilled workers in the metal industry. "About 50% of this category of workers finished two years of school, and about one-quarter went to school for only one year (as a rule these were self-taught)."[46]

Table 5: Standard of education of fitters inthe Putilov Works, 1918-1920

Degree of education	Duration of instruction in years	Number of workers absolute	in %
Illiterate	0	42	6.1
Literate without finishing school	1	173	25.3
Parish schools, etc.	2	21	3.1
Two-class schools town or country	3	340	49.6
Three-class schools District schools	4	45	6.6
Four-class schools town	5	38	5.5
More than four-class school	6 or more	3	0.4
Literate with unknown level of education	–	23	3.4

Source: Iu. S. Kulyshev and V. I. Nosach, *Partiinaia organizatsia i rabochie Petrograda v gody grazhdanskoi voiny 1918-1922 gg.* Leningrad, 1971, p. 270.

Can one conclude that the workers in Kostroma were above the national average in education, or did the club there attract a special public, that is, those of the proletariat who already had more education and were socially and politically active? A commission enquired into the level of culture and spare-time activities of the working population of Kostroma in 1919. Over 7,000 people were questioned. More than 50 per cent of those questioned had hardly any knowledge at all of reading or writing. When asked if they were improving their knowledge, more than 70 per cent answered in the negative, whereas of the 1,877 people who wanted to improve their education not one was completely illiterate. All had attended some school (usually the lower primary school) and only 260 people had no completed school education. On the other hand, all those who were illiterate or almost illiterate, with only few exceptions, answered that they did not want to improve their education. With reference to participation in leisure-time cultural activities, the following picture appeared:

Table 6: Workers' attendance at cultural institutions (1919)

| Number of visits (1 month) | MEN | | | | WOMEN | | | |
	lec-tures	meet-ings	theater concert	cinema	lec-tures	meet-ings	theater concert	cinema
1-3	508	904	297	365	465	1,096	405	555
4 or more	183	217	130	325	125	151	155	339
no informa-tion	62	113	44	66	112	211	86	122
none*	2,089	1,608	2,371	2,086	3,527	2,771	3,583	3,213
Total	2,842	2,842	2,842	2,842	4,229	4,229	4,229	4,229

*The survey showed that 1,224 men and 2,234 women attended no events at all.

Source: I. I. Beliaev, "Komissiia fabrichno-zavodskikh predpriiatii po kul'turno-prosvetitel'noi rabote sredi shirokikh mass," *Sbornik Kostromskogo Proletkul'ta*, No. 1, 1919, p. 103.

Those who made the survey come to the conclusion that "the figures show clearly that far too little is still being done in the way of penetrating the everyday life of workers in matters of culture."

Unfortunately, there are no broad data available about the educational and social structure of members of individual clubs for the time before 1920. In Kostroma it may be concluded that the club as an institution for spare time activities primarily attracted the more politically conscious, better educated workers. As the comparison with the urban working population there made clear, the club members were in possession of an elementary, but above-average education, and the majority felt themselves motivated to enquire into new fields of knowledge and experience. The conclusion that principally politically active and more highly skilled workers were the driving force in the clubs is supported by analogous surveys about political activity at a factory level. These come to the conclusion that the establishment of factory committees or trade union institutions was also organized by the more experienced, skilled workers.[48]

Role of clubs in the everyday life of urban industrial workers

As there exist hardly any contemporary empirical inquiries about the social situation, concrete working conditions, spare-time activities, and cultural activities of the urban working class during 1917-1921, only an attempt can be made at a summary of the role of factory clubs in the everyday life of the workers during the period of War Communism. This attempt is founded on scattered pieces of statistical information, the daily press, and biographies of workers.

Workers' clubs were to a great part founded by spontaneous initiatives within the factories, and later often taken into the organizational structure of central authorities. By looking at the programs on which these clubs were based, one can conclude that organizations like the Bolshevik Party, the trade unions, and Proletkul't made great efforts after the October Revolution toward the systematic building of clubs. In these early days only Proletkul't had the means to follow its conception more consequently.

It became obvious, however, in the practice of the clubs, that the claim to a universal expansion of knowledge and abilities within the proletariat was not realized immediately or easily. Neither the organizational framework nor the educational situation of the club members allowed for such an extensive process. In equipping and organization, factory clubs were dependent on the initiative of single factories. This explains how strongly the existence and programmatic trends of the clubs were influenced by the general everyday planning of its members. The catastrophic situation of food supplies had an immediate effect on the practice of the clubs in the centers, the practical topics dealt with, and caused the timetable of the club to be modified and adjusted to the daily rhythm of members who were dependent on the acquiring of food. The migration of industrial workers out of the centers, as well as the rebilleting actions within the towns, caused great fluctuations in the number of members and even the dissolution or establishment of clubs. The fluctuation of active members especially in 1919 does not therefore necessarily mean that there was a decline of interest in a club by the workers, but was more the fault of the specific economic and social general conditions which only left limited scope for spare-time cultural activities.

In the course of the civil war, workers' interests in the clubs shifted accordingly: the overpowering aspect of acquiring food gained in importance, so that Proletkul't remarked rightly that in the clubs "canteens are more important than theaters." In the face of the breakdown of public services and transport communications, the exchange of information, advice and assistance, discussions, and agitation were shifted to the clubs. Hunger, cold, material anxiety, and cramped living conditions led to the clubs' taking over the function of "a second home." As all private restaurants, cafés, and places of amusement had been closed after the October Revolution, the value of the clubs as a meeting-place for companionable hours is not to be under-estimated. Especially for young people, this aspect played an important role.

In the conditions during the civil war, the clubs could hardly offer more than superficial agitation and improvisation instead of the intended extension of basic knowledge. Even if "light entertainment" was predominant in the clubs, their function still consisted of more than providing a cheap diversion from the monotony of everyday life. At least one could find here the possibility to break down barriers concerning social contacts; to discover new fields of experience and forms of expression primarily in the sphere of art; and to learn the spirit of solidarity and discover common social as well as private interests and to develop these further.

The fact that workers, in spite of, or rather because of, their extremely difficult living conditions could still have the energy to perform in their club theaters, to write poems, to draw pictures, to do amateur handiwork, to take part in discussions or even to learn the alphabet, is evidence of a great willingness to learn and a readiness to accept new experiences and social forms. It illustrates the new creative, impulsive atmosphere which had its roots in the revolutionary political development of the year 1917. This "pioneer spirit" expressed itself in the clubs as spontaneous agitation through the use of artistic means. In this connection one must pay attention to the often-cited large number of mass theater productions, in which the revolutionary experiences of the proletariat were reconstructed by artistic means and which were for the most part prepared within the clubs.[49] Even if the claim expressed by the Proletkul't to develop a specific proletarian art in the clubs was realized only to a very small extent, one can state that the mere active confrontation, the gradual discovering and taking into possession of the sector of art by wide circles of workers established a new quality in revolutionary culture.

All in all, the period from 1917 to 1921 can be described as the "spontaneous" phase in the history of the Soviet workers' clubs. During this phase, because of the weaknesses of central planning, organization, and control, there existed room for new experiences which opened up dimensions previously unknown to the workers. Here, in the clubs, possibilities were offered to incorporate single interests into a social context; that is, to overcome individualism in behavior and consciousness by discovering common perspectives and using the clubs as a medium for collective action.

University of Kassel

Appendix I.

The ten commandments for club members

1. The club is the foundation for your development, as it trains and strengthens your class-consciousness.
2. It helps you to experience and understand important events in your country as well as in the whole world and guides you towards the salvation of our time — towards communism.
3. It develops your personal initiative and makes you a conscious, resolute worker of the Soviet Republic.
4. It develops in you a feeling of community and collectivity and teaches you to honor work and working people more than before.
5. Honor your club and don't allow yourself any kind of rough behavior, uphold cleanliness, order, and organization.
6. Don't waste your reserves on spiritual forces, but develop and deepen them: register for a scientific club circle, whether it be courses in Marxism, history, literature, drama, choir, or music.
7. Don't mistake the workers' club for the old, bourgeois club where one played cards, danced, and drank. The workers' club offers you sensible entertainment: concerts, opera, performances, literary evenings, productions, lectures, discussions about various subjects.
8. Don't waste your time on stupid and empty pastimes, but go to your club and sharpen your wits.
9. Don't put all the blame on your club if you see that it doesn't work well. Don't forget that every member must make his contribution to the common work. If the club is bad, not only the administration

is at fault, but the members general council, which allows disorder, abuse, and slovenliness in your club.

10. Don't say that the Soviet power economizes on expenses for your further education: The central department finances the clubs, and all performances. Concerts, lectures as well as scientific and artistic attractions are free of charge for club members.

Source: "Desiat' zapovedei dlia chlenov kluba," in *Revoliutsionnye vskhody*, nos. 7/8, 1920, p. 14.

Notes

[1]H. Pridik (ed.), *Des Bildungswesen in Sowjetrussland. Vorträge, Leitsätze und Resolution der Ersten Moskauer Allstädtischen Konferenz der Kulturell-Aufklärenden Organisationen vom 23-28 Februar 1918.* Annaberg/Erzg., 1921.

[2]T. A. Khavina, *Bor'ba kommunisticheskoi partii za Proletkul't i rukovodstvo ego deiatel'nost'iu 1917-1932 gg.* Leningrad, 1978, p. 41; A. K. Kolesova, *Deiatel'nost' rabochikh klubov po kommunisticheskomu vospitaniiu trudiashchikhsia v 1917-1923 gg.* Moscow, 1969, p. 81.

[3]W. Suess, *Der Betrieb in der UdSSR. Stellung, Organisation und Management 1917-1932.* Frankfurt, Bern, 1981, p. 40; S. A. Smith, *Red Petrograd: Revolution in the Factories, 1917-1918.* Cambridge: Cambridge University Press, 1983, pp. 80ff.

[4]*Kluby Moskvy i gubernii. Spravochnik.* Moscow, 1925, pp. 20f.

[5]D. Grille, *Lenins Rivale. Bogdanov und seine Philosophie.* Cologne, 1966; Z. A. Sochor, "Modernization and Socialist Transformation: Leninist and Bogdanovite Alternatives of the Cultural Revolution." Unpublished Ph.D. dissertation, Columbia University, 1977; K. M. Jensen, *Beyond Marx and Mach: A. Bogdanov's Philosphy of Living Experience.* Dordrecht, Boston: Reidal, 1978; G. Gorzka, *A. Bogdanov und der russische Proletkult. Theorie und Praxis einer sozialistischen Kulturrevolution.* Frankfurt, New York: Campus, 1980; K. Maenicke-Gyoengyoesi, *Proletarische Wissenschaft und sozialistische Menschheitsreligion als Modelle proletarischer Kultur. Zur linksbolschewistischen Revolutionstheorie A. A. Bogdanovs und A. V. Lunacharskijs.* Berlin, 1982; D. G. Rowley, "Millenarian Bolshevism: Empiriomonism, God-Building, Proletarian Culture." Unpublished Ph.D. dissertation, University of Michigan, 1982.

[6]See, for example, "Proletarische Kultur. Schwerpunktthema" in *Ästhetik und Kommunikation*, Beiträge zur politischen Erziehung, nos. 5/6, 1972; P. Gorsen and E. Knoedler-Bunte, *Proletkult. System einer proletarischen Kultur. Dokumentation*, vols. I, II. Stuttgart, 1974; I. L. Aronchik, *Kritika V. I. Leninym teorii 'proletarskoi kul'tury' (proletkul'tovshchiny) i sovremennost'.* Moscow, 1963; V. T. Ermakov, *Istoricheskii opyt kul'turnoi revoliutsii v SSSR.* Moscow, 1968; V. V. Gorbunov, *V. I. Lenin i Proletkul't.* Moscow, 1974; G. G. Karpov, *Lenin o kul'turnoi revoliutsii.* Leningrad, 1970; L. A. Pinegina, *Sovetskii rabochii klass i khudozhestvennaia kul'tura 1917-1932.* Moscow, 1984.

[7]Gor'bunov, *Lenin*, p. 59; CGA RSFSR, f. 2306, op. 15, d. 272, ll. 9-9.

[8]CGALI, f. 1230, op. 1, ed. khr. 802, l. 11.

[9]CGALI, f. 1230, op. 1, ed. khr. 802, l. 12; Kolesova, *Deiatel'nost'*, p. 63.

[10]CGALI, f. 1230, op. 1, ed. khr. 795, l. 2.

[11]*Shestoi s"ezd RSDRP(b). Protokoly.* Moscow, 1958, p. 191.

[12]I. I. Gordeev, "V virche vremeni," *Moskovskie bol'sheviki v ogne revoliutsionnykh boev.* Moscow, 1976, p. 192; *Gudki. Ezhenedel'nik Moskovskogo Proletkul'ta*, no. 3, 1919, pp. 30f.; *Rabochii klass Sovetskoi Rossii v pervyi god diktatury proletariata. Sbornik dokumentov.* Moscow, 1964, p. 328.

[13]V. I. Lenin, "Rechi na zasedanii Moskovskogo komiteta partii ob organizatsii grupp sochuvstvuiushchikh 16 avgusta 1918 g.," *Polnoe sobranie sochinenii*, vol. XXXVII, Moscow, 1974, pp. 46f.

[14]"Iz protokola soveshchaniia sekretarei raionnykh komitetov KRP(b) Moskvy ob organizatsii agitatsionykh otdelov, 17. 9. 1918 g.," *Rabochii klass*, pp. 317ff.

[15]See *Pervyi Vserossiiskii S"ezd Professional'nykh Soiuzov, 7.-14.1. 1918.* Moscow, 1918.

[16]"Ustav VTsSPS, 11.1. 1918," *Pervyi Vserossiiskii S"ezd*, p. 377.

[17]M. N. Potekhin, *Petrogradskaia trudovaia kommuna 1918-19 gg.* Leningrad, 1980, p. 116.

[18]GAMO, f. 186, op. 1, ed. khr. 317, l.4, cited in Kolesova, *Deiatel'nost'*, p. 59.

[19]*Petrogradskaia obshchegorodskaia konferentsiia rabochikh klubov.* Petrograd, 1920, p. 32.

[20]*Materialy po statistike*, 2nd ed. Petrograd, 1920, p. 100.

[21]"Khronika Proletkul'ta," *Proletarskaia Kul'tura*, nos. 13/14, 1920, p. 86.

[22]N. Kazimirov, "Biblioteki i kluby," *Biulleten' Tsentral'nogo Statisticheskogo Upravleniia*, no. 46, 5 April 1921.

[23]S. Krivtsov, "Khronika Proletkul'ta," *Proletarskaia Kul'tura*, no. 3, 1918, p. 32.

[24]CGALI, f. 1230, op. 1, ed. khr. 1515, l.23.

[25]See, for example, "Raionnye kluby," *Gorn*, nos. 2/3, 1919, p. 126.

[26]Cf., the regional reports in "Khronika Proletkul'ta," *Proletarskaia Kul'tura*, nos. 15/16, 1920, pp. 73-85; "Plan organizatsii Proletkul'ta," *Proletarskaia Kul'tura*, no. 6, 1919, pp. 27 f.

[27]CGALI, f. 1230, op. 1, ed. khr. 121, l.57.

[28]"Tezisy k dokladu tov. Iadvigi—organizatsionnyi vopros," *Petrogradskaia obshchegorodskaia konferentsiia*, p. 135.

[29]See "Khronika Proletkul'ta," *Proletarskaia Kul'tura*, no. 6, 1919, p. 31; nos. 7/8, 1919, p. 68; "V provintsii—Proletkul'ty," *Proletarskaia Kul'tura*, nos. 15/16, 1920, p. 76.

[30]"O klubnoi otchetnosti," *Petrogradskaia obshchegorodskaia konferentsiia*, p. 136.

[31]"Konstruktsiia otdelov Moskovskogo Proletkul'ta," *Gorn*, no. 5, 1920, pp. 86 f.

[32]*Vneshkol'noe obrazovanie*, nos. 6-8, Petrograd, 1919, p. 75.

[33]"Primernyi ustav kluba Proletkul'ta. Prilozhenie no. 1," *Proletarskaia Kul'tura*, nos. 7/8, 1919, p. 66.

[34]For a definition of "collectivism" in A. Bogdanov's writings, see Gorzka, *Bogdanov*, pp. 134 ff., 208 ff.

[35]"Kul'turno-prosvetitel'naia rabota," *Gorn*, no. 5, 1920, p. 77.

[36]*Sbornik Kostromskogo Proletkul'ta*, no. 1, 1919, p. 37; Potekhin, *Petrogradskaia*, p. 116.

[37]I. Kubikov, "Petrogradskie rabochie kluby v revoliutsionnyi period 1917-1918 gg.," *Vestnik Kul'tury i Svobody*, nos. 3/4, 1918, p. 55.

[38]*Gorn*, nos. 2/3, 1919, p. 126; "Klubnyi otdel," *Gorn*, no. 5, 1920, p. 88; T. V. Kuznetsova, "K voprosu o putiach resheniia zhilishchnoi problemy v SSSR," *Istoriia SSSR*, no. 5, 1963, pp. 141 ff.; T. A. Remizova, *Kul'turno-prosvetitel'naia rabota v RSFSR 1921-1925*. Moscow, 1962, p. 241.

[39]*Vneshkol'noe obrazovanie*, no. 1, 1918, p. 13; nos. 2/3, 1919, p. 61; "Klubnye nedostatki," *Revoliutsionnye Vskhody* (Zhurnal proletarskich klubov), nos. 3/4, Petrograd, 1920, p. 15.

[40]Maria A. Rastopchina, one of the founders of this club, published a series of brochures and articles on methodological questions and experiences of workers' clubs; see M. A. Rastopchina, *Kak ustroit' i vesti rabochii sotsialisticheskii klub*. Kostroma 1918; M. A. Rastopchina, *Kul'tura nasha. So znameni 1-go Rabochego Sotsialisticheskogo kluba*. Kostroma 1919; M. A. Rastopchina, *Rabochii i krest'ianskii klub. Materialy kursov podgotovki rabotnikov*. Kostroma 1920.

[41]S. A. Smith, "Spontaneity and Organisation in the Petrograd Labour Movement in 1917," *University of Essex: Discussion Paper Series, no. 1, 1984, p. 16;* K. T. Dieckmann, *Die Frau in der Sowjetunion*. Frankfurt, 1978, pp. 80ff.; *Zhenshchina i byt*. Moscow, 1926.

[42]"Khronika Proletkul'ta," *Proletarskaia Kul'tura*, nos. 7/8, 1919, p. 68; nos. 9/10, 1919, p. 59; nos. 15/16, 1920, p. 83.

[43]*Sbornik statisticheskikh svedenii po Soiuzu SSSR 1918-23 gg*. Trudy tsentral' nogo statisticheskogo upravleniia. Moscow, 1924, vol. XVIII, p. 53.

[44]*Ibid*.

[45]Iu. S. Kulyshev, and V. I. Nosach, *Partiinaia organizatsiia i rabochie Petrograda v gody grazhdanskoi voiny 1918-1920 gg*. Leningrad, 1971, p. 265.

[46]Kulyshev and Nosach, *Partiinaia organizatsiia*, pp. 267 f.

[47]I. I. Beliaev, "Komissiia fabrichno-zavodskikh predpriiatii po kul'turno-prosvetitel'noi rabote sredi shirokikh mass," *Sbornik Kostromskogo Proletkul'ta*, no. 1, 1919, pp. 102 ff.

[48]Smith, *University of Essex: Discussion Paper*, p. 10.

[49]Cf., R. Fueloep-Miller, *Geist und Gesicht des Bolschewismus. Darstellung und Kritik des kulturellen Lebens in Sowjetrussland*. Zurich, Leipzig, Wien, 1926, pp. 192 ff.; J. Gregor, and R. Fueloep-Miller, *Das russische Theater—sein Wesen und seine Geschichte mit besonderer Berücksichtigung der Revolutionsperiode*. Zurich, Leipzig, Wien, 1928, p. 105; J. Paech, *Des Theater der russischen Revolution. Theorie und Praxis des proletarisch-kulturrevolutionären Theaters in Russland 1917-1924*. Kronberg, 1974, pp. 123 ff., 322 ff.; G. I. Il'ina, *Kul'turnoe stroitel'stvo v Petrograde, 1917-1920 gg*.

Leningrad, 1982, pp. 140-154.

Russian and Soviet Economic Penetration of North-Eastern China, 1895-1933.

Felix Patrikeeff

Russian economic penetration of China has long served as something of a riddle. In terms of sheer scale and audacity, the misguided attempt at creating a "Yellow Russia"[1] in China's north-eastern corner surpasses anything that other European countries dared dream of in conducting their commercial affairs from the "little Europe" of the concessions and colonies dotting the China coast.[2] Yet Russia's sprawling railway zone (with its areas of free trade and showpiece settlements) had its beginnings in a treaty system founded on fairly equal bases[3] and spawned little of the entrepreneurial thrust normally associated with the China trade. These contradictory images of the origins and course of Russian economic imperialism have resulted in inferences of it as a distinctive entity. Mark Mancall, in juxtaposing the Kiakhta and Canton trading systems, observes of early commercial relations at Kiakhta, one of two settlements to which border trade was limited under the terms of the Kiakhta Treaty (1727):

> The Russians did not seek entry into China [through the Kiakhta System]...nor to force concepts of free trade on the Chinese, concepts the Russians themselves held, at best, only weakly; the Chinese, in turn, did not insist on the all-importance of Chinese customary forms of this intercourse, as they did at Canton.[4]

To this image of harmony might be added that of Rosemary Quested's "matey" Russian imperialist as a phenomenon quite separate from his more imperious counterparts:

> It may be hypothesized that, notwithstanding the evidence for increasing racial seclusion after the Russo-Japanese war, the Russians could still thereafter mix better with Asians at certain levels — usually when it was politically or commercially desirable — than other Western imperialists of this period.[5]

The question then is whether Russian imperialism should be interpreted as an innately benign form, and if so is this conclusion entirely compatible with the obvious (and professed) scale and scope of its undertakings in Manchuria? In the end, the peculiarities observed in the

Russian presence in North-Eastern China may have to be explained not by a search for innate characteristics of the Russians themselves, or their trading relations, but by such factors as the effect of physical distance, absence of a consistent policy and the failure to integrate economic activity sufficiently with political objectives. Rather than "matey" Imperialism, a more suitable epitaph to the Russian phenomenon in North-Eastern China would be "Bezalabernyi" Imperialism.[6]

While the style of Chinese relations with Russians may be regarded as qualitatively different to that of their relations with other powers, the restrictions on the freedom of Russians to trade outside the immediate zones of advantage were similar to those governing other Western states.[7] Had Russia desired to do anything to improve these trading terms, it is unlikely that it would have had the means to pressure China into improving them.[8] The Russian Empire's Far Eastern limits were strained enough with the problems of securing and developing Siberia and the Maritime Province. The imbalance in China's favor is most graphically demonstrated by attempts at colonization undertaken by Russia and China of the Russian Far East and Manchuria respectively. In the 300 years of Russian rule in Siberia, the population there had barely reached 15 million by the outbreak of World War I. In Manchuria the population had increased six-fold in less than 30 years.[9] By the 1920s the results of this were further reinforced: the Russian territory, although able to support its own food production, was almost completely dependent for its food from European Russian and Manchurian exports of grain and cattle. Manchuria, on the other hand, was by then producing food for its own needs, plus surpluses (particularly wheat) for export.[10] The link of steel, which was to draw together the Russian Far East with the fertile plains of North-Eastern China into a single productive entity, instead served as a brittle bridge spanning an underdeveloped Siberia.

In Manchuria itself, the factor of distance, both historical and physical, worked against the Russians in that it allowed them, at least initially, the freedom from commercial competition that the treaty ports and China proper would not. Under the sheltering wing of the Ministry of Finance, the pockets of "Russianess" were allowed to take root, but not long enough to blossom fully. The insularity of the Russian presence is best demonstrated by its response to forays by Western firms into the Manchurian markets in the early 1900s.

When an Anglo-American tobacco firm sent a network of agents into Northern Manchuria with advertising posters and free samples of cigarettes to carry out a sales campaign, they encountered a market still served by large quantities of Russian tobacco products. It was noted that the rival products they encountered were cheap cigarettes under names such as "Siren" and "Kazakh," which showed no signs of conforming to the tastes or needs of the Chinese market. Also, Russian *papirosy* were seen to have a limited market as the Chinese saw them as a way of using less tobacco.[11] That the Russian manufacturers and traders of these goods could be so far out of touch with local requirements seems to reinforce the view that there were local requirements and that there were strong elements of ethnocentricity present from the start. That they came into sharper focus with the Russo-Japanese War seems to be a function of the shock imparted by the war on the Russians in Manchuria. Their extended claims both to "Russianess" and their "colonial" status served simply to draw them closer together as a community in bringing their pleas to the attention of the Russian government. It was largely an attempt to revive the shelter provided earlier by Witte's "paternal capitalism." The war forced the Russian community in Manchuria to retrench, consolidate on the advantage provided by the Chinese Eastern Railway (CER), and begin to think about commerce on a broader, more keenly contested, scale.[12] Along with the sense of siege and isolation experienced by the native Russian population came a flood of criticism of local Russian trade, of the gap between European Russian manufacture and the Chinese markets, of the untapped potential that Manchuria represented as a center of trade.[13]

Witte's vision of a gradual development of Russian commercial interests in Northern Manchuria, taking the least line of resistance in dealing with China's authorities, may have had a chance to take shape, had the Finance Minister's power base not been usurped by the more threatening and beligerent Bezobrazov clique in 1903. To his credit, Witte saw the brittle and fragile nature of Russian economic activity in the region. He saw that progress could only be achieved through "patient, long-range policy, dependent on a feeling of security for the morrow..."[14] and that the adoption of the militaristic forms of Western imperialism could only endanger the evolution of an enduring Russian edifice in the Far East. Combined with (and indeed contributing to the success of) the harder political line that replaced Witte's blueprint was the sudden fall in investment provided by Russian heavy industry. After the slump of 1900, industry could no longer supply the funds that flooded eastward in the 1890s. Even if the funds were available for the further development of the Russian Far East, the political opposition to such investment would have been great, if not prohibitive.[15]

In its place was the short-sighted policy of consolidation and rule in the image of a quasi-military outpost. The new policy was disdainful of Chinese fears, Japanese aspirations, and Western commercial jealousies.[16] More importantly, it was oblivious to the inability of a fragile

Russian infrastructure in China—created with the long-term in mind—to resist the short-term onslaught of anxious neighbors and rivals. Investment in the railway continued to grow steadily, but this became viewed largely in strategic terms. This investment, in spite of its scale, provided little encouragement to Russian commercial flair or the conquering of new markets. A report from an agent of the Ministry of Trade and Industry, commenting on the state of Russian trade in Kirin, observed that Russian goods there were plentiful, but that there was not a single Russian warehouse in the settlement. He also noted that the CER ran a commercial agency there which was open only during the summer months. "It would be useful," he concluded, "to open the premises in the remaining months as a repository to Russian trade for samples of our goods, by which Chinese buyers could decide on orders."[17] By 1914 the CER had become bureaucratized and estranged from the task of spreading Russian commercial influence in Manchuria. Instead it competed (with razor sharp margins) with the South Manchurian Railway for primacy as a conduit for Manchurian exports.[18] Harbin, rather than being the center of Russian economic influence and the main distribution point for Russian goods for the whole of China, had become a processing center for Manchurian raw materials destined for transhipment through Russia itself.[19]

The inability of Russian exporters, local Russian businesses and the railway to work hand-in-hand had led to lost chances and unrealized commercial potential in the areas opened by the railway, where Russia had a clear advantage. It was a state of affairs that forced the Harbin Stock Exchange Committee to publish a plea to the Russian authorities for decisive measures to be taken in support of its trade and traders in Manchuria. The pamphlet registers a sense of isolation and a feeling of desertion felt by the "native" Russian population of Manchuria. It points out that trade and industry came into being in Manchuria "at a time when Russia's goals were completely different [and] all forms of enterprise were encouraged by representatives of the Central Government, many of whom had visited the Far East."[20] In a situation where the Russian share of Northern Manchuria's import market is inexorably slipping, the committee points to Southern Manchuria "where everything is organized with such calculation that monopolies in all fields of economic activity belong solely to Japanese interests."[21] This yearning for a return to Witte's priorities of "trade and industry always in the front"[22] disguises slightly the fact that Witte's scheme for extending Russian economic control through Manchuria, and indeed North China down to Peking, always had at its heart expansion via the CER and the Russo-Chinese Bank and not the direct farthering of Russian traders' interests *per se*.

This policy had not altered significantly once Witte had lost the reins of effective control of Russian Far Eastern policy. What had developed, and the committee's comments seem to underline this, is the growing divergence in outlook between the CER, the Bank, and Russian commerce and industry in the region.

Once the idyll of the sheltered formative period had been shattered by the Russo-Japanese War, the Russians in Northern Manchuria were forced, mainly by commercial pressures from the south, to take stock of their role in the Far East. Although they continued to see themselves as a Russian colony, it became increasingly clear that their success would depend on individual commercial initiative rather than as the favored charges of Russian policy in North-Eastern China. Given the wide range of enterprise and trade that the Russians explored,[23] it might be concluded that there seemed to be no shortage of such initiative or an eagerness to prosper. Why this corpus of entrepreneurship did not take root may be explained by the unwillingness of the Russian authorities to shift their focus sufficiently from the CER to small-scale commercial presence as a basis for the spread of Russian economic influence. In spite of the triumph of Bezobrazov's crude form of economic imperialism over Witte's "gradualism" as the basis for Russia's Far Eastern policy, a distorted form of Witte's dictum of "railway and bank first" remained at the core of the scheme of development for Northern Manchuria.

The imbalance of this policy came into sharpest relief in two main areas: the chronic shortage of capital that plagued Russian businesses in the region, and the failure of European Russian manufacture to make sufficient inroads into internal markets there. Both created grave, and eventually insurmountable, weaknesses in Russia's economic hold on Northern Manchuria. The paucity of capital was the result of the Russian authorities' inability to see past the strictures of a rigid finance structure (which placed emphasis on CER/Bank-generated enterprise) to the cultivation of a more broadly based network of credit institutions. This situation was not eased by foreign banks operating from Harbin, whose attitude to Russian business—in anything other than soya bean exports—was at best cautious. In the case of the Hongkong and Shanghai Banking Corporation (HSBC), which became the most powerful of the banks through its early involvement in the bean trade,[24] substantial borrowing was made extremely difficult for almost all Russian businessmen. For many of the larger Russian business houses, their unavoidable financial entanglements with the CER became increasingly a liability. The Railway would often deal in pronotes with these companies, which in turn attempted to use them as security with banks. The banks' attitude to such forms of guarantee, particularly after the 1917

Revolution, grew more cynical: "These [pronotes] are only paid at due date when there is any cash in the till, which is nearly akin to when the moon turns green."[25]

For smaller Russian firms wishing to deal in goods in the interior, the chronic lack of funds meant that their operations had to be run on a shoestring, with little room for miscalculation. The traders' position in this respect was not helped by the tangle of customs duties, agency administrative charges, and differences in forms of payment that were involved in moving goods inland. In Kirin province after 1908, for example, the duty on vodka was silver based, while that on tobacco remained in the local bronze currency.[26] More perplexing still was the fact that duties in Manchuria as a whole had the habit of appearing in sudden, quite unexpected ways.[27] If these extra costs were not provided for, could not be met, the shipments would be confiscated, thus tying up stock and capital. Besides the straightforward scheme of duties (there were over 120 main categories by 1922[28]), the conduct of trade was made more difficult still by the cost of indeterminate obligations of provincial governments to the central government in China and the random imposition of "military taxes" by local military authorities.[29] To this must be added the difficulties experienced by traders in securing a steady flow of suitable merchandise from sources in Russia, which were largely indifferent to trade with North-Eastern China. This was an area in which the Russian authorities could have done more but failed to intervene. Furthermore, there was little encouragement by the Russian authorities of its own industries and traders to adopt more aggressive methods in defending existing, or developing new, markets in the region. In 1913 Russian exports of kerosene to Manchuria fell dramatically after a major Russian exporter had reached an agreement with the Asiatic Petroleum Co. not to compete with Standard Oil in Southern Manchuria. Not only did this cause a fall in the total Russian export of kerosene, but, as a government agent for trade put it: "This hasn't prevented American kerosene from making greater and greater inroads into the Northern Manchurian market."[30]

By the time of World War I Russia's share of exports to China stood at a meager 3.8 percent of the total, compared with 3.48 percent in 1910. After a brief rise to 4.8 percent, with the Russian Revolution the figure fell to below 1 percent.[31] Even in Manchuria itself, Russia's share of the import market continued to rise only in value; its overall share had, as early as 1912, fallen to 17 percent.[32] So serious were the problems of solvency (and the predicament of Russian imports) that the few years before the Russian Revolution were littered with pleas to the central authorities in Russia on behalf of Russian business in North-Eastern

China. The Stock Exchange Committee of Harbin, for example, in their petition suggested five measures to bolster Russian business in the region. All five points concerned the creation of credit institutions.[33] The pleas went unheeded, and Russian interests were left at the mercy of foreign capital to conduct business on the brink. Funds, when they could be found, came in the form of short-term loans at prohibitively high interest rates.[34]

The contradictory characteristics in the relationship between Russia and its Manchurian "colony" stood in direct contrast to Japanese policy in Southern Manchuria. There, investment was matched by a balanced combination of encouragement (and shelter) of enterprise and entrepreneurial thrust, backed by a well-organized banking system and home industry. This combination, by contrast, was particularly potent in its ability to seize opportunities in markets and the purchase of troubled foreign enterprises. Gerasimov gives a vivid example of how the Japanese were able to employ "roving capital" to its fullest effect. The Shcherbin Distillery at An'da Station was subjected to an unexpected military tax of 10,000 Tsitsihar Dollars. The owner and his partner could not raise the money and were consequently imprisoned. They had no choice but to sell the enterprise to Japanese interests at a substantial loss.[35]

To have expected a similar pattern of penetration and condolidation from Russian policy is, perhaps, unrealistic. The Russian trade policy in Manchuria conformed closely to the country's general attitude toward trade. Before 1914, the Russian government involved itself little in trade, and foreign commerce was conducted according to principles of private trade, with the state simply concluding trade arrangements and operating customs duties. It was not until after that year that the state involved itself actively in the country's foreign trade, while the first attempts at foreign trade planning, organized large-scale stockpiling for exports and purchase of imports came only with the Provisional Government.[36]

The revolution brought virtually a complete collapse of trade figures. Hardest hit, in this respect, was the steady evolution of Vladivostok as a conduit for Manchurian exports. Before World War I nearly 80 percent of exports were via Vladivostok and the Russian land frontier at Manchouli Station. By 1920 its position had been taken by Dairen, which was handling 80 percent of exports and had tightened its grip further on imports.[37] Siberia, which had been dependent on food supplies from Manchuria, became more so. Demand for grain frequently sent this commodity rocketing in price.[38] The black market, which had quickly re-established itself after the closure of the 50-verst duty-free zone in January 1913,[39] developed momentum as the Russian side of the border drifted into a chaotic state. There also was an economic counter-penetration of Russian territory. This culminated in the extension of foreign capital into the Siberian and Maritime regions: the intervention in 1918 was an ideal time to consolidate financial services for exporters in Vladivostok itself. The potential that the Hongkong and Shanghai Bank Corporation, for example, saw in the port was evident as late as October 1924, when a Bank official wrote: "Everything seems to point towards Vladivostok becoming the commercially important port foreseen by its original founders. The great drawback is the uncertainty of the political situation."[40] The HSBC operation in Vladivostok was to endure well into the Soviet era.[41] With the sharp rise of the Manchurian bean trade, the importance of keeping lines of finance and communication open between Manchurian trade and Vladivostok became a matter of semi-official policy on the part of the Soviet government.[42]

In Manchuria the process of establishing a Soviet economic foothold was tortuous, as evidenced by the difficulties encountered in wrenching control of the CER zone from the death grip of General Horvath's "regime." The task was made no easier by the Soviet advocacy of a reconstruction of its activities in the area, "...but with new principles of co-operation with the Chinese rather than the pattern of exploitation set during Tsarist times."[43] This formula would prove difficult to square with the exigencies of countering the practices of less altruistic commercial competitors in the region. Equally, it provided a strong political weapon for the Chinese authorities in their efforts, between 1924 and 1929, to assume full control of the CER.

The conditions of re-entering North-Eastern China were exacerbated by the presence of a new element — that of the Russian émigré society — in an already complicated political fray. Many who composed this group had experienced years of gradual impoverishment. Their numbers were bloated by large the number of refugees finding their way across the northern borders of China.[44] Resources available to this political rag-tag, particularly the new arrivals to the Harbin area, were few; a factor which tended to heighten animosity towards their former homeland. Ironically, the increasingly hard times for the Russians coincided with the spectacular rise of the Manchurian economy. This is at least in part explained by the concentration of the foreign banks on the bean trade, largely to the exclusion of many other forms of commercial activity. The exports of beans, indeed export trade as a whole, was securely in the grasp of a small number of foreign (but not Russian) trading companies,[45] and little of the profit was ploughed back into Northern Manchuria.[46] The polarization between Soviet Russians and émigrés showed itself mainly in the atmosphere of mutual suspicion and recrimination that prevailed. Institutional channels were available to the émigrés for their resistance to Soviet activities, the most important being their numbers in CER employment,[47] and those employed by the Chinese Maritime Customs.

Although the origins of a state monopoly and co-ordination of foreign trade may be traced to wartime conditions, with the introduction of a general foreign trade plan and the Supply Committee of the Ministry of Commerce and Industry, the initial steps taken by the Soviet government were tentative. Nationalization of foreign trade was instituted on 23 April 1918 but there was no specification of which organizations were to conduct trade on behalf of the state. Nor was there any firm trade machinery devised until 1920, when decrees were passed transforming the Commissariat of Commerce and Industry into the Commissariat of Foreign Trade. It was only in October/November 1925 that joint stock companies, limited liability companies and syndicates were formed and the People's Commissariat of Foreign Trade merged with the People's Commissariat of Home Trade into a single People's Commissariat of Trade.[48] This realignment was mirrored in the pattern of trade with China, 1925 marking the first major expansion of trade, particularly Soviet exports, since 1916.[49] Although the rise was still well under the 1916 level, this belies the change that occurred in the style of trading that showed itself at about this time. Perhaps the most striking examples of the new entrepreneurial flair which appeared are those of the Dal'bank and Dal'gostorg activities in the bean trade. In the case of Dal'bank, its operations began to show keenness during the liquidation of the Russo-Asiatic Bank. By the end of 1926 it had secured an active financial role in over half of Harbin's bean-oil refineries and bean mills, and by 1929 all bean processing operations in the entire region had at some stage received its credit.[50] Dal'gostorg had, within the space of a few years late in the 1920s, become one of five companies monopolizing the bean export trade.[51] Both Dal'bank and Dal'gostorg showed an aggressive commercial edge which had been the preserve of foreign banks and trading companies until then.

Such inroads into local commerce are particularly striking given the level of suspicion prevailing in China as a whole about the real motives of Soviet agencies operating there.[52] An opportunistic style of business was also to be seen in the activities of Soviet exporters to Manchuria, but here the results were far more modest, with the general emphasis being on the import trade. Although the Soviet commercial initiative worked meticulously at preventing any political connotations being attached to its work in North-Eastern China,[53] the association by implication of Soviet advisors farther south after 1925 was difficult to avoid. It allowed Chinese authorities greater leeway in exerting pressure on the Soviet position vis-a-vis the CER. This pressure, in turn, helped to reveal further anomolies in Soviet policy in China. When Soviet officials began to take a tougher line against the apparent Chinese encroachment on their rights within the structure of the Railway's management, the head of HSBC's Harbin Branch observed that "Soviet Russia as the champion of foreign rights in China is something very strange and totally unexpected...."[54]

No less difficult a task for the Soviet authorities was the problem they inherited from Tsarist Russia, namely how to incorporate their activities in North-East China into a general development of the Russian Far East. The Ussuri Railway, a system running parallel to the CER, remained underdeveloped and underused. The territory through which it ran had natural resources, but their exploitation was difficult and costly. Only a branch line of the Ussuri (connecting Suifenho [Pogranichnaia] with Nikolsk and Vladivostok) was found to be profitable,[55] and then only marginally so.[56] There were no straightforward solutions to this problem. Attention instead was increasingly directed to the further development of Vladivostok as an export point for Manchurian produce.[57] The growth of commercial relations between Vladivostok and Northern Manchuria was lucrative in the short term, but its foundations were not on safe ground. The enhanced commercial role of the port was based largely on the soya bean trade and was increasingly dependent on a smooth working relationship with the CER. The imbalance in this pattern of development suffered a double blow. In 1929 the Soviet authorities were no longer able to maintain an adequate grasp on the situation in Manchuria and resorted to military solution. That in itself undermined the steady economic gain that the Soviet Union had enjoyed in the region since 1925.[58] The repercussions of the conflict on Northern Manchuria were severe. Foreign banks shut down their operations when hostilities broke out and did not resume their normal credit work until early the following year. By then the effects of the world slump had reached Manchuria. The commodity that suffered most was beans, with prices going down sharply until January 1931 when they were 135 percent lower than in September 1929.[59] Even at these prices there were few buyers abroad. With the collapse of the soya bean trade, the CER's major source of revenue vanished. The Soviet Union had, through its successful military action in 1929, restored an active partnership in a crippled concern.

It is a fitting epilog that the eclipse of Soviet political and economic influence in North-Eastern China, which began at this time, coincided with the start of a major export initiative by the Soviet Union. An intelligence report from Dairen warned in 1930 that in Manchuria:

> Even the foreign merchants with whose imports these goods compete, admit that the Soviet merchandise is of good quality considering the prices for which it sells, and, as a matter of fact, if the present situation furnishes an example of what Soviet Russia may be able to do when she shall have completed her ambitious industrial program, the foreign merchants in Manchuria are likely to find themselves facing the most serious competition which they have yet seen.[60]

The Far Eastern Crisis of 1931 initiated a political and economic process to ensure that this would not find an enduring form in the region. However, in the report is a faint echo of a response to the observations and suggestions made seventeen years earlier on how a firm Russian grip on North-East China's economy might have been secured.

St Antony's College, Oxford

Notes

[1]Recognized in its foetal form by Rosemary K. I. Quested in her seminal work on Russians in Manchuria, *"Matey" Imperialists? The Tsarist Russians in Manchuria, 1895-1917.* Hong Kong: Centre of Asian Studies Occasional Papers and Monographs, no. 50, University of Hong Kong, 1982, pp. 155-159. Those who are studying the *terra incognita* of Russian presence in Manchuria owe a great debt to Dr. Quested's pioneering work on the subject.

[2]Quested cites a figure of 479.6 million rubles having been spent on schemes in Manchuria up to 1903 (p. 155). Nikolai N. Liubimov, in his *Ekonomicheskie Problemy Dal'nego Vostoka (Vostochnaia Kitaiskaia Zheleznaia Doroga)*, Moscow, 1925, suggests that, inclusive of interest charges, over 400 million rubles were spent on the railway alone (p. 7). By January 1907 this figure had risen to over 750 million rubles (*ibid.*). By the late 1920s the figure had reached 1044 million rubles (representing nearly 40 percent of the foreign investment in railways in China as a whole). M. Frizendorf, *Severnaia Man'chzhuriia: Ocherki Ekonomicheskoi Geografii.* Khabarovsk, 1929, p. 157.

[3]Mark Mancall, "The Kiakhta Trade," in *The Economic Development of China and Japan*, ed., C. D. Cowan. London, Allen and Unwin, 1964, p. 23. Mancall reminds us that the Treaty of Nerchinsk (1689), the first signed by China with a non-Asian power, may be regarded as being favorable to the Chinese because it forced the Russians to leave the Amur river basin area. Similarly, the Kiakhta Treaty, and the style of trade that it institutionalized (which Mancall contrasts with the Canton—or Treaty Port—system), may be seen as the Chinese response to increased pressure from Russian traders in the border region, with its object to limit severely rather that to encourage trade with Russia. In this document too China was technically at an advantage as nothing was said of Chinese traders entering Siberia. See "Sino-Russian

Trade," *The Chinese Economic Monthly*, vol. III, no. 6 (June 1926), pp. 232-236.

[4]Mancall, *Kiakhta Trade*, p. 48.

[5]A tentative conclusion offered (especially on the period up to 1905) in Quested, *"Matey" Imperialists?*, pp. 330-331.

[6]This might be translated as slovenly or disorderly. As with many Russian words, the original conveys the intended meaning better than its translation.

[7]See, for instance, *The Chinese Economic Monthly*, pp. 232-236; A. E. Gerasimov, *Kitaiskie Nalogi v Severnoi Man'chzhurii*. Harbin, 1923.

[8]Mancall, *Kiakhta Trade*, p. 23.

[9]Gerasimov, *Kitaiskie Nalogi*, p. 102.

[10]A. E. Gerasimov, "Ocherki Ekonomicheskogo Sostoianiia Raionov Verkhov'ev r. Sungari," *Vestnik Man'chzhurii*, no. 10, 1929, p. 55.

[11]Ministerstvo Torgovli i Promyshlennosti. Otdel Torgovli, *Po Voprosu o Polozhenii Russkoi Torgovli i Promyshlennosti v Man'chzhurii*. Petrograd(?). 1914, pp. 20-21.

[12]*O Polozhenii Russkoi Torgovli i Promyshlennosti v Man'chzhurii*. Zapiski Kharbinskogo Birzhevogo Komiteta, Harbin, 1913, pp. 8-9, 13.

[13]Ministerstvo Torgovli, *Po Voprosu*, pp. 1-3.

[14]Cited in B. H. Sumner, "Tsardom and Imperialism in the Far East And Middle East, 1880-1914" (Raleigh Lecture on History), *Proceedings* of the British Academy, vol. XXVII (1940), p. 14.

[15]*Ibid.*, pp. 19-21.

[16]Best summed up in new Minister of the Interior Plehve's statement of 7 May 1903 to the special council: "Russia has been made by bayonets not diplomacy...and we must decide the questions at issue with China and Japan with bayonets and not with diplomatic pens." Cited in *Ibid.*, p. 14.

[17]Ministerstvo Torgovli, *Po Voprosu*, p. 28.

[18]Just how sharp the margins were can be seen from the examples of October 1912, when the CER tariff was 1.5 kopeks per pud higher than that of the SMR. Despite a good harvest, which should have increased traffic by 3.4 million puds in soya beans, the difference in tariff resulted in a reduction of 670,000 puds. *Ibid.*, p. 37.

[19]*Ibid.*, p. 34.

[20]*O polozhenii*, p. 9. The document refers specifically to Witte and snipes at the changing attitude of the CER.

[21]*Ibid.*, p. 8.

[22]Sumner, *Proceedings*, p. 12.

[23] See *Vestnik Man'chzhurii* and *Ekonomicheskii Biulleten'* for full survey of activities.

[24]See Felix Patrikeeff, "Prosperity and Collapse: Banking and the Manchurian Economy in the 1920s and 1930," in *Eastern Banking: Essays in the History of the Hongkong & Shanghai Banking Corporation*, ed., Frank H. H. King. London, Athlone, 1983, pp. 265-278.

[25]*Ibid.*

[26]Gerasimov, *Kitaiskie Nalogi*, pp. 21-22.

[27]*Ibid.*, p. 24.

[28]*Ibid.*, p. 22.

[29]*Ibid.*, pp. 19-20.

[30]Ministerstvo Torgovli, *Po Voprosu*, p. 52.

[31]Aleksandr V. Marakueff, *Foreign Trade of China and its Place in World Trade.* Harbin, 1927, pp. 64 and 66.

[32]Ministerstvo Torgovli, *Po Voprosu*, p. 43 (figure refers to Harbin).

[33]*O Polozhenii*, pp. 14-15.

[34]In 1913 the interest rate (including brokerage was about 18 percent. Fixed assets, on the other hand, had a return of 15 to 20 percent gross. *Ibid.*, pp. 6-7.

[35]Gerasimov, *Kitaiskie Nalogi*, pp. 19-20.

[36]Alexander M. Baykov, *Soviet Foreign Trade.* Princeton: Princeton University Press, 1946, pp. 4-6.

[37]Dairen's share of the import market had grown from 68 percent (prior to WWI) to 92.5 percent (in 1920). A. A. Neopihanoff "The Development of North Manchuria," *Chinese Economic Journal*, vol. II, no. 3 (March 1928), pp. 264-265.

[38]"Flour Market in North Manchuria," *Chinese Economic Bulletin*, vol. XI, no. 33 (1927), pp. 16-18. When demand made itself felt in Siberia, prices for wheat from the Heiho region would shoot from $0.70-$1.00 to $2 per pud. This was to have a serious (and chronic) effect on Chinese flour mills in Heiho. Competition between the main mills was cutthroat, upping the purchase price of grain and forcing down the price of flour when it went to market (frequently the wheat was purchased from farmers at $1.50-$1.80 and sold as flour at a little less than $2.00 per pud).

[39]Russian flour milling, which was hardest hit by the closure, took the lead in this by constructing warehouses on the Chinese bank of the Amur to allow transport of flour to Russian soil as contraband (or as baked bread). Ministerstvo Torgovli, *Po Voprosu*, p. 40.

[40]HSBC Archives, S/O Files, Minter to Wood, 22 November 1924.

[41]HSBC closed its office finally on 30 September 1925. The territory was starved of financial services, reflected in a bank officer's comment in late 1924 that "The officials at present are ready to do practically anything to get us to stay in Vladivostock [sic] and would no doubt like us to launch out in all directions. If we could be certain that we should not be subject to expulsion from the country at probably only a moment's notice we might take up some of the attractive line of business offering." *Ibid.*

[42]In January 1924 the manager of the Ussuri Railway informed the manager of HSBC, Harbin Branch, that he knew "positively that any interference with the Bank in Vladivostok is made by the local authorities without sanction from headquarters." HSBC S/O, Knox to Baker, 1 January 1924.

[43]N. Sizov "Ekonomicheskoe Polozhenie Severnoi Man'chzhurii," *Novyi Vostok*, no. 6, 1924, p. 147.

[44]An indication of the numbers—and chaos—involved may be seen in the

following: between 1912 and 1918 the Russian population in China increased from 45,000 to 59,719. In 1919 that figure rose to 148,170, falling to 144,413 in 1920, 68,250 in 1921, and rising again to 96,727 in 1922, after which it remained at approximately 80,000. In 1919 and 1920 the total number of Russians in China rivalled closely the largest foreign population, that of the Japanese (171,485 in 1920). For Manchurian figures, see Quested, *"Matey" Imperialists?*, pp. 221-222, 276, 289.

[45]HSBC S/O, Baker to Wood, 22 November 1922.

[46]See Patrikeeff, "Prosperity and Collapse" in *Eastern Banking,* for a more detailed discussion.

[47]Witness the Soviet attempt to break the émigrés away from the CER through Order 94 (1 July 1925), which dismissed all employees who were not Soviet or Chinese citizens. The Chinese authorities countered this by giving stateless Russian employees Chinese papers. The number of émigrés working for the Railway, therefore, remained high. See George E. Sokolsky, *Story of the Chinese Eastern Railway.* Shanghai, 1929, pp. 48-50.

[48]Baykov, *Soviet Foreign Trade*, pp. 7-17.

[49]Exports from the Soviet Union increase from 8,612,000 Hk Taels in 1924 to 11,844,000 HkT in 1925 (or from 0.85 percent to 1.25 percent of total trade). Marakueff, *Foreign Trade*, pp. 66-67.

[50]Patrikeeff, "Prosperity and Collapse" in *Eastern Banking,* p. 275.

[51]*Ibid.*, p. 269.

[52]The China Coast press was quick to pick up the slightest bit of evidence to suggest ulterior motives for Soviet commerce. In the summer of 1923, for example, the Hong Kong newspaper *South China Morning Post* published an article about Centrosoiuz being more a political institution disseminating "violent Bolshevik propaganda" than a co-operative trading society. The HSBC, which had financed a small shipment of furs to New York for them, made its position plain: "One reason [for business with] them last year was that they were reported to me as keeping out of politics in Harbin, and I have not heard otherwise since. Probably there is too much chance of trouble with the Whites. We have on occasions to deal with Bolsheviks...but we don't want to have anything more to do with the militant type than we can help." HSBC S/O, Baker to Knox, 5 June 1923.

[53]Reports on marketing of manufactures, *Ekonomicheskii Biulleten'*, 1925-1926.

[54]Just how far some Soviet officials were integrated into capitalist society in the North-Eastern provinces is shown, albeit in anecdotal form, by the following report from a Maritime Customs official seeing off Manchouli's Soviet Consul (who was returning to the Soviet Union): "He is generally very popular with all the officials here and his departure is regretted. He had a hearty send off, in fact as he remarked to me on the platform — the only people who were not present were the working classes." Official Report, Assistant in Charge of Sub-port, Manchouli, 3 June 1927.

[55]HSBC S/O Report, Wood to de Courcy, 26 July 1929.

[56]Liubimov, in *Ekonomicheskie Problemy*, concludes that only the development of the Maritime Province, in industry or agriculture, would satisfy the needs of the Ussuri Railway (p. 11). The province's industry was too weak, however, to allow the railway

to turn in a profit (between 1922 and 1925 the number of firms in the region rose from 110 to 176, all small) (p. 47).

[57]Its main function was to serve the Manchurian export market (in beans). But as Liubimov remarks: rolling stock filled with North Manchurian surpluses reaching Vladivostok would return to Suifenho empty. Dairen had captured much of the Manchurian import traffic. *Ibid.*, p. 11.

[58]In 1928 alone exports were up by 38 percent and imports by 33 percent, *Ekonomicheskii Biulleten'*, no. 1, 1929, p. 3.

[59]Evgenii E. Iashnov, "Kriziz Sbyta i Man'chzhurskoe Sel'skokhoziaistvo," *Ekonomicheskii Biulleten'*, no. 2, 1931, pp. 5-7.

[60]Henry W. Kinney Memorandum, Dairen, 18 December 1930, pp. 1-2.

Sovietization of the Shtetl of Eastern Poland, 1939-1941

Ben-Cion Pinchuk

The small town, or *shtetl* in Yiddish, was the predominant urban element in the eastern provinces of the Polish Republic, annexed by the USSR in the Fall of 1939. These provinces had been the core of the tsarist Pale of settlement with its very high percentage of Jews. The region itself was predominantly a backward agricultural country with only scattered spots of modern urban development. For large sections of the local population, the shtetl fulfilled all the functions of a town. The purpose of the present paper is to detect the changes that took place in the small towns and its Jewish population in former Eastern Poland during the twenty-two months of Soviet rule.

The shtetl of 1939 reflected the civilization of its inhabitants as well as the economic level and cultural evolution of the surrounding agricultural population. This "overwhelmingly agricultural region was a backward area with poor transport and little contact with the outside world. The peasant of the Polesian marshes, for example, still traded in barter almost exclusively."[1] Crop production for local consumption was still the predominant form of agriculture in the eastern regions of Poland. Many of the peasants lived below "any reasonable subsistance level."[2] Eastern Galicia, which made up with the Kresy the Soviet share in the partition of Poland, was not much better off. Rural life there had changed little for centuries. Poor soils and small plots made for an impoverished peasant population. Thus, the area that was acquired by the USSR constituted one of the more backward regions in Europe.[3]

"A Jewish island in a non-Jewish ocean"; that was often the characterization of the shtetl by its inhabitants and neighbors. While here and there one could find exceptions, the Jews constituted the dominant urban element in the small towns of Poland's eastern provinces. Quite frequently they had an absolute Jewish majority and almost always they constituted the largest ethnic group.[4] The Jews were also the majority among the business owners and artisans in the small town.[5] Therefore the shtetl had definite Jewish characteristics. Synagogue, and *Mikveh* (ritual bath), *Beth-Midrash* (study-prayer house) and *Kheder* (elementary religious school) as well as other Jewish institutions were prominent features of the shtetl's landscape. So were the Jewish houses. They could easily be distinguished from those of their non-Jewish neighbors. The complexion and attire of the shtetl Jews were visibly different from those of the gentile as was their clothing. Sabbath and Jewish holidays determined, to a large extent, the rhythm of economic activity in the small town. Shops were closed on the Sabbath and no transactions were made on the Jewish holidays. Friday night candles, Jews rushing to the bath on friday noon or Khanukah candles shining for eight nights in the cold long winter evenings, and many more external manifestations of Jewish life gave a "Jewish" character to many small towns of eastern Poland.

Economically, the majority of the shtetl Jews occupied themselves with commerce, crafts and services for the surrounding peasant population. In spite of the influx of Polish settlers into the eastern provinces and their engaging in business and administration in the urban centers, the Jews still constituted over seventy percent of the commercial population[5] and over 50 percent of the crafts.[6] The predominance of the Jews in commerce and crafts was even more pronounced in the small towns that attracted but few Polish settlers. Shtetl Jews in the eastern provinces of the Polish Republic suffered, like their co-religionists in other parts of the country, from the anti-Jewish policy of the government in the thirties. The official discriminatory policy of the authorities contributed to the accelerated impoverishment of the Jewish population. The standard of living was very low and many were helped by charitable organizations. The younger generation faced a grim future with few prospects of earning a living in their native towns.

A basic feature of the Jewish shtetl community was the presence of autonomous organizations. The *Kehilla*, the general communal organization, embraced the entire Jewish community. Polish authorities granted it the right to levy taxes, and it was in charge of many of the religions, social and educational functions of the community.[7] Besides the general *Kehilla* organization, the shtetl had a great number of voluntary educational, charitable and political organizations. Many Jewish educational institutions were found even in the small towns of the eastern provinces. These included religious (*Kheders* and *Yishivot*) as well as secular Yiddish, Hebrew and Polish schools. Voluntary charitable organizations took care of different aspects of welfare: handling money donations, visiting the sick and destitute, offering help in arranging weddings, and providing food and lodging for the orphans. The elaborate philanthropic network was assisted by generous donations from overseas shtetl emigrants. Divisions within the Jewish community found their expressions in a multitude of political movements and parties. These ranged from the extremely orthodox to the completely secular, as well as Zionist and socialist parties that offered their solutions to the problems of Polish jewry. The result of this multitude of institutions, organizations, parties, etc., as well as the size of the shtetl, was an intensity of social intercourse and a strong sense of Jewish identity and cohesiveness. Intimacy and intensity of multi-faceted Jewish life were among the most impressive marks of the Jewish shtetl community.

Twenty-two months of Soviet rule changed radically the shtetl community, its internal structure, way of life and even to some extent its external appearance. The new rulers pretended to transform the entire political, economic, social and cultural structure of the local population. Sovietization meant an attempt to change the structure of the annexed territories to conform to the regime existing in the USSR at the time. All of the ethnic groups living in the provinces underwent radical changes in their way of life. The Jewish shtetl communities, because of their social and economic idiosyncracies, as well as the traditional attitude of Soviet communism towards Jewish nationality and religion, suffered mortal blows to their very existence as a distinct ethnic-religious entity. Soviet policy destroyed within a short period the very basis of a separated and distinct Jewish existence.

Economically the shtetl did not change its basic role. Modern urban centers did not develop within the rather short period of Soviet rule. Hence, the small town continued to provide services to the surrounding agricultural population. The quantity of services undertaken by the new regime was much larger than that of its Polish predecessor. The scope of state activities in the fields of education, health, welfare, entertainment, propaganda, etc., was much enlarged in the new Soviet territories. Quite naturally, the network of small towns spread throughout the region served as centers of the Soviet apparatus established in the area. Yet, while the basic function of the shtetl in the local economy had not changed, its internal economic structure was completely transformed. As mentioned above, the vast majority of the Jewish shtetl belonged to the lower middle-class of independent small shopkeepers, peddlers, and artisans. That class was destined to disappear according to some of the basic tenets of Soviet communism.

After a very short transitional period, that lasted approximately until January 1940, the new rulers pursued a systematic policy of eliminating private commerce and at the same time forcing the artisans into newly formed cooperatives.[8] The high concentration of shtetl Jews in occupations defined by the regime as "unproductive" or even as "class enemy," made their adjustment to the new economic system particularly painful. No conscious attempt was made by the Soviet rulers to facilitate the transition to the new order, nor did they take into account the pecularities of the Jewish economic structure; hence the extraordinary hardships encountered by large sections of the shtetl Jews, particularly in the initial stages of building the new regime. There were those who, in spite of great efforts on their part, could not find their place in the Soviet economy. The more affluent, the old, and certain professions such as lawyers, and the cultural-religious intelligentsia, found it very difficult to earn a living. However, they constituted a minority among the Jewish shtetl community.[9]

Statistics on the developments in the annexed territories are completely missing. Nevertheless, one can reach sound conclusions as to the broad trends, and draw a quite reliable portrait of what happened. The impression one gets is that, by and large, the majority of shtetl Jews eventually found a place in the new economic system. This was particularly true of the majority of the poor and of the young in the community. The expanding Soviet bureaucracy and services absorbed many shtetl Jews. All legal discrimination, that denied Jews under the old regime access to government and public jobs, was now abolished. While Jews were still informally discriminated against in jobs of political importance or high visibility, it affected only few. In lower and middle-ranking jobs, particularly those that required some literary or professional training, Jews were accepted. This occurred because the local Ukrainian and Belorussian populations quite frequently lacked the necessary educational qualifications, while the Polish population was resentful towards the new rulers and not trusted by them. Many former shopkeepers and employees in commercial establishments found jobs in the consumer cooperatives and in the highly bureaucratized supply network established by the Soviet authorities.[10] Without open coercion, but rather through a combination of economic pressure and enticements, large numbers of artisans were forced to end their independent and frequently precarious existence and join the newly formed establishments. There were also artisans who found employment in government factories and enterprises.[11]

The young shtetl generation, those in their late teens and twenties, who had faced a bleak future in anti-semitic Poland, adjusted best to Soviet rule. Study opportunities formerly closed to Jews by the *numerus clausus*, government jobs and professions formerly denied, became accessible for the first time. "The youth of the shtetl literally bloomed," noted an inhabitant of Lubach, and he was echoed by many others from different parts of the new Soviet territories.[12]

Integration into the Soviet system cost the shtetl Jewish community dearly, especially in terms of Jewish identity and community cohesiveness.

The opposition of Soviet communism to any expression of Jewish nationalism, and Moscow's denial of the desirability of a separate and distinct Jewish ethinc-religious existence, had a long history before 1939. The goal of the Stalininst line that prevailed in the thirties, was to assimilate individual Jews, as fast as possible, into the surrounding Soviet society. At the same time, the regime tried to eliminated institutions and organizations of every kind that facilitated and expressed Jewish distinctiveness. Stalinism, in its attempt to impose on the peoples of the USSR a monolithic centralized regime, strove to achieve complete integration of the Jewish community into the Soviet state, while completely disregarding its peculiarities and problems.[13]

Centuries of extraterritorial existence as a distinct ethnic-religious entity resulted in the evolution of an elaborate and intricate structure of autonomous institutions and organizations in the Jewish community. Adherence to basic tenets of Judaism and the autonomous institutional system provided the framework for the continued collective existence of the Jewish community. For the individual Jew they gave a sense of security, direction and purpose. Soviet rule destoyed almost overnight the institutional-organizational structure of Jewish collective existence. The elaborate system of formal and informal organizations and institutions (secular, religious, political and cultural) disappeared almost completely within a short time after the entry of the Red Army into the Polish eastern provinces. A much smaller religious system, and a denationalized educational network that used Yiddish as the language of instruction, were the only Jewish collective expressions left in the shtetl. At the same time, much attention was paid to imbuing the shtetl community with Soviet ideology, values and norms.

Political parties of the former regime had no existence in the communist state. The numerous political organizations that existed in the shtetl, reflecting socio-economic and ideological differences within the Jewish community, dissolved almost spontaneously. Whether extreme Orthodox or secular Zionist, liberal or social democrat, none was tolerated by the new regime. The Jewish community was aware of that attitude. Official party organizations ceased to meet; the leaders either fled abroad, went into hiding, were arrested or exiled by the Soviet authorities.[14] The communist party and its youth movement, the Komsomol, replaced the former political organizations for adults and youth. Jews and non-Jews were, at least formally, included in the same political movement. Jewish autonomy suffered the same fate as its political organizations. Its heart, the *Kehilla*, with its dependent religious, educational, welfare, and subsidiaries, was dissolved. Its right to levy taxes was abolished, its leaders disappeared in one way or another, and its official status was rescinded with the abolition of the Polish legal system.[15] The leadership either ran away, hid, or was systematically removed by the Soviet authorities. For the first time in shtetl history, there existed no organization that expressed the collective identity of the Jewish community. In time of trial, the individual Jew had nowhere to turn for collective deliberation, advice and action.

On the face of it, religion fared better under the communist rulers. People were allowed to practice their religions and the religious functionaries were usually left alone. Some synagogues were confiscated and used for other purposes, yet many were left for the believers.[16] In spite of the lack of overt, certainly large-scale, suppression of religion, there was a drastic decrease in all forms of religious observance. It was made abundantly clear to the shtetl community that religious practice was considered by the new rulers as an act of defiance and would certainly be a serious obstacle to success in Soviet society. Anti-religious propaganda demonstrated, particularly to the young, that success in the new system meant staying away from overt religious observance. A drastic decrease in all forms of religious observance could be noticed in the shtetl. The young stayed away from the synagogue, which became a refuge, mainly of the older generation.[17] It should be noted that for many shtetl Jews, the coming of the Soviet regime accelerated rather than created the process of secularization. For many of the younger generation, the hold of tradition and religion was too weak to deter them from taking advantage of the new opportunities opened by the Soviet rulers.

In the field of education, the communist authorities provided a Soviet substitute to the former system. The declared policy was to provide every ethnic group with schools in its "mother tongue." Primary and secondary schools in Yiddish, using the phonetic script, were formed in the many small towns of the former Polish provinces. Hebrew, the study of Jewish history and the Bible were removed from the curriculum. The language of instruction, and highly selected and purged literary texts were the main Jewish elements in the new school system. The schools served as centers of indoctrination against Jewish religion and ethnicity. Even in this form the de-nationalized school system showed clear signs of decline in the second year of Soviet rule. In many small towns with large Jewish communities, and even Jewish majorities, Yiddish schools became Ukrainian, Belorussian or Russian institutions.[18]

Demographically, the small towns of the former Polish provinces underwent little change. There were no large-scale population movements in either direction. Time was too short for that. By and large, the Jewish population remained the dominant ethnic element. Yet the shtetl changed and lost much of its Jewish character. Gone were the external landmarks that characterized the shtetl for many generations. The market place, the small shops, the artisans' workshops and stands all disappeared with the establishment of the Soviet economic order. Frequently, the market place turned into a square with a newly erected statue of one of the Soviet heroes. The few synagogues that still opened their doors for prayer and study were just a poor reminder of the many Jewish public and religious buildings that dominated the shtetl. Sabbath and the many Jewish holidays ceased to be public events that determined the economic rhythm of the shtetl. When celebrated at all, they were confined to the privacy of homes, away from the ever watchful new rulers.

The changed external appearance reflected more profound transformations that took place in the life of the Jewish shtetl community. The old economic order was destroyed and with it, the independent Jewish small shopkeepers and artisans. However, even under the Soviet economic system, most shtetl Jews remained in the services that the small town supplied to the surrounding countryside. Jews were still absent from direct production, agriculture and industry. The very rich among the shtetl Jews disappeared, but they had been very few. Albeit, at a low standard of living, the majority found its place in the new economy. The younger generation found the Soviet system more open and promising than anything they had known before. To succeed in the Soviet state many were ready to abandon religion and the traditional way of life. This willingness was not new, it had been only drastically accelerated under the transformed conditions. Religious observance was an obstacle for advancement in the USSR, and the shtetl Jews knew it. The result was the dramatic decrease of all forms of religious observance, which was still widespread before the Soviet annexation. The de-nationalized Yiddish schools, that served mainly as vehicles of anti-religious and anti-national indoctrination, were poor substitutes for the many religious and secular teaching institutions that had existed before. Assimilation, rather than the continued collective existence of the Jewish community, was the goal of the communist rulers and the schools had to serve that aim.

Destruction of the elaborate system of Jewish autonomy in the shtetl was the most basic transformation introduced by the Soviet regime. For the Jewish community it was a structural change that threatened its very existence as a distinct collective entity. Centuries-old institutions and organizations that facilitated the existence of the Jewish community and preservation of an individual's Jewish identity, were destroyed overnight. In June 1941, on the eve of the German invasion, the small towns in the former Polish provinces still had a very high proportion of Jews among their inhabitants, but gone was the intimacy and cohesiveness of the community. The shtetl had lost much of its Jewish character while its

Jewish community had lost its instruments of expressing its distinct identity and assuring its further existence.

Haifa University

Notes

[1]A. Polonsky, *Politics in Independent Poland, 1921-1939.* New York: Oxford University Press, 1972, p. 5.

[2]J. Taylor, *The Economic Development of Poland, 1919-1950.* Ithaca: Cornell University Press, 1952, p. 79.

[3]*Ibid.*, p. 24.

[4]R. Mahler, *Yihudei Polin bein shtei milkhamot olam* (Jews in Poland between the Two World-wars: a Socio-Economic History on a Statistical Basis). Tel-Aviv, 1968, pp. 28-36.

[5]B. D. Weinryb, "Polish Jews under Soviet Rule" in P. Meyer *et al.*, *The Jews in the Soviet Satellites.* Syracuse: 1953, p. 331.

[7]H. M. Rabinowicz, *The Legacy of Polish Jewry. A History of Polish Jews in the Interwar Years, 1919-1939.* New York: 1965, p. 121.

[8]N. P. Vakar, *Byelorussia.* Cambridge, Mass.: 1956, pp. 162-164.

[9]A major source for this article were the almost two hundred *Memorial Books* for the Jewish communities in the Eastern provinces. On the economic hardships of the initial stages of sovietization, see among others: *Sefer Zikaron Dubno* (Memorial Book of Dubno). Tel Aviv, 1966, p. 646; *Pinkas Kleck* (Kleck's Book). Tel Aviv, 1959, p. 85; *Grodno: Entsiklopedia shel galuiot* (Grodno: An Encyclopedia of the Diaspora). Jerusalem, 1973, pp. 139-140; *Pinkas Slonim* (The Slonim Book), Vol. II. Tel Aviv, 1962, p. 34. Also, *Shoat Yehudei Polin.* Jerusalem, 1940, pp. 58-93, which contains contemporary reports on territories occupied by German and Soviet forces.

[10]*Rishonim lamered, Lachwa* (The First to Rebel, Lachwa). Jerusalem, 1957, p. 37; *Sefer Stryj* (Book of Stryj). Tel Aviv, 1962, p. 161; *Geven amol a Yiddish Shtetl Lubach* (There was once a Jewish Shtetl Lubach). Tel Aviv, 1971, p. 35; *Sefer izkor likhilat Sarny* (Memorial Book of the Sarny Community). Tel Aviv, 1966, p. 79.

[11]*Janow al yad Pinsk* (Janow near Pinsk). Jerusalem, 1969, p. 225; *Kleck*, p. 90; *Stryj*, p. 161; *Sarny*, p. 79.

[12]*Lubach*, p. 40. Also *Sefer Zikaron likhilat iwie* (Memorial Book of the Iwie Community). Tel Aviv, 1968, p. 381; *Sefer Ilia* (Ilia Book). Tel Aviv, 1962, p. 317; *Sefer Zikaron likhilat Lipnishok* (Memorial Book of the Lipnishok Community). Tel Aviv, 1968, p. 135.

[13]Z. Gitelman, *Jewish Nationality and Soviet Politics*, Princeton: Princeton University Press, 1972, pp. 485-510.

[14]P. Shwartz, *Dos iz geven der onheib* (This was the Beginning). New York, 1943, p. 330; *Sefer Lida* (The Lida Book). Tel Aviv, 1970, pp. 256-260; *Shoat Polin*, p. 36; Weinryb, p. 330.

[15]A. Zak, *Knecht zenen mir geven* (We were Slaves). Buenos Aires, 1956, vol. I, p.

79; *Sefer Sokolovka* (Sokolvka Book). Jerusalem, 1968, pp. 343-344; *Shoat Polin*, pp. 43-44; *Grodno*, p. 505; *Sarny*, p. 75.

[16]*Janow*, p. 225; *Kleck*, p. 90; *Stryj*, p. 161; *Sarny*, p. 79.

[17]*Sefer Mir* (The Book of Mir). Jerusalem, 1962, p. 586; *Sefer Volozhin* (The Book of Volozhin). Tel Aviv, 1970, p. 532; *Janow*, p. 320; *Lachwa*, p. 37; *Iwie*, p. 295; *Lubach*, p. 38.

[18]*Sefer Zikaron Dubno* (Memorial Book of Dubno). Tel Aviv, 1966, pp. 649-650; *Iwie*, p. 389; *Kleck*, pp. 92, 86; *Lubach*, pp. 33-34.

The Russian Revolution and Stalinism: A Political Problem and Its Historiographic Content

Michal Reiman

A discussion has been revived in recent years about the relationship between Lenin and Stalin, between the Leninist and Stalinist periods. The impulse has come mainly from non-conformist, dissident literature and, more particularly, from Russian literature published in exile. This discussion differs from those of earlier years. After the Twentieth Party Congress (1956) not only left-wing but even liberal historians tended to separate Lenin from Stalin, place them and their respective periods in a different light, and to describe their relationship as one of contradiction. A different tendency predominates today: the Leninist period is being compared to the Stalinist period, the differences between Lenin and Stalin are being evaluated as insignificant. The roots of Stalinism are thought to lie in the 1917 October Revolution and the seizure of power by the Bolsheviks. This is not an entirely new tendency; in earlier years it was propounded by a group of authors who regarded Stalinism as a variant of a totalitarian system. Now this view is widely accepted in the non-conformist movement of the Soviet bloc countries. It has been supplemented by new lines of argument, and this has given it greater strength and impact.

It is not difficult to detect the causes of these changes in the political literature. The 1950s and 1960s had been strongly influenced by hopes for positive changes in the USSR; Stalinism was thus able to appear as a merely transitory phase in Soviet history to be overcome sooner or later. In the 1970s, however, the Brezhnev era revealed the fallacy of such hopes. An anti-Stalinist concept did not gain the upper hand. The Soviet system proved incapable of undergoing more thorough socio-economic, let alone political, reforms. The dynamics of development of the USSR slackened considerably, while politically motivated repression increased. In addition, foreign policy took on visibly imperial features (Czechoslovakia 1968, the Sino-Soviet conflict, Afghanistan, Poland, etc.).

The new stage in the discussion on the Russian Revolution, on Lenin and Stalin and the respective periods, has a distinctly political background. Mounting criticism of Soviet communism, present and past, is evident not only in the conservative and liberal but even in left-wing literature including its Eurocommunist component. Political aspects inevitably lead to a host of biased interpretations, exaggerations, inaccuracies or even deliberate distortions; but the fundamental trend of the discussion deserves close attention.

The point of departure in dealing with the complex of questions raised in the present discussion is the approach to the October Revolution, its nature, significance and outcome. The first problem one must examine is the approach of the Bolsheviks to that revolution, since it determined the character of the policy and the actions of the Bolsheviks during the Leninist as well as the Stalinist periods, and the complex arguments and logical procedures which were used to justify and support this policy and these actions.

It is well known that at the outset the Bolsheviks regarded October 1917 as a socialist revolution. This was an article of faith. Doubts about the fundamental course of the revolution were not tolerated. This gradually placed a firm seal not only on Bolshevik but on all political thinking at the time, on the concepts and categories which have prevailed ever since in the assessment of the revolution. It is, however, interesting to see how this concept came about.

Original Marxism — and the Bolsheviks were a Marxist party — maintained that a socialist revolution was determined by a high degree of development of the forces of production and by the exhaustion of the possibilities offered them by capitalism. Russia, however, was a country at a rather backward stage of capitalism, by European standards. Soviet historiographers do speak, with hindsight, of an intermediate stage of capitalism and of a relatively advanced capitalist imperialism[1]; but it is worth remembering that such conclusions do not change the nature of the basic assessment. As regards social labor productivity, Russia was far behind the foremost capitalist states; however, since the time of the Russian Revolution capitalism has seen further radical developments without exhausting its possibilities.

The methods by which the Bolsheviks arrived at their conclusions about the socialist character of their revolution is revealing from our point of view. The history of Russian Social Democracy, and thus of Bolshevism, began roughly in the middle of the 1880s when a bitter struggle flared up again between the *Narodniki* (Populists) and the Marxists on whether Russia had embarked, or would embark, on a capitalist road. In the 1890s Lenin was among those actively involved in this controversy.[2] On merit, the Marxists who spoke of the development of capitalism were right; but it must be pointed out that a mere twenty of twenty-five years before the 1917 Revolution the consequences of capitalist development in everyday life were not evident enough to make a complex system of demonstrating the thesis unnecessary.

It is a fact, however, that capitalist relations were to make exceptional progress in the subsequent twenty years. This changed the image of Russia visibly. The new development did not last long enough to modify the entire productive, social or cultural structure. There was no divergence of views about the backwardness of the country among politicians of all the decisive trends. The Social Democrats—both Bolsheviks and Mensheviks, with the exception of Trotskii whose "permanent revolution" reckoned with a transition to socialism—agreed that the impending revolution in Russia would be bourgeois-democratic. They differed mainly in their evaluation of its driving forces: the Mensheviks looked ahead to the rule of the liberal bourgeoisie, the Bolsheviks to a revolutionary democratic rule of the workers and peasants.[3]

The Bolsheviks changed their position only in the course of the 1917 Revolution. The reasons were sufficiently clear; they were formulated by none other than Stalin, on behalf of Lenin, at the Sixth Congress of the RSDWP (B) in August 1917:[4] While it was true that capitalism had developed to a small degree, the foundations of the capitalist organization of production had been shaken to such an extent that state intervention in the economic sphere would be essential. The degree of political freedom that had been attained would facilitate action, and the workers were widely organized. The seizure of power would amount to a socialist revolution and it would be an unforgivable mistake and pedantry not to exploit this possibility.

The Bolsheviks had naturally realized at the outset that in a take-over motivated in this way the attainibility of its socio-economic objectives would remain an unanswered question. The matter had not been discussed in greater detail because it had been assumed that the problem would be solved by revolutions taking place in a number of more advanced countries, which the Bolsheviks anticipated in the immediate future. A deeper reflection was not to take place until after 1923 when it had become evident that the prospect of an early world revolution was not realistic.

The awareness of Russian backwardness remained very strong in the party, yet to admit the impossibility of building socialism in an isolated Russia would have amounted to declaring that the Bolshevik policy in the revolution had been mistaken or that the victims of the cruel civil war had died in vain. The notion of building socialism in one country, defended by Stalin and N. I. Bukharin, prevailed in the end. It necessarily hinged on the premise that Russia had all that was needed to build socialism, and that the ideas about Russian backwardness in the previous version were wrong. This was the essential content of a bitter struggle between the party leadership and the left opposition (Trotskii, G. E. Zinoviev, L. B. Kamenev), which ended in 1927, ten years after the October takeover.[5]

This development of Bolshevik thinking reached its climax in 1936. In the midst of a wave of political terror and trials of former party leaders, Stalin declared that the foundations of socialism had been created in the USSR; the Soviet Union had entered the phase of completing the construction of a socialist society and the gradual transition to a communist society.[6] In the course of a mere forty years or so Bolshevik thinking had undergone quite a remarkable change: from providing evidence of the existence of capitalism in Russia, it had come to provide evidence of the existence of socialism in that country.

The road along which Bolshevik thinking had advanced suggests that, in assessing the character of the revolution and the subsequent development of society, both Lenin and Stalin were motivated in equal measure by an interest in seizing, maintaining and consolidating power. Their evaluation of the socio-economic realities and the application of these realities in practical policies were subordinated to this interest. The attitude towards these realities and their nature thus became the central problem of Bolshevik policy.

The 1917 Russian Revolution was a peculiar combination of an immature bourgeois revolution of modern times and a plebeian revolution. In October 1917 this combination was untied in favor of a plebeian revolution.[7] The influence of modern times on this revolution can also be detected in what became its special feature: that it was headed by a party with a clearly socialist program.

If one uses the term in its original sense, the October overthrow was not a socialist revolution because Russia was lacking the conditions necessary to carry out such a revolution. Moreover, Russia and, subsequently, the USSR were on the threshold of a long period of maturation of their economy, social structure and culture, which has not been entirely achieved even today. The 1917 overthrow was not a socialist revolution because post-revolutionary Russia and the USSR have been unable to escape the social effects of their immaturity, a new polarization of poverty and wealth, the growth and institutionalization of a new social differentiation; unable to avoid the revival of brutal forms of social and political oppression.

I disagree with the view, occasionally expressed in the present discussions, that October 1917 was a tragic historic derailment brought about by the policy of the Bolsheviks. It reflects an unwillingness to accept history as a specific and inevitable combination of progress and regression, of positive and negative social phenomena and events, the alternation of periods of rise and decline. The October overthrow took place under conditions of profound national catastrophe caused by the collapse of the old order during the war. Its driving force consisted in part of the workers and lower urban strata, the soldiers and sailors whom the war had permanently uprooted from their former environment, as well as sections of the poorest peasant population. The ideas and interests guiding these strata were often miles removed from modern society; indeed, they were often in stark contrast to it. As a result, October 1917 not only buried the vestiges of the pre-revolutionary system but totally destroyed the hitherto unconsolidated and incompleted edifice of a modern industrial society in Russia. This gave the October overthrow its highly destructive, regressive features.

This raises the question of the true role of socialist ideas in Russia, a question that occupies a prominent place in contemporary discussions. Certain authors regard the application of these ideas as one of the decisive causes, if not the determining cause, of the development towards Stalinism; they see it as an element linking Lenin and Stalin, and as a link between the Leninist and the Stalinist eras. This opinion has one fundamental flaw: it approaches the problem mainly in a negative manner, and fails to provide a convincing answer to the question as to how and why socialist ideas were able to create the framework and permanent forms of the existence of society if they were in stark contradiction with the reality of the country.

The role of socialist ideas in post-revolutionary society was probably determined originally by two factors. The first was that the Revolution was exceptionally devastating. It destroyed from top to bottom, not only the former institutions and mechanisms of political and public life, but also the mechanisms and forms of organization of the economy and production processes, the mechanisms and forms of organization of social relations, of science and culture, the relations and ties between the nationalities and ethnic groups in the former empire. The work of destruction was completed by the civil war which swept virtually the entire territory of that empire. The most basic needs of the population could not be satisfied. Millions of people starved to death or died as a result of epidemics; further millions lived on the brink of starvation.

Society gradually became plebeian. The wealthy and educated strata were crushed, often physically eliminated, or driven abroad. The former forms of ownership relations in large-scale production were liquidated together with the social basis of their possible restoration. Society was placed in a situation where it was compelled to build the forms and mechanisms of its future existence from scratch. It had to build entirely its macrostructure as well as certain elements of its microstructure.

The second factor was that, in view of the conditions of power, only the Bolsheviks were able to undertake such a revival. One cannot regard the Bolsheviks as a mature and competent force fully aware of the peculiarities and complexity of the historical situation and tasks. They lacked practical experience, and the knowledge or habits to enable them to organize and run society; they lacked a culture of management or an adequate culture of social behavior and conduct. In most cases they even lacked elementary education. Not even the most educated representatives of Bolshevik summit – Lenin, Trotskii, Bukharin, Kamenev, Zinoviev, A. I. Rykov – possessed the necessary knowledge and experience. Their experience and knowledge were predominantly theoretical.

The Bolsheviks were a plebian party which had a plebian vision of the world, highlighted by a hatred of, and opposition to, the upper strata of society, exasperated by the cruelty of the civil war and the hostility of the surrounding "capitalist" world. This resulted in a widespread extreme rejection of everything that characterized the old society. The Bolsheviks also lacked positive ideas as to what should be put into practice. In this situation, theory and doctrinal socialist ideas began to play a unique role, unlikely to be repeated in history. They served the Bolsheviks as a singular substitute for their lack of knowledge about the real course of industrial or social processes, as well as for the lack of experience or habits regarding their organization and management. This explains the notorious attempt made in 1918-1921 to introduce communist production and distribution in a starving and totally disrupted Russia – the so-called War Communism. This meant in practice that the government confiscated foodstuffs and agricultural products from the farmers and distributed them in factories, among the workers and the working population in the towns and cities. The same distribution was to apply to industrial products which the nationalization of industry had made the property of the state. The police persecuted private trade, and it was intended in the near future to abolish money and a monetary economy.

This utopian and wholly amateurish approach to the organization and running of society could not last for long. It aroused widespread opposition, resulting in large peasant uprisings and the revolt of Kronstadt sailors in March 1921. The economic consequences were extremely serious as well. The system of War Communism collapsed while economic and social policy had to be adapted to the reality of post-revolutionary social relations. The former role of theory was substantially reduced, though theory had already influenced the shape of the basic structures and mechanisms of the newly built society as well as the forms in which this society, or rather its ruling party, perceived the accumulated problems and attempted to deal with them.

I have tried to outline the fundamental relationship between the character of the revolution and the nature of its thinking. It contained a deep contradiction—politics was deprived of the possibility to express its objective and intentions, or the character of social reality in adequate notions and categories. The contradiction underlying the nature of the revolution itself was even more relevant. The revolution had established and egalitarian, plebian model of society based on the dismantling of the pre-revolutionary forms of industrial civilization. The objectives which it had knowingly set for itself were meant to secure rapid growth and development. These objectives could not be achieved within the framework of the social relations which the revolution had originally established. Both contradictions mentioned were present, though to a differing degree, both in Lenin's era and in Stalin's. They formed the basis of the accumulation of negative social phenomena and eventually led to the emergence of the Stalinist regime.

The political literature of the 1960s and 1970s emphasized the differences marking the respective political attitudes of Lenin and Stalin. In this light, Stalin's leading position in the party could in itself appear as the point of departure towards Stalinism. More recent literature has not basically modified this stance. It has presented a harsher evaluation of the Leninist era and made Lenin personally responsible for Stalin's rise. The difference between Lenin and Stalin has thus become of little consequence.

The problem of the relationship between the Leninist and the Stalinist eras and of the political and personal relations between Lenin and Stalin is neither simple nor unequivocal. In the first place, the Leninist era is not homogeneous when judged in terms of the policies pursued. It is divided into two stages by the year 1921. Its first stage, in which the "War Communism" policy was applied, is characterized by its extreme cruelty, by the vast scale of every type of violence, by the application of bureaucratic and military methods as well as by large-scale, socially motivated, terror. A turn occurred in the second stage. The New Economic Policy (NEP) was introduced: private trade and markets were once more legalized, production was revived and the material situation of the population began to improve. The scale of socially motivated violence diminished rapidly, and society returned to peace-time conditions. It is important to point out that it was this turn—the second half of Lenin's era (1921-1922) when Lenin was already seriously ill—that provided the basis of a positive assessment of Lenin's economic and social policy.

A further circumstance is no less important: the Stalinist era was not internally homogeneous, either. The Leninist period was not followed immediately, at least not linearly, by a rise of what we term Stalinism today. Shortly after Lenin's death there was a further intensive expansion of NEP, the social situation calmed down, the material position of wide sections of the population improved, and there was greater social and legal security. NEP reached its climax in 1925, and it was only later that complications set it. The turn did not occur until 1928-1929, which marked the beginning of the actual Stalinist period. Thus, when positive assessments of Lenin's activities are made today it should be noted that the Stalinist era has, paradoxically, contributed to this being so. Without the five or six years of NEP following on Lenin's withdrawal from politics, Lenin's turn in 1921 would have remained a short-lived episode and would hardly have received major attention.

The complexity of the real relationship between the Leninist and Stalinist eras becomes even more evident if one makes an unbiased analysis of the content of the political differences dividing Lenin and Stalin in 1922. This is all the more important since various authors frequently use these differences to argue that the transition from Lenin to Stalin was a transition from a correct Leninist concept to an incorrect Stalinist one. The differences concerned three sets of questions: the nature and objectives of the nationalities policy, the concept of building socio-economic relations, and the methods of securing the internal stability of the party and its leadership. In addition, there was Lenin's unpublished proposal to remove Stalin from the post of General Secretary of the Central Committee of the Russian Communist Party (B).[8]

The nationalities question provoked the sharpest clashes, probably because the situation in that sphere offered the best opportunity for attacking Stalin's position of power. In September 1922 a commission of the Central Committee headed by Stalin worked out a proposal for the merger into one state of several Soviet Republics until then formally autonomous: Russia, Ukraine, Belorussia, and the Transcaucasian Federation. The non-Russian Republics were meant to enter the Russian Federation as autonomous formations. Lenin, who had not initially been involved in these projects because of a stroke, objected. He maintained that the proposal violated the principle of equality. He therefore recommended the establishment of a new federal state: the Union of Soviet Republics. Despite Stalin's objections, the Central Committee accepted Lenin's recommendation. That was not the end of the problem, however, because Lenin's recommendation implicitly questioned further aspects of the solution of the nationalities problem as it had been applied until then.

The Federation of the Transcaucasian Republics—Georgia, Armenia and Azerbaijan—was formed in March 1922, at a time when Lenin was too ill to participate fully in everyday political life. Its establishment was justified by the need to unify the modest resources and forces of these Republics; but real power in the Federation was in the hands of the Transcaucasian Regional Committee of the CPR(B) and the federal government. The individual Republics were deprived of the possibility of defending their own interests and solving their own problems. This produced discontent, which was particularly strong in Georgia. When it was decided to form the USSR the Central Committee of the Georgian Communist Party demanded the dissolution of the Transcaucasian Federation and the accession of the Transcaucasian Republics of the USSR. This demand seemed quite justified as there was no reason why Georgia, Armenia, or Azerbaijan should not have had the same rights as Russia, Ukraine or Belorussia. A different view prevailed in the Moscow Central Committee and in the Transcaucasian Party Committee. They insisted on maintaining the Transcaucasian Federation. The demands of the Central Committee of the Georgian Communist Party were turned down, and the Central Committee of that party resigned in protest.

Lenin was worried by developments in the Transcaucasian region. He was concerned about the brutality with which the representatives of the Central Committee of the Georgian Communist Party had been treated and was afraid that this was a manifestation of Russian great-power chauvinism. He demanded an investigation and remedy. The various commissions despatched from Moscow did not heed Lenin's intentions. This made him indignant and he blamed Stalin and several other leaders for the situation that had arisen. He intended to accuse his opponents of chauvinism at the Party Congress in the spring of 1923 but was prevented by a stroke, which finally excluded him from political life.[9]

The unresolved clash between Lenin and Stalin on the nationalities question has been widely discussed in political literature. It could have led to Stalin's departure from his post. Lenin's proposals and recommendations are generally assessed favorably. Yet these assessments often have one flaw—they do not identify the root of the matter: the concentration of power in the hands of the Central Committee and the Politburo in Moscow, which in turn severely limited the rights of the Soviet Republics and provided the basis for great-power chauvinism. Despite their great significance, Lenin's reservations about Stalin were brought to bear only on minor points.

The problem of the implementation of NEP was far more important for the future development of the social and political situation. The serious contradictions on this issue were not brought into the open or clearly formulated at the time for one reason or another, which is why they have escaped the attention of many authors. Only differences on preserving the monopoly of foreign trade were discussed. In October 1922 the Central Committee approved a proposal, backed by Stalin, to slacken the foreign trade monopoly in order to facilitate the expansion of economic relations with other countries. Lenin, supported by Trotskii, obtained the reversal of this situation since he feared that the weak Soviet economy would be placed at the mercy of foreign capital. Though this was a significant problem, it was only one of many.

A more intensive reconstruction of the economy on the basis of NEP began in the autumn of 1921 but ran up against exceptionally grave difficulties. Industrial production remained insignificant, agriculture was hit by the bad harvest of 1921, and large territories were affected by a famine that cost the country more than five million lives. Industrial enterprises had to make immense efforts and suffer great losses to master the new situation of the market. Yet the market was utterly restricted and a barter economy continued to predominate. There was no confidence in the legal system. Despite great endeavors, the government did not succeed in persuading foreign companies to place investments in Russia, while the extremely limited entrepreneurial interests within the country concentrated chiefly on trade.

Opinions on how to proceed differed widely. The government's economic positions were not seriously threatened by capitalism for the moment. The disastrous state of the economy and extreme shortages presented a far greater danger. Some Bolshevik politicians saw a way out in giving greater scope to market relations. This was designed to create a stimulus for a faster rise of production and a recovery of finance and of the currency. Proposals to slacken the monopoly of foreign trade, discussed as early as the spring of 1922, were also part of these endeavors. These proposals were opposed by another, originally weaker, group of leaders. They feared the economic consequences of adapting industry to the market and insisted on the principle of a rigid plan, i.e. on elements of a barter economy. They had an exaggerated fear of the social effects of a market economy, social differentiation and the rise of capitalist enterprises.

Lenin's attitude towards NEP was not narrow-minded; he came out against those who were warned against NEP from left-wing positions. On the other hand, he was not tempted by the purely economic advantages of a market economy but by the socio-political aspect of the matter, and by the prospect of removing the tension in relations with the peasantry.

He was afraid that under conditions of the market small-scale agricultural production might well escape the control and regulating influence of the government.

Certain essential factors in Lenin's political development which frequently escape scholarly attention deserve mention. When Lenin returned to Moscow in the spring of 1922 to resume his political activities after his illness, he became alarmed about, and opposed to plans to expand NEP which had gained ground in the party. He reacted to them by putting forward the slogan "an end to retreat." This could only be interpreted as opposing the further expansion of the sphere of market relations. He wanted the party to focus its efforts on improving the quality of the administrative and economic apparatus and on fighting bureaucracy. It was also his intention that the government should rapidly take trade under its control and thus narrow the scope of uncontrollable market processes.[10]

But Lenin's change of heart was not confined to the economy. He was also afraid that NEP might undermine the political stability of the regime. This became evident especially when economic development demanded an end to coercive methods in the economy and in social relations as well as greater legal security. Early in 1922 the CHEKA was reorganized to become the Chief Political Administration (GPU) and was to be used in future solely to combat political crimes. At the same time it lost its judicial authority, which went to the courts, and a new penal code was prepared. Lenin was anxious that the greater measure of legality should not be interpreted as political liberalization, which would have encouraged the Bolsheviks' political opponents. He insisted on the broadest possible definition of political offences and on the legal codification of terror.[11] His pressure played a considerable role in launching the police and the judicial drive against the Russian Orthodox Church in the spring of 1922 as well as in the harsher treatment of the non-Bolshevik Russian intelligentsia. It is essential to mention Lenin's share in the preparation and organization of the political trial of members of the Central Committee of the Party of Socialist Revolutionaries, which held the attention of public opinion, especially in Europe, for more than six months. Lenin demanded an uncompromising stand and severe sentences.[12] To this end he even sacrificed the negotiations then in progress on an agreement between the three Internationals: the Communist, Socialist and Two-and-a-Half. This greatly impaired the chances of an agreement between communist and socialist parties in Europe.

Lenin's pressure strongly influenced the relations of the Bolsheviks to their political opponents and adversaries. The orientation on the "final liquidation" of non-Bolshevik organized political forces was sanctioned at the conference of the Russian Communist Party (B) in August 1922.[13] This pressure did not have the same impact on economic policy, where the Bolsheviks were much more exposed to the requirements of everyday reality. This resulted in a difference of opinions which were reflected in the clash on the monopoly of foreign trade. It was never resolved mainly because Lenin suffered a stroke. He nevertheless outlined in his Testament a number of questions which set forth his correctives to NEP. Lenin supported Trotskii's proposals for a more rigid role of planning. In his article "On the Coopertive Movement" he outlined a model based on complete state control of the economy, which he described as a socialist economy. Here he again placed strong emphasis on improving the quality of the state and economic apparatus and on struggling against incompetence and bureaucracy.[14]

Lenin's concept of NEP thus shifted to the left. It created conditions for further disunity and differences with the majority group in the Central Committee of which Stalin was a prominent representative. Lenin's attack against bureaucracy caused a widespread stir and many leading Bolsheviks accepted it with barely concealed irritation. It should be remembered that Lenin never regarded bureaucracy as a phenomenon inherent in the new social system. His proposals for reinforcing the role and improving the activities of the supervisory bodies—the worker-peasant inspectorates and the party control bodies—did not go too far beyond a "struggle" against bureaucracy, which was in itself bureaucratic and could not be sufficiently effective.

Lenin's potentially most explosive proposals, however, were those advocating changes in the party. He was motivated by the fear of a split in the party. His considerations originated in the tense relations within the leadership, especially between Stalin and Trotskii. Lenin felt that they could easily be projected into the social sphere and poison relations between the two pillars of Soviet power—the proletariat and the peasantry.[15]

On the surface Lenin's reasoning appeared correct but, whatever his motives might have been, it avoided the substance of the situation inside the party. A certain dualism within the Central Committee was not only the result of relations between Stalin and Trotskii, it had been there as far back as 1917 as the product of relations between Lenin and Trotskii and between their supporters. While Lenin was there, readiness to cooperate mostly prevailed, the reason being that Lenin enjoyed considerable personal and political authority with Trotskii and his supporters. With the advance of Stalin, relations inevitably became more tense. Trotskii did not trust Stalin and was not ready for lasting cooperation. The situation would not have been much different had some other member of the Leninist faction (e.g., Zinoviev or Kamenev) taken Stalin's place.

Lenin's reasoning also distorted the situation within the party on another issue. It suggested that the positions of Stalin and Trotskii within the Central Committee were equal, but no such equality existed. In the course of a bitter struggle of factions, Lenin had enforced changes in the Bolshevik Central Committee at the Tenth Congress of the Russian Communist Party (B) in 1921 which had deprived Trotskii and his supporters of most of their power. At a time when Lenin was about to leave the political scene his faction, and hence Stalin, held an absolute majority in the Central Committee. It remained merely a question of time and of opportunity when and to what extent they were going to put the majority to practical use.

The problem Lenin tried to avoid was that his departure was bound to remove the conditions for the survival of the Bolshevik leadership in its existing composition. The leadership contained no integrating personality capable of replacing Lenin. A reshuffle of the leadership and an ensuing power struggle became inevitable. The only problem was how to make it take place, if possible, painlessly and quickly.

Lenin's evasive attitude and his inaccurate representation of the situation in the party were naturally not the result of a mere error of judgment. The contradictions within the Central Committee had isolated him and made Trotskii, anxious for changes in the leadership, increasingly his ally. Yet, if for no other reason than because of earlier developments in their relations, Lenin could not see Trotskii as a real alternative. Lenin had no substitute, and this had a decisive influence on his thinking.

Lenin's proposals reveal helplessness. To avert a split he suggested that the Central Committee should be substantially expanded and transformed into a kind of permanent party conference. This, of course, was opening the door to the application of the representation principle, favoring top bureaucrats at the expense of politicians. In addition, the Central Committee was ceasing to be a working body, certainly an operative one. Power was being concentrated even more in narrow bodies, above all in the Politburo. The contradictions within the leadership were thus becoming more serious, the very opposite of what Lenin had hoped to achieve.

The same applied to Lenin's views on individual leaders. His Testament, notes he made during his illness, contains his personal assessments of six prominent party politicians (Stalin, Trotskii, Zinoviev, Kamenev, Bukharin and G. L. Piatakov); but these assessments are not accompanied by any concrete recommendations, except for the proposal to remove Stalin from his post.   This was a very topical proposal, motivated by Stalin's unsuitability for high office (rudeness, disloyalty, capriciousness) and probably also by the recent conflict in Transcaucasia. Yet Lenin did not present his proposal to the party.   He did not even acquaint his closest collaborators in the leadership with it and made no suggestion for an alternative candidate.   His proposal did not leave the safe until after his death when it could no longer influence the situation in the party.

A closer examination of the conflicts between Lenin and Stalin does not bear out the prevailing notions about the significance of Lenin's proposals made at that time.   It would be much more correct to state that Lenin raised key problems connected with party policy without being able to propose or enforce adequate solutions.

I do not intend to relativize the connection between the Leninist and Stalinist periods or to present Stalin in a more favorable light than he deserves.   The history of the USSR cannot be observed merely through the prism of Stalinism.   There was undoubtedly a continutity between the two periods.   It is evident from such examples as the Leninist practice of War Communism and Lenin's limiting interpretation of NEP in 1922. Nor is it possible to deny that Russia in the days of both Lenin and Stalin was a rigid totalitarian-type dictatorship, and that even in the days of Lenin, but more particularly in Stalin's era, there was a growth, consolidation and stabilization of every type of bureaucratic apparatus, with a new vertical social differentiation, which was additionally aggravated from the mid-1920s onwards by Stalinist political methods.   It is equally true that the 1920s as a whole formed a separate specific period, marked by its own tendencies of development but providing scope for various development alternatives.   NEP brought Bolshevik policy closer to the reality of economic and social relations.   So much so that foreign observers appraised Soviet policy of that time as, by and large, "moderate."   Even the increasingly bitter internal party struggle did not change this.   While the struggle paved Stalin's path to unlimited power, it did not lead to fundamental changes in the basic character of economic and social life.   This clearly leads to the conclusion that when dealing with the problems of Stalinism a number of authors have exaggerated the connection between Lenin and Stalin, and between the Leninist and Stalinist periods.

The conclusion about the relationship between Lenin and Stalin and their respective policies in the 1920s outlined above naturally does not answer the question of the link between the revolution and Stalinism raised earlier on.   It is in no way superfluous to point out that the NEP period did not eliminate but merely mitigated the contradictions in post-revolutionary society already described. The contradiction was between the character of the revolution and the nature of Bolshevik thinking, and the contradiction between the immediate social impact of the revolution and the long-term requirements of society for economic development. The latter contradiction, in particular, was of exceptional importance.

In my book *The Birth of Stalinism* I noted that the development towards Stalinism was conditioned by the structural crisis of the Soviet system of the late 1920s.[16] The war and the revolution had interrupted the accelerated upsurge of Russia which had started in the years before the revolution. What had happened was the mass destruction of material and cultural values, production mechanisms and the intellectual potential of the country, followed by the restoration of the Soviet economy to the pre-war level. This occurred around 1927. This development meant that post-revolutionary society was marked by immense unsatisfied requirements. It produced strong pressure for speeding up the pace of economic growth. An additional factor was the effect of the economic upsurge of a number of advanced countries in the second half of the 1920s, which threatened to increase the relative backwardness of the USSR.

The Soviet leadership reacted to this situation by increasing the volume of investments and by an intensive policy of industrialization. This came up against structural limitations which had emerged as the product of the revolution. It was not successful in restoring wider economic relations with other countries which in the past had provided substantial investments, imports of new technology and of production know-how. This placed much greater demands on the country's internal life. Within the country the revolution had disrupted the former links between industry and agriculture; it had produced strong disharmony in the forms and pace of their development, in the people's motivation to production and in their ability to meet each other's needs. To this one must add the incompetence and improvisation which characterized many economic and political solutions. Agriculture was therefore not in a position to satisfy the increased demands of the industrialization policy.

An acute crisis broke out in late 1927, the procurement of agricultural raw materials and foodstuffs collapsed, and supplies to the cities and industry were in danger. The situation was strongly influenced by the external political difficulties experienced by the USSR, and by the unresolved struggle against the left-wing opposition. Stalin resorted to brute force. He hoped to obtain in this way the needed grain from the peasants while simultaneously crushing the opposition. This, of course, meant the end of NEP. There was a split in the party leadership and its more moderate section (Rykov, Bukharin and M. P. Tomskii) came out against Stalin's course. The crisis took on political dimensions.

These events virtually closed the period of the 1920s, the NEP era. To continue along the existing course of economic and social policy was impossible. The result was not only the transition to a new political orientation but also to the construction of a new structure of society. It meant an onslaught against the substantial achievements of the October Revolution. Collectivization abolished a situation in the villages created by the land reform. Rapid industrialization meant the brutal dismantlement of the rights of the workers, which drastically worsened their position at work and in everyday life. To counter the resistance of the population the government resorted to preventive terror, which simultaneously served as an instrument to tighten and consolidate a new labor and social discipline. Stalinism was gradually becoming a reality.

The road chosen by Stalin was commensurate with his vision of social problems and with his character as a political leader. It has been frequently pointed out in the political literature that the situation existing at the time did not rule out an alternative solution. It would nevertheless be erroneous to fail to see that the Stalinist policy developed on a specific basis: it was an attempt to overcome by radical methods the contradiction between the social results of 1917 and the requirements of development. It was an attempt to adapt the economy, social and political relations, to the prospect of speedy industrial growth, and to secure the power position of the USSR.

Stalinism was strongly marked by the plebian character of the new ruling stratum and by the ideological tradition and the armory of concepts of Bolshevism. While it adapted ideologically to the new social reality, it was not able to eliminate the contradiction between the character of the revolution and the nature of Bolshevik thinking. In the eyes of the party, the public and in Stalin's own eyes, socialist ideology remained the main means of legitimizing his actions and of trying to justify the drastic social change, brutal oppression and terror. The contradiction between theory and practice, inherent in the revolution itself, was to attain exceptional proportions.

Several authors have expressed the view that Stalinism was the logical implementation of Leninist plans, whereas the "weakness" of the 1920s mentioned earlier emerged from mere tactical maneuvering caused by inadequate strength. However, it is impossible to rationalize, with hindsight, the motives of historical personalities. The intentions and motives of their acts are historical facts, they must be carefully researched and documented, and cannot be construed arbitrarily. It is hardly possible to blame Lenin directly for social projects, political and social decisions or events which reached maturity many years after his death. And vice versa, though the lion's share in the creation of a system bearing his name goes to Stalin, one may doubt whether this system had been Stalin's intention as far back as the middle of the 1920s. The thinking of politicians has a structure different from the thinking of intellectuals. Long-term ideological plans and the motives arising out of them are rarely, and only under exceptional circumstances, able to gain superiority in this kind of thinking over the logic of events and actual social processes, of which the years 1918-1920 provide an example.

The transition from the Leninist to the Stalinist era and from the Russian Revolution to Stalinism can hardly be explained outside the framework of the contradictions of the revolution and of post-revolutionary society. This does not mean relieving historical personalities of their responsibility; but it does imply avoiding the impression that their actions are entirely arbitrary and independent of the historical context. The significant contribution of recent literature on Soviet history and Stalinism, mentioned at the beginning, lies in the fact that it frees the Russian Revolution and Lenin as a personality from further idealization. It would, therefore, be a pity if this progress were to lead to further expedient stereotypes serving momentary political requirements.

Free University of Berlin

Notes

[1] For further information about the development of Soviet positions, see K. N. Tarnovskii, *Sovetskaia istoriografiia rossiiskogo imperializma.* Moscow, 1964; for a critique of western historiography, see G. Ch. Rabinovich and V. N. Razgon, "Rossiiskaia burshuaziia perioda imperializma v sovremennoi amerikanskoi i angliiskoi istoriografii," *Voprosy istorii,* 1985, no. 2, pp. 21-32.

[2] See L. H. Haimson, *The Russian Marxists and the Origins of Bolshevism.* Cambridge, Mass.: Harvard University Press, 1966, pp. 103-105. From a Soviet point of view, see P. N. Pospelov *et al., Vladimir Il'ich Lenin. Biografiia,* 2nd ed., Moscow, 1963, pp. 29-34.

[3] B. N. Ponomarev *et al., Istoriia kommunisticheskoi partii Sovetskogo Soiuza.* Moscow, 1959, vol. III, pp. 73-121; see also: L. Schapiro, *The Communist Party of the Soviet Union.* New York: Random House, 1960, pp. 71-85.

[4] I. V. Stalin, *Sochineniia,* vol. III. Moscow, 1946, pp. 171-178.

[5] *Istoriia KPSS,* pp. 319-412; see also: R. V. Daniels, *The Conscience of the Revolution: Communist Opposition in Soviet Russia.* Cambridge, Mass.: Harvard University Press, 1960, pp. 273-321.

[6] I. V. Stalin, *Voprosy leninizma,* 2nd ed. Moscow, 1952, pp. 545-573.

[7]M. Reiman, "Spontaneity and Planning in the Plebian Revolution," in *Reconsiderations on the Russian Revolution*, ed. by R. C. Elwood, Cambridge, Mass.: Slavica Publishers, 1976, pp. 10-19.

[8]V. I. Lenin, *Polnoe sobranie sochinenii*, vol. 45. Moscow, 1964, pp. 343-348.

[9]R. C. Tucker, *Stalin as Revolutionary, 1879-1929*, New York: Norton, 1973, pp. 254-278; from Soviet point of view, *Istoriia kommunisticheskoi partii Sovetskogo Soiuza*, vol. IV, no. 1. Moscow, 1970, pp. 196-210; see also: G. A. Galoian, *Oktiabr'skaia revolutsiia i vozrozhdenie narodov Zakavkaz'ia*. Moscow, 1977, pp. 236-256.

[10]*Odinnatsatyi sezd RKP/b, Mart-aprel' 1922 goda.   Stenograficheskii otchet.* Moscow, 1961, pp. 10-44.

[11]Lenin, *PSS*, vol. 45, pp. 190-191.

[12]M. Jansen, *A Show Trial under Lenin: The Trial of the Socialist Revolutionaries, Moscow 1922*. The Hague: Nijhoff, 1982; see also Lenin, *PSS*, vol. 45, pp. 141-144.

[13]*Pravda*, 8 and 9 August 1922.

[14]Lenin, *PSS*, vol. 45, pp. 369-372.

[15]Lenin, *PSS*, vol. 45, pp. 343-348; see also Moshe Lewin, *Lenin's Last Struggle*. New York: Vintage Books, 1970, pp. 77-89; Michal Reiman, "Stalin pered zakhvatom vlasti" in *Vremia i my*, no. 83 (1985), pp. 224-233.

[16]M. Reiman, *Die Geburt des Stalinismus. Die UdSSR am Vorabend der zweiten Revolution*. Frankfurt/M., 1979, pp. 193-206.

Party Opposition to Stalin (1930-1932) and the First Moscow Trial

Pierre Broué

From Sochi, on 25 September 1936, J. V. Stalin and A. A. Zhdanov addressed a telegram to the other members of the Politburo stating:

> Yagoda has definitely proved himself to be incapable of unmasking the Trotskyite-Zinovievite bloc. The OGPU is four years behind in this matter.[1]

The same charge was formulated in the resolution approved by the February-March session of the Central Committee of the All-Union Communist Party (Bolsheviks):

> The People's Commissariat of Internal affairs has fallen behind at least four years in the attempt to unmask these most inexorable enemies of the people.[2]

Everybody is aware today that there was not, in the thirties, a "terrorist bloc" of "harmful activity, diversion and espionage of the Japanese-German-Trotskyite agents" carried out by the Old Bolsheviks and defendents of the Moscow Trials. But recent discoveries, first in the Trotskii Papers (former "closed part") in the Houghton Library, then in the Nicolaevsky Collection in the archives of the Hoover Institution at Stanford, have taught us that in 1932, that is to say four years before the trials, a "bloc of the oppositions" was organized, which was initially a "Trotskiite-Zinov'evite bloc" and that it was destroyed, without its presence being realized by the routine repression of its members. This evidence suggests that the existence of such a bloc was discovered only during the investigations in preparation for the First Moscow Trial. The charges against the so-called "terrorists" in the First Moscow Trial were really charges against the members of this "political bloc," depicted as a "terrorist bloc" by the procurator and the defendants themselves.[3]

The first document found in Trotskii's archives is an undated (Fall 1932) report by Trotskii's son, Lev Sedov, written in chemical ink, informing Trotskii of the constitution of a bloc composed of Trotskiists, Zinov'evists, former Trotskiites called "capitulators" around I. N. Smirnov, and the Lominadze-Sten group, and that negotiations were in progress, not only with a Zinov'evist dissident group headed by Safarov and Tarkhanov, but also with the so-called "Riutin group." We also learn through Trotskii's answer to his son of a subsequent discussion between father and son about the question of the validity of the slogan "Down with Stalin!" and the relation to be developed with the "liberals" (Smirnov group) and the "rightists" (Riutin or rather the Riutin-Slepkov group). The messenger sent by I. N. Smirnov to L. L. Sedov in Berlin in 1932 was E. S. Holzman, who was to be one of the defendants during the First Moscow Trial. He was to confess later that he had met Trotskii and Sedov in Copenhagen, where Sedov had never been.

Some documents found in Sedov's Papers in Hoover cast useful supplementary light on the case. For the first time, we learn something about the man who was depicted by procurator Vyshinskii and some of the defendants as the one who brought the terrorist directives from Trotskii to the USSR, that is Iuri Petrovich Gavenis (sometimes Gaven), and Old Bolshevik working in Gosplan. Gavenis never appeared on the bench of defendants but was later shot, according to Roy Medvedev, carried out on a stretcher, after having been savagely tortured, and having refused to make a "confession." In 1936 Trotskii and Sedov denied having had any contact with him. In fact, they had. Allowed to go to Germany in order to receive medical care, Gavenis wrote to Trotskii and got an interview with Lev Sedov who wrote an account of it. Gavenis gave information about the bloc, supplementing Holzman's. He also gave information about his own "O"-group (probably Osinskii) and seems to have agreed to bring back to the Soviet Union a message to the Trotskiite group itself — in spite of his worry about the latter having been infiltrated by OGPU. The correspondence between Trotskii and Sedov demonstrates that father and son were astounded at the beginning of the trial when they saw that Smirnov and Holzman, already guilty in Stalin's eyes, did not content themselves with confessing the truth but accused themselves of fantastic crimes.[4] Sedov at first wondered whether he should tell the truth, publicly, but finally decided to deny everything, except proven contacts, which seemed to him the only way of hindering the annihilation of the defendants. All these persons can be traced in the Trotskii-Sedov correspondence under the following pseudonyms: "Ko," "Kolokoltsev" or "Kolokolnikov" for I. N. Smirnov, "Orlov" for E. S. Holzman, "Sorokin" for Gavenis. Lev Sedov was the first to understand that Gavenis had refused to confess, which explained his absence among the defendants in front of the court.

There is today a trend which appears in the Western historiography of the thirties and is best expressed by the works of J. Arch Getty. From an excellent consideration of sources, criticism of the testimonies, establishment of the lack of first-hand accounts for the "political" version of the emigres (and especially of the Menshevik historian B. I. Nicolaevsky), Professor Getty and other distinguished authors seriously question the validity of several interpretations of the internal party opposition, beginning with the Riutin affair. Before criticizing what he wrote, I must acknowledge the merit of Professor Getty who is the first and, as far as I know, the only one to have mentioned, in his own work, an article of mine which contradicts some of his views.

Here are the three texts found by the Leon Trotskii Institute team in 1980 during our investigation of the Trotskii Papers in the Houghton Library. The first is Sedov's letter written in chemical ink, date unknown, probably the end of September 1932:

> The (...) has been organized. It includes the *Zinovievites*, the *Sten-Lominadze* group and the *Trotskyites* (former "c.............."). The Safar.-Tarkhan. group have not formally joined yet—their position is too extreme; they will join very soon. Z and K's declaration about the very serious mistake they made in '27 was made during negotiations with us about the bloc, just before Z and K's deportation.
>
> The collapse of I. N. (.........), Preobrazh. and Uf. group (the three of them belonged to the center) was caused by a sick, half-distracted man. He had been arrested by accident and started talking. No document could be found at I. N.'s of the others that could be "Trotskyite literature." A few days before he was arrested, I. N. said to our informer: "X has betrayed. I am expecting to be arrested any day." Thanks to the presence of *his* Markovkin who had thoroughly informed him, he was ready. Unfortunately, I. N. did not have time to convey the information."
>
> The informer asserts there had been *no* mistake from abroad, or links with abroad.
>
> If there are any important points at issue, I will wire before Thursday (according to instructions).
>
> The collapse of the "Old People" is a bad blow but the links with the workers have been preserved.[5]

Of course, the words deleted are "bloc," "capitulators," "Smirnov." "Safar." means Safarov, "Tarkhan." Tarkhanov, "Z" Zinov'ev, "K" Kamenev, "Preobrazh." Preobrazhenskii, "Uf." N. I. Ufimtsev. "His Markovkin" seems to be an OGPU man connected with Smirnov and "the informer" is obviously E. S. Holzman. "Old People" means Grunstein, who had capitulated recently.

Trotskii answered in the middle of October:

1) My letter home had already been written before I got yours referring to Kol. The letter was obviously for the Left Opposition, in the true meaning of the word. But you may show it to the Informer in order to give him an idea of my point of view.

2) The proposal of a bloc seems to me altogether reasonable. I insist on the fact that it is a bloc and not a unification.

3) My proposal of a declaration is obviously for our fraction of the Left Opposition, in the strict meaning of the term (and not for our own allies). I don't agree with the allies' opinion according to which we should wait for the rightists to go further, as regards our fraction. Against repression, one fights by anonymity and conspiracy, not silence. A waste of time is unthinkable: from a political point of view, it would mean leaving the ground to the Rightists.

4) How is the bloc going to express itself? For the time being, mainly by mutual information. The allies inform us about the Soviet Union in the same way as we do for them about the Communist International. We must come to an agreement about a very accurate way of correspondence.

The allies must send us papers for the *Biulleten*. The staff of the *Biulleten* will commit themselves to publish the allies' documents, but reserve the right to comment on them freely.

5) The bloc does not prevent mutual criticism. We will fight unrelentingly and ruthlessly against any propaganda from the allies in favor of the capitulators (Grunstein, etc.).

6) The question of an economic program has been sketched in the last issue of the *Biulleten* and [will be] developed in the following issues.

A few questions:

1) What does the Declaration of the 18 mean (*Sots-Vestnik*)?

2) What about the Decist, Workers Opposition and other Ultra-Left groups?

3) What does the ally think of the draft of platform published in the last issue of the *Biulleten*?

4) What does he think about the problem of the Communist International (we attach the same importance to this problem as to those of the USSR)?

As to the general situation of the country, the information we get does not differ much from the image I could get through a careful reading of Russian newpapers.[6]

The conditions of secrecy maintained in Trotskii's entourage as well as his own unwillingness years later to admit the existence of the bloc are better expressed in a letter written by his secretary, Jean van Heijenoort, from Mexico to Lev Sedov in Paris on 3 July 1937, which enclosed a copy of Trotkii's letter quoted above:

> Dear Friend,
>
> Here is a copy of a letter found in the archives. It was in a "confidential" file with other odd things. There is neither a date nor any other piece of information and this is an exact copy. The original is badly type-written, it seems to be a copy of a hand-written letter. Here are a few clues given to me by my uncle.
> 1) The letter must have been written by me and sent to L. S. in Berlin.
> 2) Kol., as mentioned in it, must be Kolokolnikov, the nickname given to Smirnov by L. S.
> 3) The question of the bloc was considered in the letter, as some of the capitulators were becoming dissatisfied again with the official policy, without unifying with the Left Opposition, and far from it. The content of the "bloc" is strictly defined in the letter, and basically comes to mutual information.
> 4) The letter can be dated after the date of the meeting with H-n and that of the publishing in *Sots. V.* of the declaration of the 18.
>
> Would it be possible to find the original? Of course, we will not make use of this page with N. Y. before receiving further information from you.[7]

Of course, "H-n" is Holzman, the "declaration of the 18" the Riutin platform, *"Sots. V."* is *Sotsialisticheskii Vestnik*, "N. Y." the Dewey Commission.

At the time, when we discovered the three documents referred to above, we had only a vague idea concerning the links between the exiles and the Soviet Union. Sedov's Papers at Hoover helped us to fill the gaps in our knowledge. Trotskii's son had succeeded in organizing in the Soviet Union, as well as in several diplomatic missions abroad, a network of informants that gave him useful and serious information. This is how—years before Nicolaevsky, the *Letter of an Old Bolshevik*, and Ciliga's and Victor Serge's books—he was in possession of information concerning the activity and the content of the "Platform" of the so-called Riutin group. During the same period, he was able to explain in his own correspondence that the Riutin group was the work of rightist leaders, the "lieutenants" immediately below the "chiefs" Bukharin, Rykov and Tomskii, angry to have been "betrayed" by them. He was also informed that the inspirers of the group and the writers of the Platform were very critical of their own past attitude towards Trotskii and the Trotskiites and that they were trying to propose a combination of the two platforms: the economic program of the neo-NEP borrowed from the Right program, and the restoration of party democracy borrowed from the Left program. The Sedov Papers finally inform us that the "Rightists" were engaged in negotiations with spokesman of the bloc, i.e., with I. N. Smirnov, and that the Smirnov group was inclined to postpone any political initiative until an agreement was reached with the "Rightists."

Who were the members of the "Bloc" as it was announced to Trotskii by L. L. Sedov? Let us begin with the so-called "Trotskiites" themselves who survived, not as a true organization, but as a network of correspondents and contacts in several major towns, places of deportation and isolation. In 1932 Lev Sedov kept in touch regularly and, apparently, safely with several people in the Soviet Union. One of them has not been as yet identified: he appears in the archives under the name "Ten−sov" (beginning and end of his real last name), and the initials M. M. and T. T., as well as the pen-name "Svoj." We only know that he was an Old Bolshevik, personally well acquainted with Kote Tsintadze and V. S. Kasparova, and a former member of the Trade Mission in London in 1930. Another correspondent, publicly known as "Piotr" after the publication by *Pravda* in January 1928 of a letter to him from Trotskii, was N. N. Pereverzev, a former official of an international railway organization in Switzerland according to Ruth Fischer. A third, probably the most important, who was able to correspond with Sedov and send him secret party circulars, as well as to inform him about public events, was Kocherets, known in the Opposition as Vet., Vetter and "the Frenchman," but publicly known under the pen-name of J. Renaud, translator of the works of the French novelist and poet Louis Aragon. Among the other people involved in the underground activity of the Left Opposition were two persons from Moscow: the Old Bolshevik Andrei Konstantinov ("Kostia") and a History Professor, A. M. Shabion, who was later suspected of being manipulated by the OGPU. Many other people were active at the time, among them the former Chekist Nadezhda Ostrovskaia, and the former leader of Workers Opposition Rafail. But the first three were the people who informed Sedov and wrote to him about the declaration of Zinov'ev leaving for exile, according to which he thought that their most serious political mistake had been to break with Trotskii in 1927.

In 1931 and 1932, all information gathered from the Soviet Union indicated the "oppositionist" mood of Zinov'ev, Kamenev and their close friends, who seem to have been especially worried about Stalin's catastrophic policy in Germany, which opened the door and paved the way for Hitler and his gang. G. L. Shklovskii, who was the contact between Zinov'ev and his friends abroad, especially Ruth Fischer and Maslow, regularly brought information showing the state of mind of the former capitulators who were beginning to regret their capitulation. The Soviet Minister in Prague, Arosov, seems to have been playing a similar role.

Lev Sedov called the Smirnov group either the "former capitulators" or the "Trotskiite capitulators." Everybody had known, from 1929 on, that people in the Smirnov group had not really capitulated but were trying to fool the apparatus, and were capable of organizing themselves as an Opposition within the party: the fact was so universally known that Andrés Nin, the Spaniard deported from the Soviet Union in August 1930, explained it openly to his German comrades of *Die permanente Revolution* who printed his declaration without apparent problem.

Jan Ernestovich Sten, a Lett, and Vasso Vissarionovich Lominadze, a Georgian, had once been good Stalinist henchmen. "Young Turks," "Left Stalinists," they had already begun to organize and act as an opposition in 1929, had been unmasked in 1930 and were continuing their oppositionist activities despite public confession of mistakes and self-criticism, which induced the apparatus to call them "double dealers." In 1931, Sedov's correspondents wrote to him that Lominadze's people were very busy, not only in the Caucasus party apparatus, but also in the ranks and cadres of youth groups. Sten as well as Lominadze, Shatzkin, Chaplin and many others, had been among the leaders of the first Komsomol generation who were to be shot "en masse" during the *Ezhovshchina*.

Safarov — and Old Bolshevik from Leningrad and ex-French exile, then a specialist on the Eastern people — and Tarkhanov — a Komsomol leader and Soviet political adviser in China — were former Zinov'evists having broken with Zinov'ev after his capitulation. They had been the first group to elaborate, in 1928, a theory about the necessity of a "double face" for oppositionists as a cover for political opposition action.

We, of course, know everything necessary about the group of Leningrad "Zinov'evists," the bulk of the party before the revolution, the core of the apparatus from 1917 to 1926 in the former tsarist capital.

What about the genesis of the Bloc? All the elements in Sedov's correspondence seem to indicate that the initiative for the regrouping belonged to Ivan Nikitich Smirnov and his group of former "capitulators." If we decide to treat the official minutes of the first Moscow Trial as a palimpsest, suppressing from them all mention of terrorism, we find the story of a political evolution of political people in a changing but dramatic situation. Kamenev said that Safarov was one of the first, probably at the end of 1930, to come back and ask for a discussion. Zinov'ev told that he was contacted in 1931-1932 by several groups, among them the old groups of Shliapnikov and Medvedev, the newer groups of the "Leftists" in which he named Sten, Lominadze and Shatzkin, and even isolated individuals such as Smilga and Sokolnikov. Both Zinov'ev and Kamenev confessed that everybody at that time thought that it was urgent to get rid of Stalin and that such a fight needed the support of Trotskii. The Zinov'evite Reingold related that, during discussions at the beginning of 1932 in Zinov'ev's *dacha*, the Zinov'evists agreed that a re-unification with Trotskii was a necessity. In May 1931, as is generally known, Smirnov, on a mission to Berlin, had several meetings with Sedov and they organized together their mutual relations and communications. Ter-Vaganian state that, having become a personal friend of Lominadze, he informed him about the meetings in Berlin and possible prospects. According to the "confessions" of the defendants in August 1936, the bloc was officially formed in June 1932. Ter-Vaganian played the role of intermediary between Kamenev and Lominadze and between I. N. Smirnov and Zinov'ev. Evdokimov was deputed by the Zinov'evists to meet the "Smirnovites" in Mrachkovskii's compartment in a railway station in Moscow. Finally, during a meeting held in Zinov'ev's Illinskoe *dacha*, the Zinov'evists decided to enter the bloc. Several weeks later, Holzman brought this information to Sedov, then brought back from Berlin to Moscow Trotskii's answer, probably supplemented by a message brought by Gavenis.

It was the beginning of the bloc, but also its end. Curiously enough, the bloc did not die of its own death. It was not broken as such by the OGPU. It withered away without having been formally broken. The first to fall were Zinov'ev and Kamenev, accused of having been informed of the content of the Riutin-Slepkov platform without denouncing it and its authors to the authorities. Expelled from the party once more, they were deported. At the same time, Riutin himself was arrested and imprisoned, and Slepkov was deported. Smilga was required to leave Moscow where he was welcoming too many visitors. About two months later, denounced by a member of his group who was probably mentally ill, Smirnov was arrested. In a similar fashion, Sten was forced to leave Moscow. Ter-Vaganian, Ufimtsev, Preobrazhenskii, Grunstein, Livshitz, and about 100 to 150 former "capitulators" were arrested. The Zinov'evist leaders, assembled in Bogdan's flat, decided that their number one task was to struggle for their reintegration and that the activities of their group within the bloc had to be stopped.

We have every reason to believe that at the time the OGPU and Stalin did not know about the existence of the bloc. Smirnov was indeed sentenced to ten years for having had "contacts with abroad," but not for having inspired a "bloc." People involved in the bloc or in contact with it, such as Lominadze, Safarov, Tarkhanov, Mrachkovskii, Safonova and Shatzkin, were neither expelled nor deported. Among the Trotskiites, Konstantinov was arrested because he spoke too much at a dinner about Stalin's general policy and was denounced, but he was not identified as a "Trotskiite." Shabion was arrested for having spoken too much about Thermidor during a lecture. The others—Pereverzev, Kocherets, N. Ostrovskaia, Rafail—were not arrested for months, and were arrested only because of the activity of their own group. If the OGPU and Stalin's press did not mention a "bloc" at the time, it was only because they did not know anything about the past existence of such a bloc. It seems likely that the investigators mistook the "Opposition bloc" for the Riutin group which was also in its own way a bloc of Right and Left Oppositions although led by the former. Everything indicates that I. N. Smirnov did not utter a word about the bloc during the period 1933-1936. In any case, Lev Sedov considered that, with the exception of Preobrazhenskii—who recanted for a second time—all the members of the Smirnov group, having left the Left Opposition in 1929, returned to it in 1932. In a report to the International Secretariat in 1934, he wrote that they were again full members of the Left Opposition.

Only during 1936—before, during and after the first Moscow Trial—would everybody formerly involved in the bloc be arrested, tried and executed or shot without trial; among them were people who had been spared in 1932-1933. Summoned by the authorites, Lominadze shot himself in a car. There were probably only two survivors of the bloc in the early forties, Konstantinov and Safarov, who were to die near Vorkuta. But at the time, and probably from 1935 on, after the mass arrests of Old Bolsheviks and the beginning of severe interrogations, the OGPU and Stalin knew everything about the bloc.

I think that they knew about it in 1935, not in 1933. On this point I disagree with Professor Getty. He writes that it is well known that Trotskii's entourage was deeply infiltrated by OGPU men "planted" by Soviet service around both Trotskii and Sedov.[8] But it is not possible to accept such assertions on the ground of such generalities. One must say who was who, which one was an agent, an informant, and check what was really possible. And we now know who the agents were. At the time when the bloc was formed, the two most important were the Sobolevicius brothers (in 1932 they were known in Europe as Roman Well and Adolf Senin, later in the United States as Dr. Robert Soblen and Jack Soble), but they were on the verge of a break, suspected of being what they were, i.e., Stalinist agents. It is unlikely that they would have been informed of such an event in these circumstances. Who else? Professor Getty puts forward the name of Zborowski.[9] But our investigation demonstrates that Zborowski had not yet met Sedov in 1932 or 1933 or even in 1934 and that he met him for the first time in 1935. Moreover, there is no evidence that the collaborators of Trotskii had been informed of the existence of the bloc; this includes close associates such as van Heijenoort. Pierre Frank, another of Trotskii's secretaries, in 1932 probably brought to Prinkipo Smirnov's report without knowing its content. In 1982, half a century later, he refused to believe his own eyes when presented with the documents, asserting that "Sedov would have told him everything," whereas the evidence is that he did not know what Sedov knew. We have every reason to believe that Stalin was not informed about the 1932 bloc before 1935 and perhaps then only through the "confessions" of imprisoned victims.

At the time of the first Moscow Trial, the best way to the truth went through an investigation or rather a counter-investigation magnificently done by the Dewey Commission and the work of several American intellectuals that demonstrated that the charges of terrorism, sabotage, espionage, etc., against the Old Bolsheviks were simply and solely frameups. The verdict of the Dewey Commission, *Not Guilty*, was a big step forward, a big step in the direction of the truth, against the lies, slanders and complicities which abounded throughout the world. I think it necessary now to apply a systematic doubt to the denials of people like Sedov who we know were not guilty of what they were accused of, but were morally obliged to deny everything. In 1936, Sedov decided to acknowledge publicly that he really met Smirnov in 1931, and reduced their interview to an ordinary talk about the current economic situation. But he energetically and categorically denied the earlier existence of the bloc that he announced to his father with pride and joy in 1932. In October 1936, in his *Red Book*, he admitted that there might have been, in 1932, some revival of the groups which had long ago capitulated, but stated that such a revival should not be exaggerated because it did not go beyond personal meetings and pious intentions. It must be understood today that the charge of "terrorism" was at the time founded upon the "existence" of a "Trotskiite-Zinov'evite bloc": acknowledging its existence would have meant for Trotskii and Sedov a surrender to the OGPU of new friends and allies. The Old Bolsheviks' defense went through Trotskii's and Sedov's denial. Today there is no reason whatsoever to believe their tactical denial and, above all, to believe it in its integrity and its totality. In the late thirties both men were fighting for their lives and honor, for the lives and honor of their comrades-in-arms, and were not ready to surrender their allies for the sake of the truth.

In fact, the Trotskii-Sedov correspondence, as well as the Sedov correspondence generally speaking, demonstrates that many people among the Old Communists, the "connaisseurs" of the Soviet Stalinized world, thought that the charge of terrorism had been added to a real framework made up with a chronology of real facts and events. It is easier for an investigator who tries to present as "terrorist" a "political" bloc, to use an exact chronology of meetings, agreements, trips and so on and to put into them another content. Victor Serge, who was personally acquainted with all the defendants in the second trial, wrote to Sedov that he thought it necessary to discover real "discussions" and real "grouplets" as the only way to throw some light on what he thought to be more "provocation" than "lies." One example will be enough to demonstrate the necessity of such an investigation: Procurator Vyshinskii mentioned in the third trial as a "Trotskiite agent" a Russian engineer named Reich, who later became, according to him, a Danish citizen under the name of Johanson. Trotskii and his friends denied any knowledge of a Dane, formerly named Reich and now called Johanson. However, we can find in the list of subscriptions to *Biulleten Oppositsii* in Denmark the name of Reich, also called Jacobsen. We must admit that a bit of truth was hidden behind the false charge.

Professor Getty and probably some other scholars refuse to take into account the Nicolaevsky version of the Kirov affair. Getty correctly underlines some of the contradictions in its presentation, the great number of second-hand sources, the variations through the years, and so on. He shows that we have no serious reason to believe that S. M. Kirov became a partisan of the "liberalization" of the Soviet regime. The legend of a "liberal" Kirov then became a propaganda trick in the time of N. S. Khrushchev and the so-called "revelations" of the so-called "de-Stalination" which was far from being a mere revision of history. Getty insists that Trotskii, who was a qualified "kremlinologist," never considered Kirov as an adversary of Stalin, but, on the contrary, as a brutal bureaucrat without any political physiognomy of his own.[10] I find some of Professor Getty's assertions not at all convincing, but I will challenge him not on the basis of his interpretations, but on the basis of evidence. In the Sedov correspondence in the years preceding 1936, we find, before the publication of the famous "Letter of an Old Boshevik" and Nicolaevsky's commentaries,[11] some letters — particularly one from an Austrian communist — giving information about Kirov's murder, the suspicious role of the Leningrad OGPU, rumors about the implication of Stalin, and so on. In 1936, Sedov wrote to Trotskii that he has been informed of Muscovite rumors according to which Kirov had been in touch with "the Right" and tried to ease his own relationship with former Oppositionists. The former Soviet journalist Zavalichkina, in her unpublished memoirs, related how Kirov received in Leningrad the former Trotskiite L. S. Sosnovskii after his capitulation.[12] Through her, one can finally understand that the official version according to which the conspirators who plotted Kirov's murder met regularly under the cover of a common work on the history of the Leningrad Komsomol, cannot but conceal a part of the truth. These people were probably meeting in order to work together on a historical project; but the fact that they were working on such a project is not indifferent. Kirov must have sought a rapprochement with the Zinov'evists by ordering a historical work in which they were to appear as the heroes of Komsomol history in Leningrad at least.

We are confronted with more important data. In March 1978, we registered a testimony of an old French Communist, Marcel Body, who has since died. He was reputed to be reliable, a man of good memory and perfectly honest. He wrote in a little anarchist paper that Kirov had sent to Paris an emissary who had an interview with Sedov:

> At the beginning of the summer of 1934, a friend of mine (...) told me that a friend of her brother-in-law, Dr. Levin, a practitioner in the Kremlin, had arrived in Paris and wanted to meet me. An appointment was made and the conversation suddenly became so important that I was amazed. Dr. Levin had just informed me of Kirov's intimate thought. It was the thought of a moderate who wanted to put an end to internal stuggles as well as to an internal policy of this huge country. According to Kirov, they should go back to a more humane policy, closer to what Lenin had advised at the time of NEP and give up the cruel collectivization of the countryside (...) "Kirov wants internal democracy to be re-established in the party and a free expression of every tendency." "Including the Trotskyite tendency?" I exclaimed. "Yes," he answered, "including the Trotskyite tendency." "And including Trotsky's return to the USSR?" "It must be considered." I rang up Sedov (...) to let him know. Sedov questioned Kirov's friend and confidant for three hours.[13]

In spite of the trust that everybody had in Marcel Body, we did not take his testimony into account and only registered it: *testis unus, testis nullus.* In 1980 we looked for some confirmation in the Trotskii Papers: no trace. Trotskii and Lev Sedov were experienced conspirators and probably did not write one line or destroyed any document on that. However, we think we have found an oblique confirmation in a report written by Sedov to his own comrades about the situation of the "Bolshevik-Leninists" in the Soviet Union after Rakovskii's and Sosnovskii's capitulation.[14] Evoking the crisis in the USSR in the preceding years, he wrote that in the Soviet Union itself "very responsible comrades debated the question of Trotskii's return." And we must confess that we are unable to imagine which "very responsible comrades" could have been debating such a question at that time except Kirov and the likes of him, whoever they were.

One might suppose that I disagree with Professor Getty on every aspect of that important question. That is not true. I think that, in fact and in the last analysis, we are very close in our conclusions. I think that the new data concerning the "Opposition bloc," the organization of two Communist blocs of Oppositions, the attempt to unify the Communist Opposition, definitively destroys all the legends and preconceived ideas about an all-mighty, blood-thirsty, machiavelian Stalin. The Soviet Union in the thirties was passing through a serious economic and political crisis. Stalin was more and more isolated and many people, including some from the ranks of privileged bureaucracy of which he was only the best expression and the unifier, began to think about the necessity of getting rid of him. The Moscow Trials were not a gratuitous crime committed in cold blood, but a counter-stroke in a conflict which was really, as Trotskii wrote, "a preventive civil war."

Only people who really believe that the regime founded by the October Revolution was not subject to degeneration and aimed from the beginning at being an absolute monolith, without any possibility of opposition and only a vague and remote future pro-capitalist dissent, who believe that Soviet history rests on the basis of a strict predetermination that germs of Stalinism were already growing in Lenin's brain—in one word, people who believe that scientific precepts for history are of no value when applied to Soviet history—only these people will reject a conclusion which explains the trials by the political crisis rather than by the so-called "essence" of so-called "Communism."

University of Grenoble

Notes

[1]Cited in Khrushchev's Secret Speech (25 February 1956), *The Anti-Stalin*

Campaign and International Communism. New York: Columbia University Press, 1956, p. 26.

[2]Based on Ezhov's report "Lessons flowing from the harmful activity, diversion and espionage of the Japanese-German-Trotskyite agents." *Ibid.*, p. 27.

[3]See Pierre Broué, "Trotsky et le Bloc des Oppositions de 1932," *Cahiers Léon Trotsky,* no. 5, 1980, pp. 5-38.

[4]I am preparing, an edition of the Trotskii-Sedov correspondence from 1931 to 1938, for the Hoover Institution Press, with documents from the Hoover Institution, Harvard College and the International Institute for Social History in Amsterdam. This work was in the beginning prepared with the late Jean van Heijenoort.

[5]Trotskii Papers, bMSRus 13-1, 4782.

[6]*Ibid.*, 13905 c & 1010.

[7]*Ibis.*, 13905.

[8]J. Arch Getty, *Origins of the Great Purges: The Soviet Communist Party Reconsidered, 1933-1938.* Cambridge: Cambridge University Press, 1985, p. 121.

[9]*Ibid.*

[10]*Ibid.*, Appendix "The Assassination of Kirov," pp. 207-211.

[11]Composed by Nicolaevsky, "The Letter of an Old Bolshevik" was first published in *Sotsialisticheskii Vestnik*, nos. 23-24, 22 December 1936, pp. 22-23; and nos. 1-2, 17 January 1937, pp. 17-24.

[12]A. Zavalichkina, "Iz Vospominanii Sovetskogo Zhurnalista: vorkrug ubiistva Kirova," (Nicolaevsky Collection, Hoover Institution).

[13]Marcel Body, "Pages d'Histoire et de Sang," *Le Réfractaire*, no. 37, March 1978.

[14]This report, written in French, will be published in no. 24 of the *Cahiers Léon Trotsky*, in December 1985, from a copy in the Jean Rous archives. Another copy, unsigned, is in the Shachtman Archives, Tamiment Library.

Stalinism and Institutionalization:
The Nature of Stalin's Regional Support

Graeme Gill

Studies of the Stalinist political structure have generally been characterized by a focus upon the control aspects of that structure. An emphasis upon the highly centralized, tightly organized aspects of Stalinism has been common not just among those who have subscribed to the totalitarian thesis but also among those scholars for whom the totalitarian paradigm has been less persuasive. However, while highly centralized aspects and strong notions of centralized control are easy to point to in the Stalinist structure, we should not assume that such control was the most characteristic feature of the structure in practice as opposed to aspirations. Indeed, it is possible to argue that the Stalinist system may better be characterized not by the strength of its controls but by the weakness of them. The crux of this argument lies in the low level of institutionalization of the internal mechanisms of the party.[1] The party did not operate as an efficient machine in the period prior to World War II with the result that institutional procedures for the structuring of the activity of lower level party members were extremely weak. Consequently, the institution's capacity to exercise tight, on-going control over party members was limited.

This question of the strength of institutional controls is raised by the main thrust of the accepted explanation for Stalin's rise to personal power. The heart of the accepted wisdom is the ability of Stalin and his lieutenants to manipulate personnel procedures in order to ensure that his supporters occupied positions of responsibility throughout the political structure.[2] This enabled him to stack party bodies with his supporters and thereby to overwhelm the opposition. This argument has a good deal of merit. However, it does assume that the party's personnel mechanism was a smoothly operating machine which Stalin and his lieutenants were able to manipulate to build up the ranks of their supporters. But as analysis will show, at least prior to the achievement of Stalin's unchallenged personal dominance on the eve of the war, that machine was anything but a smoothly operating organism.

At the outset, it should be emphasized that Stalin's control, through his supporters and assistants, over the personnel mechanism is not in question. It is the nature of the relationship between those appointing personnel to positions and those who are appointed which is at issue. If the personnel mechanism could not be used to move established supporters of Stalin into positions of power, as will be argued below, the accepted explanation becomes significantly weaker. It may be bolstered by the argument that the act of appointment itself is a means of establishing a supportive, patron-client relationship, but while this may be true, the act of appointment devoid of any other linkages is a weak basis upon which to build an enduring political relationship.[3] Solid clientelist support which could sustain a leader through difficult times in the face of severe challenges is unlikely to be generated through appointment alone. Stalin's position throughout the 1920s and 1930s may thus be due less to his ability to build up a solid clientelist base at the middle levels of the party than it was to the more conditional support offered by political leaders at these levels.

The ability to use the personnel mechanism to promote established supporters into positions of responsibility throughout the party apparatus was dependent upon the efficiency of that mechanism. More precisely, it required adequate and up-to-date personnel records at the center, a regularized system of decision-making on personnel questions, and an effective means of ensuring the implementation of those decisions at lower levels. Fundamental to the operation of such a system was the existence of stable, regularized institutional links between central party organs and those at lower levels. All of these were essential to the development of the party as a strong, institutional structure. However, between the revolution and the war the party was not to develop in this way.

The party as an organizational structure was under continuous pressure during the pre-war period. The source of pressure of most relevance to the question of the structuring of personnel procedures was the fluctuating nature of party membership. Between 1917 and the eve of the war, in round figures the party increased in size almost 142 times: 1917 – 24,000; 1924 – 472,000; 1930 – 1,677,910; 1935 – 2,358,714; 1940 – 3,399,975.[4] But these figures tell only part of the story. While the total party membership rose in the way these figures indicate, the total number entering the party was actually greater than these figures suggest because at the same time large numbers were leaving the party. Throughout the period, party ranks were depleted by death and by voluntary withdrawal. In addition, as a result of a succession of campaigns designed to get rid of undesirable elements, there was a large-scale forced effluxion from party ranks. The following campaigns were mounted during this period:

1919	re-registration of party members
1920	re-registration of party members
1921-22	official chistka
1924-25	verification of government cells and educational institutions
1925-27	verification of village cells
1928	heightened levels of vigilance among government officials and management and in local organs
1929-30	official chistka
1933-34	official chistka
1935	verification of party documents
1936	exchange of party cards
1936-38	terror/Ezhovshchina

There are no accurate figures for those who left the party during these campaigns. What is clear is that the overall membership level of the party was in a continual state of flux throughout this period with large numbers of people leaving party ranks at the same time that others were flocking in.[5] Maintaining accurate membership records in the face of such a continually changing situation was an administrative task of major dimensions. It was further complicated by the need to keep track of party members who, while not leaving the party, shifted their place of residence or were transferred in their work. Particularly during the early part of the Soviet period when the mass transfer of communists was common, this constituted a very heavy administrative burden.

The high level of membership fluidity created significant problems for the party's administrative structure. Keeping track of the multitudinous membership changes would have been a daunting task for a bureaucratic system which was fully established and operating, but for party organs in the early years of Soviet rule, trying to establish their control in a war-ridden and devastated society, often characterized by a shortage of administrative talent and perhaps even of literate officers, and with only a minimum of office management procedures worked out, the task was well-nigh impossible. The difficult conditions in which the party organs below the central level developed had serious implications for the development of an administrative regime in the party and for the shaping of their own modes of operation. These are discussed below. More particularly in personnel matters, it meant that there were serious deficiencies in the personnel records and registration procedures of most party organs.

The construction of an effective personnel management system was dependent upon the existence of a comprehensive and up-to-date register of all party members. Without such a register, rational decisions about personnel placement and the best disposition of party forces could not be made. During the pre-war period, a number of attempts were made to build up an effective, on-going system of registration in the party. Party-wide re-registrations of party members were announced in 1919 and 1920[6] and party censuses were conducted in 1921-1922 and 1927.[7] The introduction of the *nomenklatura* system in 1923[8] and the revision of the nomenklatura lists in December 1925[9] and possibly 1928[10] constituted further opportunities for some systematization of party personnel records. The *chistki* of 1921-1922, 1929-1930 and 1933-1934, the verification of party documents of 1935 and the exchange of party cards of 1936 provided further scope for setting party records straight. Lower party organizations were bombarded by the center with letters, circulars and instructions in attempts to introduce a standardized system of registration throughout the party and to ensure that party registers were kept up to date. The structure of local committees was, on occasion, also amended in an effort to strengthen personnel work.[11]

The success of these efforts to construct a systematic registration system should not be exaggerated. The domestic housekeeping arrangements of party organs at lower levels were undeveloped and lacking in system, and this applied as much to the personnel area as it did to other aspects of party work. It is not surprising that membership records of individual party organizations during the initial years of Soviet power could differ from the actual number of members by as much as 80 percent.[12] The results of the initial party re-registration were disappointing. According to a letter from responsible Central Committee Secretary, V.M. Molotov, and Uchraspred head Lisitsyn, in August 1921, the registration of responsible workers in the party had not really got going because of the general lack of organization, an absence of appropriate organizations to carry out the task, and the existence of different forms and systems of registration both between and within guberniia committees.[13] Despite the claim that the re-registration had been completed satisfactorily by early 1923,[14] critics claimed that it was often carried out in a purely formal way, with some people incorrectly listed as responsible workers and others incorrectly excluded.[15]

The most important step forward in the construction of a regularized, party-wide, personnel system was the institutionalization of the *nomenklatura* principle in 1923[16]. Although there were early problems in standardizing this system between party levels and across the country as a whole,[17] this established the framework for the systematic distribution of party forces, which necessitated a regularized structure of membership registration. But the problem with this framework is that it relied upon the cooperation and capacities of the lower level party organs and their leaders. The development and continued operation of a systematic process of party registration remained dependent upon adequate record-keeping at the lower levels of the party and the regular transfer of the information stored there to the central organs. The problem was that the standard of registration at the lower levels remained deficient.

Throughout much of this period, but particularly during the early and mid-1930s, the inadequacy of lower level registration procedures was a common theme in the press. Party organs were accused of failing to pay sufficient attention to the need to have an accurate registration of party members. Party leaders were said not to be aware of the real state of their organizations, with their membership records being as much as 50 percent at variance with real membership figures. Some members transferred into another party organization while remaining registered in their original organization; some possessed more than one party card; some party committees had on their lists individuals who should have been on the *nomenklatura* lists of other committees; and many party organizations were characterized by large numbers of "dead souls."[18] High levels of turn-over and mobility of party workers were attributed, in part, to poor placements as a result of inadequate knowledge of the individuals concerned by the party organs responsible for their appointment and to an over-reliance on established officials because of the paucity of knowledge of other potential responsible party workers.[19] Even when local registration procedures were not as deficient as these criticisms seem to suggest, there was frequently a problem in regularly informing the center of personnel changes, so that even if local records were up-to-date, those at the center were likely to be significantly behind actual developments.[20] Deficiencies of this sort in the registration procedures of lower level party organs, added to the problem of keeping higher levels constantly abreast of personnel changes at the lower levels, meant that the administrative basis upon which the *nomenklatura* system rested was much weaker than most observers assumed.

The problems created for the establishment of a regularized personnel system by the deficient nature of lower-level registration were exacerbated by the problems encountered in constructing an efficient personnel mechanism at the center. The establishment of a personnel apparatus began at the Eighth Congress with the formal creation of the Orgburo and the Secretariat. The latter was to consist of seven departments of which one, the Records and Assignment Department (Uchraspred), was to collect personal data and statistics on all party members in order to provide the basis for appointments, transfers and job postings.[21] During 1920 Uchraspred took a first important step toward establishing a register of responsible workers by setting up a card system of responsible workers at the guberniia level.[22] The card system was established in September 1920,but administration of it was divided between two sections of Uchraspred — the registration section and the statistical section[23] — an administrative arrangement which cannot have improved the chances of creating an integrated personnel mechanism. This registration system was superseded by a new and more complex one in early 1922. It was claimed at the time that the new system would not destroy the existing one,[24] but it is difficult to believe that the introduction of the new system would not, at least initially, cause some disruption and confusion to central personnel management. Indeed, during the early years of its operation, an efficient and ordered internal regulative milieu was in evidence in Uchraspred. The problem of bringing about the internal ordering of Uchraspred's administrative responsibilities was complicated by the heavy workload it had to bear (particularly in the light of its responsibilities for processing the results of the party census as well as its personnel distribution functions), by the absence of clear institutional boundaries between its responsibilities and those of Orgotdel (the Organization and Instruction Department of the Secretariat) on the one hand and of the Orgburo on the other, and by staffing problems. One indication of the state of Uchraspred's internal work was given by V.P. Nogin at the Eleventh Congress.[25] He reported that the files in Uchraspred had massive gaps in them and, when there were files on individuals, they often had insufficient information to enable the decision-makers to make a realistic evaluation.[26] The central registration system early in the 1920s was clearly inadequate to underwrite a regularized, impersonal personnel system.

The smooth development of a personnel system at the center was hindered by further disruptions during the 1920s. A major new form of registration, which involved some rationalization of central records, was completed in March 1924.[27] Further adjustments would have been necessary to keep registration in line with subsequent changes to the *nomenklatura* arrangements of the Central Committee. In addition, other minor refinements and adjustments were made from time to time.[28] Such tinkering with the registration procedure can only have increased the sense of uncertainty and ambiguity in personnel affairs. Such uncertainty was exacerbated by the re-ordering of the secretarial apparatus in 1924, a re-organization which involved, among other things, a merging of Uchraspred with the organization section of Orgotdel, thereby bringing together responsibility for the supply of personnel to lower levels with the more general supervision of the activities of the lower organs. The new body was called the Organization-Assignment Department, or Orgraspred.[29] A further element of uncertainty stemmed from the high level of mobility of workers in the party apparatus; of the 767 people working in the apparatus at the time of the Fourteenth Congress, 704 had changed their jobs in the preceding eighteen months.[30]

Further major changes were made to the central personnel apparatus during the 1930s. In 1930, as a result of Orgraspred's inability to meet the increased demands for cadres stemming from the First Five-Year Plan, personnel matters were restructured. This took the form of splitting Orgraspred into two separate departments, the Organization and Instruction Department which was concerned with the distribution of personnel within the party, and the Assignment Department which was responsible for personnel in administrative-economic and trade union spheres.[31] The final structure was not approved by the Orgburo until 7 May 1932,[32] a delay which may reflect difficulties in bringing the reorganization to fruition. This was changed again in January 1934, shifting the basis of organization away from that of function which had applied since 1930 and onto an "integrated production-branch" basis. This change involved the splintering of responsibility for personnel between a number of different departments of the Secretariat; personnel in agriculture, industry and transport henceforth became the responsibility of, respectively, the Agriculture, Industry and Transport departments. Although personnel within the party remained the responsibility of a single department – the Leading Party Organs Department which was itself subject to a further reorganization in September 1935[33] – the absence of a single career path meant that the question of party personnel became excessively complicated because of this division inside the Secretariat.[34] In practice, however, power over cadres tended to flow to the Leading Party Organs Department, a tendency recognized in 1939 by yet another reorganization which restored the functional principle by concentrating power over all personnel in a newly-established Cadres Directorate.[35]

Between the formal establishment of the Secretariat in 1919 and the outbreak of the war in 1941, the organ designed to handle personnel matters at the center thus underwent four major organizational transformations plus a number of more minor organizational adjustments. In addition, the registration process was subject to a variety of attempts at reordering and restructuring. The frequent changes at the center reflect the unsatisfactory way in which personnel matters were conducted at this time. The reorganizations themselves were bound to produce administrative confusion and inefficiency, at least in the short run. Moreover, the fact that they were carried out is in itself an expression of the discontent which party leaders had with the conduct of personnel affairs throughout the period. Clearly a smoothly efficient personnel regime was not established in the party before the war.

The absence of an efficient personnel regime inside the party during this period does not, of itself, disprove the argument that Stalin was able to get to power by placing his supporters in positions of importance throughout the political structure. His personal secretariat, about which there is little hard information,[36] may have had its own personnel files and mechanisms. If so, however, it is doubtful that these would have been more extensive than those of the party center, even if Stalin had what amounted to a direct link into the regional party apparatus, as one scholar has argued.[37] It is more probable that Stalin's lieutenants relied mainly on regular party sources for much of their personnel data and information. In any case, the absence of an efficient personnel regime stretching throughout the entire party structure does not mean that a regime embracing the most important positions in the structure (extending to the guberniia level) did not exist from an early time. From 1922-1923 the party center had records of incumbents of guberniia level positions, even if such records were occasionally incomplete and somewhat out of date. Furthermore, from at least this time, the center could impose a candidate on a guberniia party organ if it so wished. This was the crucial level within the party; the guberniia party secretary dominated the appointment process at lower levels and thereby was the major influence in the construction of the local power apparatus and in the shaping of regional delegations to party congresses and other gatherings. Control over the filling of these positions was therefore potentially of great importance for anyone like Stalin with aspirations to consolidate his power at the apex of the system.

The inadequacy of central records meant that the decision-makers initially had little hard official data upon which to base rational decisions about personnel distribution. Such decisions must have been made principally on the basis of personal knowledge of potential incumbents or in substantial ignorance of their backgrounds and possible political affiliations. Certainly the situation would have improved as record-keeping improved, but even so the sort of material which was included in official records was unlikely always to be a reliable guide to an individual's future policy orientations. Thus, if Stalin's cronies did seek to place his supporters in positions of power throughout the structure during the early years of Soviet power, a development which was unlikely prior to the election of Molotov, N.M. Mikhailov and E. Iaroslavskii as Central Committee secretaries at the Tenth Congress, their success must have been restricted by the limits imposed by the extent of their personal knowledge.

Given the problems posed by deficiencies in the record-keeping system and the limits of personal knowledge and acquaintance, Stalin's supporters in the central apparatus could make judgments about the political reliability of office-holders principally on the basis of their performance while in office. Did they support Stalin's positions or oppose them? It is clear that, in his rise to the top, Stalin was able to count on the support of a significant number of leaders at the sub-national levels of the party. Such support, usually attributed to the creation of a clientelist machine, is explicable in terms of the structural position within which middle-level leaders found themselves. Indeed, the factors structuring their position were evident even before Stalin could wield substantial influence in the process of personnel selection with the result that even if he had been able to appoint supporters in the way in which the accepted explanation suggests, those individuals would have been encouraged to act in the way they did by the objective circumstances in which they found themselves.

A major feature of the situation in which middle-ranking leaders found themselves immediately after October was the immense pressure placed on the party as an organizational entity. In most areas party organizations were not robust and had been unable to develop their internal procedures on a regularized basis prior to coming to power. As a result, their actions often tended to be *ad hoc* in nature as they struggled to carve out for themselves a leading role in local political life in the midst of social and economic dislocation and civil war. Central to the development of the party as a strong institution was the generation of an efficient administrative regime inside the party organization. This involved the development of an apparatus which was capable of effectively maintaining the life of the party by carrying out the sort of basic housekeeping functions which are essential to any organization of this type. Measures for maintaining regular communication between different parts of the organization, for convening meetings, for making adequate provision for those meetings, for the translation of decisions into action, for verification of the implementation of decisions, and for maintaining contact with higher and lower level party organs were all essential to the development of a strong organizational and administrative framework inside the party. This task was complicated initially by competition from other bodies — soviets, the CHEKA, committees of the poor, military councils, food detachments and special plenipotentiaries from the center — all operating in the same area as the nascent party committee, all owing their institutional allegiance to bodies other than the party committee and posing a direct challenge to the authority and institutional integrity of the party organization. The challenge of the soviets was particularly important during the initial years of Soviet rule as in many areas personnel flowed out of the party committees and into the soviets so that the latter effectively swallowed the former.[38] Even after measures were taken at the center to strengthen lower-level party organs,[39] many still faced a daunting task in establishing and enforcing their authority over rival organizations. Some institutional confusion, characterized by claims of overlapping jurisdictions, remained.

The rapid party growth during the early part of the period also imposed significant pressures on the party structure. Party organs had quickly to develop an efficient mechanism for administering personnel matters, for registering party members and for keeping the resulting records up to date. However, the enormous fluidity of the membership noted above imposed immense strains upon the weak organizational structure, which in most instances was simply unable to cope with the weight of demands made upon it. The shortage of administrative experience, and often talent, among many party members could only exacerbate this problem.

Another source of pressure on local party organs was the sort of demands made upon them from above. In many parts of the country, particularly during the period of War Communism, party organs had to function in an atmosphere of popular hostility. Yet in such a situation, party organs were confronted with demands from above which, even in more favorable circumstances, would have been difficult to fulfill. The problem for lower-level party organs was not just that demands from above were extravagant in their expectations, but that often they were made in a form which was non-specific. Broad instructions could be couched in ideological terms which may have had a degree of specificity for the ideological *cognoscenti*, but for the ordinary local party secretary who often had a very low level of ideological literacy, such terms were often almost meaningless. Such an absence of specificity also created an ambiguity in criteria for success: if the aims and outlines of a particular policy were vague, it was very difficult to reach judgments about whether that policy had been implemented satisfactorily or not. A similar result could occur even when instructions were specific because of the center's propensity to send out a number of instructions on the same topic but with the detailed directives varying. Party organizations were thus under continual pressure to perform but in a situation in which criteria for success were uncertain. Indeed, such criteria could shift as perceptions at the center changed and with them policy priorities.[40] Moreover, in such an environment, the consequences of failure could be severe, at least in career terms and, during the civil war, in terms of one's life as well.

One effect of these cumulative pressures on the party organization at the middle levels was to encourage a centralization of power at these levels at the expense of the rank-and-file. This was symbolized in the weakness of plenary assemblies and their control over their executive bodies; few plenary meetings of party bodies were held as power became concentrated in executive organs or in the local secretary personally.[41] Many secretaries were able to concentrate a large number of official positions in their own hands.[42] One delegate to the Ninth Congress described the situation which prevailed at the lower levels in many areas as a "dictatorship."[43] But what was particularly important about this centralization of power was the form it took. Very often it cut across institutional boundaries and resulted in the formation of what came to be called "family groups." So called "familyness" or "groupism" combined with the much criticized "localism"[44] to produce a local power structure the existence of which had significant ramifications for the way in which the party developed.

The essence of this phenomenon was the establishment of control over a local area by a group of individuals combining together principally to establish and maintain that control, including the fending off of excessive outside interference. The group could represent the coming together of the leaders of various public organizations in the region, perhaps the local leaders of the party organization, Soviet, trade union and CHEKA, and may therefore constitute a coalition of local bureaucratic interests. Or it could take the form of a personality-centered power faction in local politics, with supporters grouping around a prominent leader, shoring up his position and consolidating themselves in positions of influence within the region under his control. Familial relations could be important in the creation of such a structure.[45]

While the generalized pressures on the party apparatus noted above were important for the centralization of power, certain aspects of the conditions of the time were significant for structuring the centralization of power in this way. One such aspect was the material hardship evident during the early years of Soviet rule. The strains imposed on the economy by the years of war against Germany, the revolution, the civil war and the policy of War Communism had been massive and were reflected in substantial economic disruption and hardship. Throughout most of Russia, and particularly in the rural areas, luxuries were non-existent and the bare essentials of life in short supply. Food shortages were widespread, reflected most graphically in the famine of 1920-1921. Under such conditions life was hard and survival a constant struggle. One way of maximizing one's chances of survival was to get into a position of authority so as to be able to ensure that when goods were available one got access to them. The grim struggle for survival thus encouraged the development of family groups and led to a situation in which such groups were clearly set off from the rank-and-file party members by the style and standard of living which they enjoyed. In many areas this was characterized by a sufficiency of many things which were in short supply elsewhere, a relative wealth amid general paucity, and although in absolute terms such leaders may not have been wealthy[46] the access to goods which their position gave clearly constituted a source of privilege.

Such localized power groupings were also stimulated by the magnitude of the tasks imposed upon local leaders at this time. Faced with the need to establish an effective administrative apparatus in a short period of time against a background of extremely unfavorable social and economic conditions, with existing administrative arrangements and procedures inside the party at a primitive stage of development, it is perhaps little cause for surprise that local leaders should rely on personalized networks in an attempt to establish control in their particular region. Far better to work directly with people, without the complicating intermediation of artificial organizational structures and constraints, and preferably with people of long acquaintance. A reliance upon such personalized networks clearly short-circuited potential bureaucratic hold-ups and enabled local leaders to come to grips with problems directly without having to worry too much about formal bureaucratic considerations.

The effect of this was reinforced by the nature of the demands stemming from above. With demands that were very difficult to implement and with severe penalties for failure, local leaders sought to structure a situation which would provide them with some protection against threats from above. Formal, bureaucratic procedure and working according to the book were not high on the central leadership's list of criteria in judging the performance of local elites; they were more interested in the successful implementation of policies than in the means whereby those policies were implemented. There was, therefore, no benefit to be had from working through highly formalized organizational structures. The interests of the local elite were best served by the establishment of a system which either would facilitate the successful implementation of the tasks set down from above regardless of administrative injunctions or would afford them some protection if they did not. In terms of task fulfillment, many saw this to lie in the network of personalized relations. In terms of protection, too, a personalized network was useful. Control over the main institutions in the region meant control over the main channels of communication to Moscow and an absence of local institutional conflict which might draw unfavorable attention to the region and could even occasion central intervention. Consolidation of control in the region by a family group also meant that the local leadership could direct the course of local elections and thereby ensure that there was no challenge from below to that group. As history was to show, the defence provided by a localized power grouping was by no means perfect, but it was probably the most for which the local elite could hope.

The establishment of control by a local elite did not mean that the party as a structure failed to develop. The legitimacy of the local elite's position depended upon its occupation of the leading party positions in the region with the result that the local party organization could not be allowed simply to die. The party structure, its organizational machinery and its "legislative" wing, did develop, but they often worked very weakly. The bulk of the work often was conducted by the local elite through the non-bureaucratic channels which were the sinews of the family group networks. Rather than structuring the political activity of the local elite, as strong institutions would have done, the local party organization was more an instrument of that elite, to be used as an instrument for the achievement of the elite's desires rather than as a forum within which issues of policy were resolved. The party structure thus could not develop any integrity or coherence as an institution. Furthermore, power as it was exercised tended to be extra-bureaucratic, residing within the local networks of personal relations which were, effectively, excrescences upon the party structure, rather than within the formal organs of the party where it was meant to be.

The power local elites were able to exercise encouraged ambitious people who were not members of the elite to seek to seize control by ousting the incumbent leading group. So called "group conflict" was common at the lower levels during the early years of Soviet rule. Official spokesmen gave various typologies of the types of groups which could be involved in such conflict. At the Tenth Congress, N.N. Krestinskii argued that squabbles for influence in the local party structure occurred between different groups of workers, uezd and guberniia organs, worker-dominated and intelligentsia-dominated parts of the guberniia committee and peasant rural and proletarian organs.[47] At the Eleventh Congress, G.E. Zinov'ev argued that such clique disputes tended to be based on age, country vs. city, party vs. soviet, economic councils vs. trade unions, and food supply committees vs. economic councils.[48] Stalin gave yet another typology at the Twelfth Congress: locals vs. recent arrivals (usually returning soldiers), proletarians vs. intellectuals, young vs. old, center vs. provinces, nationality vs. nationality.[49] In such struggles, the aim was usually to capture sufficient local support to oust the incumbents, although it was not uncommon for local protagonists to enlist the help of the center, either directly or indirectly. The center was often all too eager to become involved, either for factional reasons linked with the struggle for power at the apex of the party or in order to bring about an improvement in methods of work within the party itself.[50]

However, the overthrow of one local elite did not necessarily lead to any structural change in the way in which the party operated at this level. Usually it meant simply the replacement of one personalized network by another. Over time the norms and conventions governing political action structured the situation such that the ability of the party's organizational structure to generate strong organizational norms was limited. Once personalized networks had become established as the main medium through which politics were played out at this level, it was difficult for incoming elites to act differently. Despite some pressure from the top for the strengthening of the party's organizational norms and procedures, the extra-bureaucratic focus of power represented by the family groups and the essentially instrumental nature of the party apparatus remained unchanged. What this meant in practical terms is that power at the sub-national levels of the party tended to remain largely in the hands of family groups throughout the 1920s and 1930s.[51]

Throughout these decades, attempts were made to strengthen the party's organizational norms, principally through the generation of administrative regulations and orders designed to structure the party's internal procedures. These took the form of circulars, letters, instructions and directives issued throughout the party by the Central Committee. Paradoxically, while such administrative regulations and the tightening of central control which they seemed to imply posed a threat to the continued power and position of local power elites, certain aspects of the nature of these regulations actually encouraged the growth of family groups. Three characteristics of the regulations are significant.

The first characteristic was the essentially contingent nature of the regulations. Traditionally, the Bolsheviks had approached rules and laws in an essentialist way. What was important about them was not what they said but whose interests they served; results produced were more important than formalistic interpretations. A similar attitude existed with regard to the relationship between task fulfillment and administrative regulation. While the value of the latter was seen to lie in its contribution to the development of a smoothly functioning bureaucratic structure, it was at no time to stand in the way of the achievement of the political aims to which the party was committed. Although this received its most positive affirmation during the civil war when all efforts were turned to the military conflict without regard for institutional boundaries, prerogatives or sensitivities, it was carried through into peacetime as one of the party's basic operating principles. The continued calls from above for the achievement of specified tasks and for the fulfillment of instructions and the complaints about lower-level organizations failing to carry out instructions, reflect an ethos in which the emphasis was upon task fulfillment, if need be at the expense of administrative considerations. Formal, administrative regulations were binding only when they did not hinder the achievement of officially-prescribed tasks; when they did get in the way of task fulfillment, they could justifiably be ignored. Of course there was a considerable amount of ambiguity here for lower-level leaders. The ultimate judgment about when a decision could be ignored and when it could not lie with the central authorities and could be subject to considerations over which the local leader had no control. An administrative regime which was considered contingent in this way could not develop the sort of normative authority that was essential if the party was to emerge as a strong organizational structure.

The second characteristic of these regulations was the gap in them relating to security of tenure for political office-holders. Formal party rules made no reference to security of tenure for formally elected party positions except indirectly by specifying the frequency with which party bodies were to meet. However, the nominal security provided by the provisions relating to meeting frequency was undermined by the center's rights to appointment institutionalized through *nomenklatura*. The growth of appointment from above as the principal pillar of personnel policy without any attendant formal security of tenure for those subject to this, created a very uncertain environment within which sub-national party leaders had to function. This was particularly the case where the central leadership had high expectations of task fulfillment along with a propensity to call for the achievement of tasks which were difficult to fulfill and rendered even more so by the way in which they were projected. In effect, what this meant was that sub-national leaders were in a very vulnerable position: they could at any time be confronted with excessive demands from above without any institutional buffers to protect them against the wrath of their superiors should they fail to satisfy exaggerated expectations. This sort of uncertainty encouraged informal power groups both to facilitate task fulfillment and to provide some protection.

The third characteristic of the emerging regulative milieu relates to the institutionalization of the appointment process through the *nomenklatura* principle. The importance of this has tended to be seen in terms of its national-level implications. However, it can also be seen as a potent instrument for the consolidation of local power on the part of local elites by formally according this level the right to make a range of political appointments within its own area.   Since the number of positions necessary for the creation of a localized political machine was very much smaller than was necessary for a similar organization at the national level, the problem of the inadequacy of records was less significant.

After the undermining of Zinov'ev's position in Leningrad in 1926, it was clear that none of these personalized local power factions could withstand a concerted effort by the central authorities to bring them down.   However, this should not be interpreted as evidence of the establishment of a highly integrated party structure in which localized power cliques either had no place or were submerged into a nationally-integrated power faction based on the General Secretary. While the centralized appointment system left sub-national leaders vulnerable, the efficiency of this for the building of a broadly-based political machine (as opposed to removing individual power cliques) was hampered by the physical problems of maintaining close communication between the center and all party organs,[52] by the deficiencies in the registration process which lay at the heart of the personnel system, and by the weakness of the administrative regime in the party.   These obstacles to the creation of centralized control gave sub-national political elites more room for maneuver than the *nomenklatura* system seemed to suggest and later observers have believed.   While sub-national leaders clearly had to watch their step because of the possibility of central intervention leading to their displacement, the center's inability to keep tight, continuing control over them means that the central-sub-national relationship may better be seen not in terms of the construction of a tightly-knit political machine around Stalin, but of a relationship in which there was a good deal of bargaining and flux.   The remainder of this paper will attempt to set out briefly the terms in which this unspoken bargain may have been constituted and to chart its course over the 1920s and 1930s.

It is easy to see what each side — the sub-national leaders and Stalin and his supporters — sought to gain from an agreement.   In their own way, both sides wanted security.   Stalin needed the support of the sub-national political leaders.   Without them and the disciplined voting blocs they brought to party fora, Stalin would have been unable to defeat the successive opposition groups in the Central Committee and the party congress.   The lower-level party leaders sought security in the vulnerable position in which they found themselves, and they hoped to secure this by providing the support Stalin needed.   Indeed, this was the other logical response to vulnerability: the creation of an alliance with a higher level protector. This was an alliance from which each expected to gain; neither was a total captive of the other. If the expectations of either side were disappointed, the alliance would come under strain.

Crucial to the emergence of this alliance was the conflict between two of the operating principles of the party: the filling of office by election and by appointment. The power of the sub-national leaders, and the very existence of the family groups, rested upon a denial of the principle of free election as the means of filling responsible positions in the region. Appointment and cooptation were the primary currency of the family group. As a result, charges about the decline of democracy in intra-party life, about the atrophy of election and the growth of appointment, constituted a direct challenge to their continued power and position. Although a more prominent element of the platform of some opposition groups prior to 1929 than of others, these groups included in their demands a call for a widening of party democracy, the extension of the electoral principle, and the restriction of the use of appointment in personnel matters. Criticisms of "bureaucratism" were the staple fare of these groups as they marched toward political doom, even if in some instances such charges were tinged with a good measure of hypocrisy. Such criticisms tended to drive together those threatened by them: the sub-national leaders and those at the center who ran the personnel mechanism and who supported Stalin.[53] Few were as forthright as the local secretary at a party conference in the Urals who accused the Right of being out to "get the secretaries" by blaming them for all that went wrong and questioning their mode of election.[54]

The vulnerability of political life at the middle and lower levels of the party structure was increased by another sort of uncertainty during the 1920s — that created by the prevailing fear in leading circles of the effects of petty bourgeois infection on the party. Concern about the effects of seizing power in a predominantly peasant country had been present in leading Bolshevik circles since October 1917. This concern remained throughout the 1920s but was manifested in a different way, principally through a concern that responsible positions in the party were filled by people with appropriate class backgrounds. Attempts to impose a minimum period of party membership for incumbency of responsible posts was one way of reacting to this. Another was through the conduct of campaigns to extirpate "unhealthy" elements. The purge of 1921-1922 was directed at "non-communist elements," principally among white collar groups.[55] The verification campaigns of the middle 1920s were also directed principally at the quality of the membership, a question given increased significance by NEP and the dangerous implications it was believed to embody. The purge of 1929-1930 formally was directed against alien elements, against "all non-communist, corrupt, alien, bureaucratized and self-seeking elements and hangers-on who take a functionary's view of their duties."[56] These successive campaigns, although they usually caught members of the opposition in their web,[57] were officially directed against alien elements in the party. Although individual party leaders at lower levels could fall into this category, the group as a whole was not threatened nor was their power base. However, the same cannot be said for the campaign for self-criticism which unrolled in 1928.

Intra-party criticism had been an element of party thinking from the early years of Soviet power, but it was never a prominent theme.[58] In the period before the Fifteenth Congress in December 1927, Central Committee Secretary Molotov built upon his call at the Fourteenth Congress for a re-animation of lower-level party bodies[59] by attacking the way in which the rights of lower-level plenary assemblies of the party to elect leading organs frequently were undermined by the machinations of local leaders. Molotov was not calling for free elections without guidance by local leaders. The latter were still to guide the deliberations of the plenary assemblies and to prevent "accidental" candidates from being elected. But this sort of vague demand on the part of Molotov created a new sense of uncertainty for sub-national party leaders because any increase in the role of the rank-and-file along the lines which seemed to be implied by Molotov's comments, threatened the type of control exercised by the local power cliques. This uncertainty was heightened by the self-criticism campaign.

Although the origins of the self-criticism campaign were officially traced back to the Fifteenth Congress,[60] the campaign really got under way with the Central Committee's appeal on self-criticism to all party members dated 2 June 1928.[61] The appeal declared that the party had already done much to organize self-verification and self-criticism from above, but that what was needed was a "powerful wave of creative self-criticism from below" in order to eliminate "bureaucratic suppression, the 'mutual guarantees' of accomplices, *chinovnik* obsequiousness, petty tyranny, ignoring the interests of the masses and petty bourgeois calmness." Without self-criticism there could be no guarantee that there would be no future Shakhty, Artemovsk or Smolensk scandals, nor could the apparatus be cleansed from kulak-capitalist elements. As well as calling for a strengthening of party work among the masses and an improvement in the quality of work and the social composition of the leading organs of the party, the appeal included four measures of particular significance: the freedom of intra-party criticism without independent thought and criticism being labelled a deviation or rowdiness; the full election of party offices including the possibility of the removal of any secretary, bureau or committee; the imposition of full penalties on wrong-doers in the party; and the need for communists to set an example for the masses and to avoid "domestic decay" which can lead to domestic matters being structured in an unacceptable fashion. From the outset of the campaign, Stalin was personally associated with it.[62]

The self-criticism campaign was presented as a central aspect of the party elections at the end of 1928.[63] Not only were local party organs carefully to examine their own work, but individual non-party workers were also called upon to evaluate the performance of the party organ in question. The electoral principle was to be implemented fully in party elections, although higher organs were to exercise "correct and businesslike leadership" at lower levels by working against unsuitable candidates. But elections were not to be replaced by appointment, unwanted candidates were not to be pressed on organizations, there were to be no elections by list, no prior discussion of candidates for elective organs in the bureau or among the *aktiv*, and no violation of voting procedures. Criticism and self-criticism were to be given full rein as party organs ensured widespread discussion of individual candidates in order to establish the will of the party organization concerned.

This sort of campaign posed a direct challenge to the power and position of sub-national leaders by making them appear accountable to rank-and-file party members and even to workers who were not party members. The response to this challenge on the part of many was to protect their positions by frustrating the implementation of the measures called for from above.[64] But the pressure on lower-level leaders did not disappear; it was maintained throughout 1929 by the continuing attention of the party press on deficiencies in local party organizations[65] — a form of publicity which all-too-often portrayed party leaders as incompetent or corrupt — and by the high turnover of sub-national party leaders in 1929-1930.[66] In the light of such attacks, it is perhaps not surprising that there was a significant level of enthusiasm among sub-national leaders for the collectivization drive: here was a chance to demonstrate their true worth.

However, if the sub-national leaders had hoped that this sort of pressure would be submerged in the waves of enthusiasm for the "great transformation," their hopes were disappointed. The escalating targets imposed from above placed increased demands for achievement upon lower-level party functionaries. Despite the unreality of many of the targets, sub-national leaders were expected to meet those targets with a minimum of difficulty. In the face of such unrelenting demands from above, these leaders also had to face concerted popular opposition from below. It was upon their shoulders that the weight of the success of the whole operation depended. Yet, little official consideration was given to their plight. Official spokesmen were critical of their performance, continually encouraging them to increased efforts to realize the party's aims. Stalin's "dizzy with success" article is the best-known instance of an official article reflecting the impossible position these leaders found themselves in.[67] The impression of "scapegoatism" was difficult to avoid. For many in sub-national leadership positions who realized from personal experience what a close-run thing collectivization had been, the view of an insensitive and unsympathetic national leadership which had begun to emerge with the self-criticism campaign must have been strengthened. Such a perception would have encouraged sub-national leaders to seek to strengthen their local power bases in the face of hostility from the center.

This impression can hardly have been shaken by the events of the early and mid-1930s. The *chistka* of 1933-1934 was officially directed at ensuring "iron proletarian discipline in the party and cleansing the party's ranks of all unreliable, unstable and hanger-on elements,"[68] a target which came to include, among others, those who questioned party decisions by suggesting that they were unrealizable, those who were self-seekers and embezzlers of public property, and those who sought their own personal ends through party office.[69] All of these categories fitted sub-national leaders whose personalized control over their regions transformed those areas into administrative fiefs, especially in the light of the complaints about lower-level performance during the collectivization campaign. This pressure was maintained at the Seventeenth Congress where Stalin emphasized the need for the verification of the implementation by lower bodies of party decisions.[70] This theme is also reflected in the comments by other speakers about the failure of lower level party organs to carry out central party decisions.[71] Despite such pressure, sub-national leaders at the middle levels of power were substantially able to protect their family groups and their power bases by deflecting the *chistka* away from their supporters.[72] Nevertheless, resentment resulted and may have been reflected in the rumors about the strength of opposition to Stalin at the Seventeenth Party Congress in January 1934.

The level of attack on sub-national leaders increased in 1935-1937. Throughout these years, the leaders came under direct attack. They were castigated for the primitive and slipshod nature of their administrations, for failure to carry out party policy and decisions, for being isolated from the masses, for familyness and for insufficient vigilance against enemies of the party.[73] These charges were made against the background of the verification of party documents in 1935 and the exchange of party cards in 1936. The former officially was prompted by the desire to bring order out of the administrative chaos which reigned at lower levels, a purpose which clearly was consistent with a strengthening of central controls and a reduction of local autonomy which subverted aspirations for a centralized administrative machine. The latter was meant, in part, as an exercise whereby increased vigilance and discipline would be brought to bear to cleanse the party of elements more "passive" than "hostile."[74] Important, too, was the heightening emphasis upon "enemies of the people" associated with the assassination of S.M. Kirov in December 1934. Within this context, charges of unsatisfactory leadership were easily transformed into the sorts of charges which brought individuals within the web of the unrolling terror leading to the Ezhovshchina.

The culmination of this tension, and therefore the final smashing of the agreement between Stalin and the existing sub-national leaders, came in 1937. Part of the campaign for vigilance which had accompanied the measures of 1935-1936 and continued into later years was a re-emphasis on the theme of criticism-self-criticism.[75] This appeal over the heads of the sub-national leaders to the party rank-and-file reached its apogee with the introduction of new electoral regulations in March 1937.[76] As well as injunctions against voting by list, the regulations called for the election of *all* responsible party positions by secret ballot and the open discussion and criticism of potential candidates at party meetings. In the equivalent regulations introduced the following year, a significant change was made: party secretaries and members of executive committees at all levels were to be elected by open ballot.[77] The initial position on secret ballot had been justified on the grounds of the scope it gave for increased criticism within the party. Its amendment came amid charges of inadequate leadership of elections resulting in the gaining of party office by inappropriate people. This charge may reflect the fact that no city or regional party leaders were replaced in the secret elections.[78] But if city and regional leaders had been able to preserve their positions once again, despite the pressure from the center manifested in the self-criticism campaign and the secret ballot, their victory was short-lived. In the middle of 1937, the Ezhovshchina embraced the party secretaries.[79] It was those who replaced the party leaders who lost their positions in the terror who were to benefit from the amendment to the electoral law noted above, an amendment which once again provided them with a means of exerting their power over their nominal electors.

What are we to draw from this analysis? The deficiencies in the party personnel regime, added to the undoubted administrative problems of the central apparatus, suggest that the capacity of Stalin and his supporters to construct a political machine of solid supporters was much more restricted than we have thus far assumed. Nevertheless, a secretarial fraction did emerge, but it was held together less by a firm commitment to Stalin than by a commonality of objective position and, presumably, interest and perhaps, by a coincidence of policy views. Sub-national leaders were caught in the tension between two power bases: one stemmed from localism and familyness, the other from integration into a nationally-focused political machine. Some were doubtless content with the second alternative, but many seem to have preferred the advantages they saw flowing from a significant degree of autonomy in local affairs. For those who sought to maximize their autonomy, every attempt by the center to improve the party's administrative regime constituted a threat to their position. However, during the 1920s, a more immediate threat appeared to stem from the positions taken by successive opposition groups. Under such circumstances, support for Stalin would have seemed the most obvious response, because at the national level, he was the head of the organization most vulnerable to the sort of charges they were laying. He was, therefore, the leader most likely to offer them protection. Even the self-criticism campaign at the end of the decade may not have shifted that support from Stalin, although it presumably would have shaken it. But what did lead to the rupturing of the relationship was the collectivization campaign and the subsequent direct assault on their position.

Of course, Stalin was able to solve the immediate political problem. Like other opposition and potential opposition forces, Stalin was able to destroy the sub-national party leadership in the great terror. But this did not eliminate the central problem posed by regionalism. This could be solved only through the development of a regularized, more efficient party apparatus. Without such a development control could only be episodic; it could not be maintained in the continuous fashion necessary for a highly centralized, efficient political machine. Without such institutional controls, the highly centralized political rule of Stalinism was much less all-embracing than it appeared.

The University of Sydney

NOTES

[1]For one discussion of institutionalization in the party, see Graeme Gill, "Institutionalization and Revolution: Rules and the Soviet Political System," *Soviet Studies*, vol. XXXVII, no. 2 (April 1985), pp. 212-226.

[2]This is not to deny the importance in the accepted explanation of such factors as

Stalin's tactical skill compared with the ineptness of his opponents, the adoption of ideological positions which were atttractive to large sections of the party, the more effective way in which Stalin was able to associate himself with the legitimizing symbol of Lenin, and the policy positions he espoused.

[3]This was shown by the experience of Khrushchev. See the general view expressed in T.H. Rigby, "The Soviet Regional Leadership: The Brezhnev Generation," *Slavic Review*, vol. XXXVII, no. 1 (March 1978), p. 23.

[4]T.H. Rigby, *Communist Party Membership in the USSR, 1917-1967*. Princeton: Princeton University Press, 1968, p. 52.

[5]The party did not always accept new members. Recruitment was suspended between December 1932 and September 1936 in connection with the purge, party verification and exchange of documents.

[6]*Izvestiia tsentral'nogo komiteta VKP(b)*, 1 May 1919, and *Spravochnik partiinogo rabotnika*, vol. I. Moscow, N.D., pp. 69-77.

[7]*Izvestiia tsk*, no. 35, 1 December 1921, pp. 14-15, and *Spravochnik partiinogo rabotnika* vi, vol. 1. Moscow, 1928, pp. 547-553 and 603-605.

[8]*Izvestiia tsk*, no. 1(59), January 1924, pp. 64-67; no. 4(62), April 1924, p. 41; and no. 1(122), 18 January 1926, p. 4.

[9]*Izvestiia tsk*, no. 1(122), 18 January 1926, pp. 2-4.

[10]A commission was charged with working out a new *nomenklatura* distribution for the Central Committee, but there is no indication of the fate of this. *Izvestiia tsk*, no. 6-7(227-228), 5 March 1928, p. 7.

[11]The most important of these followed the reorganizations of the central Secretariat discussed below.

[12]Cited in Rigby, *Communist Party*, p. 97 fn. 14.

[13]*Izvestiia tsk*, no. 32, 6 August 1921, pp. 17-18. Also see the complaints by the Ninth Conference in May 1921 and the Twelfth Congress in April 1923. *Kommunisticheskaia partiia sovetskogo soiuza v rezoliutsiiakh i resheniiakh s"ezdov, konferentsii i plenumov tsk.*, vol. II. Moscow, 1983, p. 299, and *Dvenadtsatyi s'ezd RKP(b) 17-25 aprelia 1923 goda. Stenograficheskii otchet.* Moscow, 1968, p. 73.

[14]*Izvestiia tsk*, no. 3(51), March 1923, p. 33.

[15]See the debate in *Pravda*, 17, 20, 21, 22,25, 28 July 1923 and 3 August 1923.

[16]For an earlier attempt to bring about a division of personnel responsibility, see the resolution of a December 1921 conference of secretaries of obkoms, obburos, and gubkoms which was confirmed at the Eleventh Congress. This set out a scheme for structuring the process of registration. *Izvestiia tsk*, no. 1(37), January 1922, p. 37, and *KPSS v rez.*, vol. II, p. 503.

[17]It was reported in 1926, for example, that the numbers on the *nomenklatura* of gubkoms ranged from 946 in Smolensk to 99 in Riazan. *Izvestiia tsk*, nos. 31-32(152-153), 9 August 1926, p. 8; and nos. 45-46(166-167), 22 November 1926, p. 6.

[18]See these criticisms in *Partiinoe stroitel'stvo* 18 September 1933, pp. 4-5; 16 August 1934, pp. 21-24; 4 February 1935, pp. 32-36; and 5 June 1936, pp. 26-28. Also see *XVII s'ezd vsesoiuznoi kommunisticheskoi partii (b) 26 ianvaria-10 fevralia 1934g.*

Stenograficheskii otchet. Moscow, 1934, p. 286. The chaos in local record-keeping is ably shown in J. Arch Getty, *Origins of the Great Purges: The Soviet Communist Party Reconsidered, 1933-1939.* Cambridge: Cambridge University Press, 1985.

[19]*Partiinoe stroitel'stvo*, 11 June 1931, pp. 13-14, 1-2 January 1932, p. 19.

[20]*Partiinoe stroitel'stvo*, 16 August 1934, p. 23. This also applied to party organs below the center but exercising supervision over lower organs. On the raikoms' failure adequately to supervise such changes in lower organs, see *Partiinoe stroitel'stvo*, 16 August 1934, p. 19.

[21]*Deviatyi s"ezd RKP(b) Mart-aprel' 1920 goda. Protokoly.* Moscow, 1960, p. 500.

[22]In August 1920 all gubkoms were instructed to supply a list of responsible guberniia-level workers, which all had done by February 1921. Unfortunately, only Riazan gubkom continued to inform the center of changes. *Izvestiia tsk*, no. 28, 5 March 1921, p. 13.

[23]*Izvestiia tsk*, no. 18 September 1920, p. 12.

[24]*Izvestiia tsk*, no. 2 (38), February 1922, p. 12. There were now to be fourteen categories rather than five.

[25]*Odinnadtsatyi s'ezd RKP(b) Mart-aprel' 1922 goda. Stenograficheskii otchet.* Moscow, 1961, p. 65.

[26]Uchraspred's report to the Eleventh Congress acknowledged that it was not adequately prepared for appointment-making on an individualized basis. *Izvestiia tsk*, no. 3(39), March 1922.p. 27.

[27]*Izvestiia tsk*, no. 3(61), March 1924, pp. 9-25.

[28]See, for example, *Spravochnik partiinogo rabotnika*, vol. IV. Moscow, 1924, pp. 144-149; vol. VI,no. 1. Moscow, 1928, pp. 527-528, 534-546 and 553-554.

[29]*Trinadtsatyi s'ezd RKP(b) Mai 1924 goda. Stenograficheskii otchet.* Moscow, 1963, pps. 133-134 and 808. For the organizational structure and tasks of Orgraspred, see *Izvestiia tsk*, nos. 17-18 (92-93), 11 May 1925, pp. 7-8.

[30]*XIV s'ezd vsesoiuznoi kommunisticheskoi partii (b) 18-31 dekabria 1925g. Stenograficheskii otchet.* Moscow, 1926, p. 89.

[31]For the Central Committee decision of 26 January 1930 bringing this about, see *Spravochnik partiinogo rabotnika, vol. VII, Moscow, 1930, pp. 169-171.* For explanations of the change, see *XVI s'ezd vsesoiuznoi komunisticheskoi partii (b). Stenograficheskii otchet.* Moscow, 1931, p. 82, and *Partiinoe stroitel'stvo*, no. 2(4), February 1930, pp. 3-13.

[32]*Partiinoe stroitel'stvo*, 9 May 1932, pp. 60-61.

[33]*Partiinoe stroitel'stvo*, no. 7, 15 October 1935, pp. 73-78.

[34]On the 1934 change, see *XVII s'ezd*, pp. 561-562 and 672, and *Partiinoe stroitel'stvo*, 1 January 1934, pp. 1-7.

[35]On the changes, see *XVIII s'ezd vsesoiuznoi kommunisticheskoi partii (b) 10-21 marta 1939g. Stenograficheskii otchet.* Moscow, 1939, pp. 528 and 670-671.

[36]See the two studies by Niels Erik Rosenfeldt, *Knowledge and Power: The Role of Stalin's Secret Chancellery in the Soviet System of Government.* Copenhagen: Rosenkilde & Bagger, 1978; and "The Consistory of the Comunist Church': The

Origins and Development of Stalin's Secret Chancellery," *Russian History*, vol. IX, nos. 2-3 (1982), pp. 308-324.

[37]The reference here is to the Special Sectors. Rosenfeldt, *Knowledge*, pp. 67-68, 70, 71-76, 83-84, and 95-96. According to Rosenfeldt (pp. 65-66), the records of high level personnel were found in the Special Sector in Moscow.

[38]*Deviatyi*, pp. 30-32.

[39]See, for example, *Vos'moi s'ezd RKP(b) Mart 1919 goda. Protokoly*. Moscow, 1959, pp. 428-429, and *Deviatyi, pp. 32 and 504*.

[40]For example, the shift in attitude to the middle peasant at the end of 1918.

[41]See, for example, Osinskii's comments in *Vos'moi*, pp. 166-187, and *Deviatyi*, pp. 118-124. Also *Izvestiia tsk*, no. 32, 6 August 1921, p. 8.

[42]See Zinov'ev's comments in *Vos'moi* pp. 279-280.

[43]*Deviatyi*, p. 62.

[44]See, for example, *Vos'moi*, p. 429.

[45]The instance most frequently discussed in Western scholarship is that which resulted in the Smolensk scandal of 1928. See Merle Fainsod, *Smolensk Under Soviet Rule*. New York: Vintage Books, 1958, pp. 48-52, and Olga A. Narkiewicz, *The Making of the Soviet State Apparatus*. Manchester: Manchester University Press, 1970, ch. 10.

[46]Although clearly some were. See, for example, *Desiatyi s'ezd RKP (b) Mart 1921 goda. Stenograficheskii otchet*. Moscow, 1963, pp. 227-229, and the resolution of the Ninth Conference. *KPSS v rez.*, vol. II, p. 302.

[47]*Desiatyi*, pp. 45-46.

[48]*Odinnadtsatyi*, p. 402.

[49]*Dvenadstsatyi*, p. 66.

[50]On local groups seeking to use the party purge against their local opponents, see *Odinnadtsatyi*, p. 371. For local clashes which occasioned Central Committee intervention, see *Odinnadtsatyi*, pp. 654-656. For a more extended discussion of one instance, see A.I. Mikoian, *V nachale dvatsatykh*. Moscow, 1975, ch. 2, and T.H. Rigby, "Early Provincial Cliques and the Rise of Stalin," *Soviet Studies*, vol. XXXIII, no. 1 (January 1981), pp. 3-28

[51]The most prominent of these in the 1920s were those of Zinov'ev in Leningrad, and successively Kamenev and N.A. Uglanov in Moscow. Others included G.K. Ordzhonikidze in Tiflis, S.M.Kirov in Baku, F.I. Goloshchekin in Kazakhstan and E. Iaroslavskii and M.M. Lashevich in Siberia. On the 1930s see, *inter alia*, Stalin's pointed comments at the March 1937 Central Committee plenum. I.V. Stalin, *Sochineniia*, vol. I (XIV), *1934-40*. Stanford: The Hoover Institute on War, Revolution and Peace, 1967, ed. Robert H. McNeal, esp. pp. 229-232.

[52]For example, it was declared at the Sixteenth Congress that some district organizations remained unaware of Central Committee directives. *XVI s'ezd*, p. 82.

[53]One reflection of this is the figure cited by Robert Daniels: of all delegates listed in the protocols of the Eleventh Congress, 16% of those in party work had engaged in oppositional activity by 1930 as compared to 50% of those working in other areas.

Robert V. Daniels, *The Conscience of the Revolution: Communist Opposition in Soviet Russia*. New York: Simon & Schuster, 1969, p. 170.

[54]Cited in Sheila Fitzpatrick, *The Russian Revolution*. Oxford: Oxford University Press, 1982, p. 118. Despite the existence of substantial lower-level support in the party for the Right, the image of Bukharin and those around him as unsympathetic to the plight of party secretaries found sufficient support to sustain it even before Bukharin's attack on the secretaries and their mode of selection in November 1928. At the time of the Shakhty affair in March 1928, with the split at the top of the party still concealed, Bukharin widened the web of responsibility from the specialists blamed by Stalin to include the local party secretaries. Stephen F. Cohen, *Bukharin and the Bolshevik Revolution: A Political Biography, 1888-1938*. London: Wildwood House, 1971, pp. 281, 302 and 323.

[55]See the Tenth Congress resolution and the Central Committee letter on the purge of 27 July 1921. *KPSS v rez.*, vol. II, pp. 327-328 and 438-443.

[56]*KPSS v rez., vol. IV, p. 489.*

[57]In the purge of 1929-30, opposition was a formal ground for purging. The resolution of the Sixteenth Conference explicitly referred to "concealed Trotskiists, Miasnikovites, Democratic Centralists and protagonists of other anti-party groups." *KPSS v rez.*, vol. IV, p. 490.

[58]See, for example, *KPSS v rez.*, vol. II, pp. 299-300 (Ninth Conference), 327 and 336 (X Congress) and IV, p. 208 (XV Conference).

[59]*XIV s"ezd*, p. 86 and *Izvestiia tsk*, nos. 3-4 (124-125), 31 January 1926, pp. 1-2; nos. 10-11 (131-132), 22 March 1926, pp. 3-5; nos. 47-48 (168-169), 3 December 1926, p. 6; nos. 5-6 (178-179), 14 February 1927, p. 16; and no. 16 (89), 30 April 1927, pp. 1-4.

[60]While there was no explicit decision on self-criticism at the congress, for calls for self-criticism, see *Piatnadtsatyi s"ezd VKP(b). Dekabr' 1927 goda Stenograficheskii otchet*. Moscow, 1961, vol. I, pp. 80-81 (Stalin), and vol. II, pp. 1434 and 1601 (congress resolutions).

[61]*Bol'shevik*, no. 11, 15 June 1928, pp. 3-7, and for a call for self-criticism in the light of the Shakhty affair, see the resolution of the joint CC-CCC plenum of April 1928. *KPSS v rez.*, vol. IV, p. 333. This resolution associated the Shakhty affair with "familyness" (p. 332).

[62]See, for example, his comments in April, May and June 1928. J.V. Stalin, *Works*. Moscow, 1954, vol. XI, pp. 31-42, 75-79, 102-104 and 133-144. Presumably, Stalin fostered this campaign at this time as a blow against the Right Opposition. Cohen, *Bukharin*, pp. 281-282.

[63]*Izvestiia tsk*, no. 31(252), 21 October 1928, pp. 3-5.

[64]See the charges in *Izvestiia tsk*, nos. 37-38(258-259); 31 December 1928, p. 11; nos. 2-3(261-262), 31 January 1929, p. 6; no. 10(269), 12 April 1929, pp. 5-6; and nos. 17-18(276-277), 29 June 1929, p. 2.

[65]Instances occurred in most issues of *Izvestiia tsk*; see, for example, no. 13(272), 15 May 1929, pp. 24-25; no. 16(275), 14 June 1929, pp. 13-14; nos. 20-21(279-280), 29 July 1929, pp. 10-16; no. 22(281), 10 August 1929, pp. 4-17.

[66]In the two years prior to June 1930, 80% of kraikom and obkom secretaries and

94% of okrugkom secretaries had taken up their current positions; nearly half of all obkom secretaries and two-thirds of okrugkom secretaries had been in their posts for less than a year. *Partiinoe stroitel'stvo*, nos. 11-12(13-14), June 1930, p. 34. The description of those against whom the *chistka* was directed cited in fn. 56 could clearly embrace the sub-national political leaders.

[67]Stalin, *Works*, vol. XII, pp. 197-205. Self-criticism remained a theme during 1930. See major articles in *Partiinoe stroitel'stvo*, no. 9(11), May 1930, pp. 3-7; and nos. 11-12(13-14), June 1930, pp. 21-29.

[68]Resolution of joint CC-CCC meeting, 12 January 1933. *KPSS v rez.*, vol. VI, p. 32.

[69]Reprinted in Rigby, *Communist Party*, pp. 201-202. Indeed, before the *chistka* began, it was declared to be directed mainly against "enemies with a party card in their pocket." *Partiinoe stroitel'stvo*, nos. 23-24, December 1932, p. 6.

[70]*XVII s"ezd*, pp. 34-36. Also see the resolution on the Central Committee report, esp. pp. 670-671.

[71]See, for example, I.A. Rudzutak on the purge and L.M. Kaganovich on party entry procedures. *XVII s"ezd*, pp. 285-287 and 552.

[72]See the discussion in Getty, *Origins*, pp. 52-53.

[73]*Partiinoe stroitel'stvo*, nos. 1-2, January 1935, pp. 37-38; no. 4, February 1935, pp. 32-34; no. 11, June 1935, pp. 6-11; no. 15, August 1935, pp. 8-9; nos. 19-20, 15 November 1935, pp. 49-57; no. 8, 25 April 1936, pp. 56-57; no. 10, 20 May 1936, pp. 59-60; no. 11, 5 June 1936, pp. 3-8;no. 21, 5 November 1936, pp. 58-62; no. 24, 15 December 1936, pp. 34-40; no. 4, 15 February 1937, pp. 5-12; no. 6, 20 March 1937, pp. 19-24 and 39-42. Also Stalin's speeches to the March 1937 Central Committee plenum, Stalin, *Sochineniia*, vol. XIV,pp. 185-245.

[74]*KPSS v rez.*, vol. VI, p. 300, where a contrast was drawn with the verification which was declared to be directed against "hostile" elements. The verification seems to have been accompanied by an expansion of the personnel files held at the center, with the inclusion of more information on individuals than hitherto. Rosenfeldt, *Knowledge*, pp. 185-186.

[75]Self-criticism had been mentioned by Stalin at the Seventeenth Congress as a principal means of overcoming difficulties in organizational work. *XVII s"ezd*, p. 33. It was given particular emphasis by the center when they were dissatisfied with the way in which lower-level leaders were conducting the verification during the first half of 1935. Getty, *Origin*, pp. 67-78.

[76]*Partiinoe stroitel'stvo*, no. 6, 20 March 1937, pp. 3-4. The secret ballot was directly linked with the struggle against "familyness." *Partiinoe stroitel'stvo*, no. 6, 20 March 1937, p. 16.

[77]*Partiinoe stroitel'stvo*, no. 8, April 1938, pp. 62-64.

[78]Getty, *Origins*, p. 162. This is in sharp contrast to the primary party organizations where turn-over levels were much higher. Figures on these will be found in *Partiinoe stroitel'stvo*, no. 10, May 1937, p. 30. See the discussion in Getty, *Origins*, pp. 157-162.

[79]All but three obkom secretaries were removed shortly after June 1937. J. Arch Getty, "Party and Purge in Smolensk: 1933-1937," *Slavic Review*, vol. XLII, no. 1 (Spring 1983), p. 75.

Stalinism as a System of Communication

Niels Erik Rosenfeldt

Let it be stated quite clearly from the start: Stalinism was many things. It is impossible to characterize it exhaustively by any particular label or "model".

> Stalinism was "revolution from above," but also "revolution from below".
> Stalinism was organization, but also chaos.
> Stalinism was planning, but also improvisation.
> Stalinism was initiative and innovation, but also traditionalism and backwardness.
> Stalinism was terror, but also enthusiasm.

In the course of time many Western sovietologists have helped us to understand the complexity of Stalinism. Among these are the contributors to the work published by Robert C. Tucker in 1977 *Stalinism: Essays in Historical Interpretation*. They also include researchers like Roger Pethybridge and Michal Reiman who have brought new light to bear on the social, economic and political background to Stalinism. And of course there is the group of historians, headed by Sheila Fitzpatrick, who have drawn such a richly varied picture of cultural revolution and social processes in Stalin's Russia.[1]

Several other pioneer works could be mentioned. Much has happened during recent years on the Stalinology front. For instance, a distinct revisionist trend has emerged — for better or worse. There is no doubt that this trend has helped to open up new avenues for scholarly discussions. At the same time, there is reason to fear that it may lead research on Stalinism into a blind alley.

Common to these new revisionists is the point of view that all the more traditional interpretations of Stalinism are both outmoded and over-simplified. In some respects they may be right, in others they are undoubtedly wrong. At any rate they must not be reproached for putting the old views to the test. What is deplorable, however, is the fact that the interpretations they themselves put forward often seem far more one-sided and less well-founded than the views they are criticizing. It leaps to the eye, for example, that many of the revisionist analyses barely include Stalin as an independently acting political leader. The General Secretary of the Soviet Communist Party is portrayed more or less as a willow that bends, without resistance, to any gust of wind. If we carry these interpretations to their logical conclusion, we end up, as it were, with a Stalinism without Stalin.[2]

This is where I personally opt out. On this question I entirely agree with Jerry F. Hough when he points out that "it is of course wildly misleading to suggest that Stalin was a passive barometer who was simply responding to societal pressure for change."[3] In the same way, there is little sense in regarding Stalin as the kind of man who merely spent his time mediating between other, more purposeful and impetuous Soviet leaders.[4] Research on Stalinism will make little headway if it disregards Stalin's own initiatives, motives and strategies.

Stalinism was not only the person Stalin. For obvious reasons it must be regarded as an interplay between the dynamic party leader on the one side and a complexity of variegated currents and conflicting interest in Soviet society on the other. It is precisely this interplay that research on Stalinism must attempt to throw more light upon.

From all this it will be readily understood that the following pages will contain no simple, easy-to-grasp formula on Stalinism that will miraculously explain all. The object of this article is only to look at Stalinism from a particular viewpoint. It is the author's hope, however, that this particular point of view will give new sustenance to research discussion in general and, more specifically, help to stimulate the ongoing dialogue between traditionalists and revisionists.

In what follows, Stalinism will be regarded as a communication phenomenon. The main emphasis will be placed on the administrative and organizational aspects of communication, i.e., attention will be drawn to the Stalinist system. Or put in another way, we shall be dealing with the communication channels used for all kinds of "messages" to and from Stalin.

The Theoretical Framework.

Let us first disregard Stalin and Stalinism and concentrate on communication processes in general.[5] Any organizational structure can of course be regarded as a communication system, i.e., as a network of decision centers and transmission channels which collects, receives, transmits, classifies, stores, selects and recombines information. Seen in this light, communication is more than an auxiliary operation. It is the very essence of organizational work. It conditions and determines all other activities.

Seen in this same light, it can also be maintained that anyone seeking political power must of necessity build up or gain control of a communication network, and that anyone exercising political power must work equally hard to ensure that his communication network is able to adapt to changing demands in step with the times.

In this continuous process of adaptation, those in power will need, on the whole, to receive two types of messages: 1) information on the general situation within the system itself and/or the world around it, and 2) information on what effect their own previous decisions have had, i.e., "feedback." This feedback information will enable them to evaluate how close they are to the realization of the goals they set out to achieve, what stumbling blocks have been encountered, and how urgent is the need to adapt to new and unexpected developments.

Those in power also issue various kinds of messages. Some of these aim at informing, influencing and convincing, whether the addressee is the general public or specific officials in the system. Others are in the nature of decrees and directives which formally oblige the recipient to carry out his duties in a particular way.

The form taken by the various messages has in itself a "meta-communicative" function, since it helps to tell the recipient how the sender expects the communication to be interpreted. In practice, however, the dividing line between the various forms is often rather obscure. And whatever form the information may take, there is one problem common to all who deal with communication: How effective is the transmission of information in relation to the aims that have been set?

The efficacy of any kind of information transfer will naturally be influenced by the particular characteristics of the communication system in question, be it the number of communication channels and reception centers, the procedures for the transmission of messages or the power vested in the various "gatekeepers" through whom the information has to pass from sender to recipient. The real or potential blockages in the communication system present political leaders with a number of precarious options. The leaders are often in a dilemma. The measures employed in solving one communication problem frequently give rise to a chain of new problems which in turn will have to be overcome by various other measures, and so on. In this sense, the communication system will constantly be in the melting pot.

Different systems — i.e., different combinations of decision centers and transmission channels — create different problems. In a strongly centralized system, there will normally be a marked tendency towards an overloading of the vertical communication and a similar massive pressure on the exclusive reception center at the apex of the system, where the information is processed and decisions made. Certain gatekeepers occupying key positions in the communication network will thus be able to obtain great power and considerable autonomy and may, for instance, attempt to utilize the feedback process to formulate their own demands and to assert specific political, institutional or personal interests.

The resultant risk that the communication process can be blocked or distorted will become even greater if the system also takes a distinct hierarchical form. The individual gatekeepers, who are able to influence the stream of information to and from the top of the hierarchy, will in such a case be strongly disinclined to pass on to their superiors negative information that can be used in evaluating their own performance, and similarly will tend to modify directives on the way down which might put them severely to the test. They will be afraid of not measuring up to expectations. They will act in fear of being hit by sanctions, of losing privileges and promotion prospects, or perhaps simply of having their secure daily work schedule upset. If the society they live in is also marked by considerable social and work life mobility — or if only expectations of such are present among the more important gatekeepers — then the disinclination to give oneself away will be even stronger.

How can these system-conditioned communication problems be solved? One can try to ensure unquestionable loyalty from the communication workers towards their leaders by means of propaganda and political indoctrination. But this sort of regimentation has its price: it can lead to barren standardization of information matters and a strong disinclination to try out new untraditional ideas. One can also build up a complex of various control and communication channels which more or less cover the same work areas. One can instigate a special inspection of administrative procedures or a specific control of personnel in the communication system. Again, one can form a parallel working corps of unofficial or "extraordinary" information agents who keep in close contact both with the local gatekeepers in the regular communication system and with the top political leadership, and whose job it is to pass on independent information to the top concerning all that goes on in the jurisdiction areas covered by the respective gatekeepers.

To the extent that these various communication channels would, as it were, be "competing" in informing the central leadership, the power vested in the local gatekeeper would be limited: he would know, or at least fear, that any information he might want to stop for personal reasons on the way up, would in any case reach the political top via one or more of the other communication channels. In much the same way, he wold also have to face the fact that the numerous control systems would sooner or later be bound to catch him out if he tried to avoid, alter or dilute any down-going directive.

Even this is still a long way from solving all the communication problems. To the extent that the various competing communication channels are passing the same information to the same recipients, there will still be a tendency toward an overloading of the vertical communication channels and the topmost reception center. And if the prime object is to maintain a strictly centralized political system, then the introduction of each supplementary communication channel will tend to create new, intricate control and co-ordination problems: "separatist" institutional interests can arise; certain communication channels might possibly manage to monopolize particular types of information and thereby acquire a certain degree of autonomy.

Apart from this there is the constant risk that local representatives of the various competing communication networks might see some advantage in dropping the competition element and forming one joint gatekeeper clique in relation to the top political leadership. This could create a stumbling block that not even the formation of a corps of extraordinary information agents would be effective against. Here, too, the political leaders will find themselves in a dilemma. If these information agents are too closely connected with the top political leadership, they may have difficulties in gaining the confidence of the local gatekeeper officials and thus be cut off from important information sources. If, on the other hand, these agents have too close a relationship with the local gatekeepers whom they are expected to supervise, then a complex of common interests may well develop between those doing the supervising and those being supervised, thus preventing an impartial flow of upward communication.

Finally, there is the obvious fact that it is not really possible in practice to accumulate all information at the top of the system. A certain degree of "decentralization" can simply not be avoided. This will of course be felt as a risk by centralistic-minded political leaders, but the risk can be countered by the introduction of rigorous secrecy procedures in the administration. The effects of this will be two-fold. Firstly, it will help to limit the "de-central" processing of information to cases of low secrecy-classification and thus also of minor importance. Secondly, it will allow for the creation of a communication system which ensures that only those at the very top of the system are in a position to review the situation in its totality. An extensive system of secrecy-classifications usually goes hand-in-hand with the application of the need-to-know principle, whereby even highly placed officials only have access to documents directly related to their own sphere of responsibility. The very few people who are not affected by these limitations normally have the authority to lay down the highest secrecy-classifications and to decide who are entitled to receive the classified documents concerned. They will therefore have a double advantage. Not only will they be among the best informed people in the entire political system, they will also be able to obtain for themselves a decisive gatekeeper role in relation to the rest of society.

However, even this sort of system has its built-in weaknesses. Local officials who know only part of the total picture will find it difficult to act rationally on their own initiative. In addition, if the system is highly hierarchical and based on severe penalties for errors and omissions, information will usually tend to be over-classified — a state of affairs that is not only impractical in itself but which also may bring with it a growing disrespect for "genuinely" secret matters. This problem has its roots in two sets of circumstances. Firstly, high classification usually adds importance to a case and thus gives the person dealing with it greater influence and prestige. Secondly, the risk of being penalized is normally much greater if you classify too low — thereby disclosing "state secrets" — than if you classify too high by being overly careful. Over-classification thus becomes the cautious official's way of safe-guarding himself.

This sketch of a centralized, hierarchical and secrecy-oriented communication system and its inherent problems will enable us to view Stalinism as a specific system of communication. Let us start with a few fundamental observations.

The Stalinist System.

Few will deny that Stalinism had features that were clearly centralistic and hierarchical, and that gatekeeper problems could thus result. It is also obvious that the political leadership was in possession of a variety of means which could be used to limit these problems and ensure efficient vertical communication. Ideological indoctrination, mass agitation and personality cult were all fundamental to the Stalinist system. An extensive propaganda apparatus was built up as a means of strengthening the loyalty of officials and other Soviet citizens towards the decision-makers in the center and to legitimize the right of these decision-makers to run the country on the basis of a massive information monopoly.

The political leaders had, in addition, a number of communication channels at their disposal — the Communist Party apparat, the soviet administration, the trade unions, the security service, etc. Obviously, each communication channel had its own purpose and function, but the areas they covered overlapped so to some extent they dealt with the same information. At the same time they were deeply integrated: the Communist Party had its special representation in all other institutions and was ultimately responsible for running, coordinating and controlling all the various apparats. Representatives of the security service, too, gradually established themselves in all parts of the Soviet system.

Within the framework of this complex structure, there were a number of specific control and inspection bodies, such as the Communist Party's Auditing Commission and the twin organs, the Central Control Commission and the Workers' and Peasants' Inspectorate (renamed and reorganized in 1934). Through these it was possible to supervise both the administrative procedures in the various apparats and the people they employed. Keeping a check on personnel was also done through the comprehensive *nomenklatura* system which gave the party leadership decisive influence on the appointment of leading officials in the party and state apparats. In addition, the Party Secretariat had no lack of opportunity to manipulate the elections to the competent party and state assemblies.

Furthermore, it is an unquestionable fact that the Stalinist administration was marked by a high degree of secrecy, and that rigorous instructions were in existence on how to deal with so-called "conspirative" documents. On top of this there was the all-pervading censorship of everything due for ordinary publication.

Thus on the surface, it must look as though the Soviet leaders had plenty of opportunities to break down the stumbling blocks that usually crop up in centralized, hierarchical communication systems, and as though they were also in an extremely good position to filter the stream of information to the rest of society.

The fact, however, that the Bolshevik decision-makers on the whole knew more than other Soviet citizens obviously does not mean that they started off by knowing everything — or even enough to enable them to carry out a rational policy. As we have seen, the means that political leaders normally operate with in attempting to strengthen their superiority on the information front, tend to create new communication problems as soon as they are put to use. This was undoubtedly the case in Stalin's Russia. The problems that arose in this way were many and varied and should be looked upon from different angles. They concerned in part the changing relationships between the local gatekeepers and the leading political organs *in toto*. But they also concerned Stalin's personal aim of obtaining for himself the highest possible degree of information control in relation to the rest of the Soviet leadership.

The history of Stalinism may well be seen as the story of the central authorities' unceasing attempts — not always successful — to overcome new communication problems that were rooted both in the nature of the political system and in the development of the political struggle. It is also the story of Stalin's special efforts to ensure for himself and his personal staff the role as the ultimate gatekeeper in relation to all other links of the system — central as well as local. Perhaps more than anything else, it is the story of how Stalin systematically tried to destroy all those gatekeepers who seemed to be standing in his way although, in many cases, they were a product of his own political actions. In brief, to gain an adequate picture of Stalinism as a communication system, we must also take into consideration the dynamics of the political-organizational development.

The Dynamic Perspective.

The existence of an information problem was recognized early on in the Communist Party administration. General procedures for the transmission of information were laid down in 1921 and in the years that followed a great many different methods were employed in strengthening up-going and down-going communication. Within the area of "living communication" — as it was called — great importance was attached to the sending out of "instructors" and "inspectors" from the Central Committee to the local party organizations. Representatives of local organizations frequently were summoned to Moscow to report on the situation in the provinces. These forms of personal contacts were supplemented by a manifold system of "written communication," including circulars, letters of information and instruction, "closed" (i.e., secret) letters, work reports and minutes from the respective party committees.

At the start, this system left much to be desired. In 1923 Stalin complained that "insufficient information" was preventing the realization of party policies. We both issue and receive too little information, stated the newly appointed General Secretary of the Communist Party.[6]

Much was apparently done in the following years to eradicate these weaknesses in the communication system. At the same time, the staff was increased in the party's central Information Department with the result that from then on there were also far better possibilities of processing the collected information and of passing it on to the decision-makers in condensed and systematic form.[7]

Around the middle of the twenties, work in the information sector took off in a new direction which, from all accounts, had a significant effect on further organizational development. The main stress henceforth was laid on keeping check (*proverka*) on the actual fulfillment of party directives and thus also on the gathering of special categories of feedback information. This control aspect was described as the most important part of the party's organizational activities and consequently as the most significant part of the work carried out by the party's Orgburo and Secretariat.

As stated in the contemporary party press, control work would no longer concern itself solely with the technical side of information procurement, but also with the very substance of the matter. At the same time, the control seems to have become far more purposeful and specific than previously, and to have drawn on a much greater amount of factual material. Earlier much of the collected information was reportedly left untouched, but after the general tightening of the administrative system in the mid-twenties the available facts were said to be far better utilized in the "operative work" of the party.

Improved administrative co-ordination was also sought. The Information Department of the Central Committee was given the job of coordinating the entire control work and was particularly requested to make greater use of secret material, e.g., documents emanating from the OGPU. Simultaneously, all the other departments of the central party apparat were instructed to gear their activities more directly to the question of control, in close collaboration with the Central Control Commission and the Workers' and Peasants' Inspectorate. Life for those in charge of the control work was also made somewhat easier by the introduction of a new administrative procedure: the various party offices were now instructed to set out their own detailed work schedule for the coming period. From a study of these schedules one could at least see whether the local officials were planning to fulfill the directives of the party leadership.[8]

Of even greater importance was the fact that the general scope of control was widened considerably. From the mid-twenties, the party press again and again stressed that it was no longer sufficient to supervise the party apparat itself. One would also have to keep check on how the soviet organs, the trade unions and the entire state economic sector were fulfilling the directives of the party.[9]

The explanation as to why the control problem now became a central issue can only be found in a combination of various circumstances. Around the middle of the twenties, the actual build-up of the post-revolutionary system of administration was entering its final phase. All the more important organizational instruments were now in place. Consequently, it was only natural for the party leadership to show more interest in whether these instruments were actually functioning as they were intended to do. The special character of the new administrative system stressed still further the need for control. As centralization grew, the efficiency of the system became more and more dependent on whether all citizens were pulling their weight in carrying out the tasks handed down to them from the political top. This made it vitally important to ensure that communication to and from the leading decision-makers was not "disturbed" on its way through the system.

The entire political culture of Bolshevism — with its emphasis on the right of the "conscious" to lead those less conscious — helped of course to feed this control mania. The growing economic and social problems in the late twenties no doubt also pulled in the same direction. Furthermore, the fierce struggle between the party leadership and the Opposition must have given a specially significant dimension to the problem of controlling the fulfillment of party directives: it was not only a question of overcoming general administrative stumbling blocks; it was also a question of exposing obstructions of a political nature.[10]

We must again remind ourselves that there is no getting away from Stalin: his morbid suspicion, his propensity for seeking "class enemies" everywhere, his ruthless striving to build for himself a position of absolute power. The well-known story of Stalin's way to the top of the Soviet political pyramid shall not be repeated here. Our interest, in the present context, must be mainly concerned with how, step by step, Stalin developed his own internal control and communication network.

His main basis, of course, was the post he had as General Secretary of the Soviet Communist Party. This offered him vast opportunities to exercise control of the party apparat and to influence communication processes in general. More specifically, his incontestable superiority on the information front in relation to the rest of the Soviet leadership is most likely due to the fact that he managed, at a very early stage, to fuse together the highly important "Secret Department" of the central party apparat with his own personal staff of assistants, his own personal secretariat. This Secret Department was in charge of the dispatch and safekeeping of classified party documents and functioned in addition as an exclusive service organ for the leading decision-making bodies of the party, the Politburo, the Orgburo and the Secretariat. By the mid-twenties at least, Stalin had managed to find leading posts in the Secret Department for his personal assistants who were thus given direct access to party information of the most important kind. This arrangement furthermore helped Stalin and his assistants to acquire a double gatekeeper role. On the one hand, they became able to influence the channeling of classified information down through the system. On the other, they had undoubtedly plenty of opportunities to filter information on the way up to the other leaders at the top.[11]

By means of a continuous build-up of this secret apparat, Stalin was also able to counteract the overloading of communications which usually develops at the top decision-making level in strongly centralized, autocratic systems. The Secret Department, which started in 1920 as a modest office under the party's general chancellery, apparently had become an independent department, with up to several hundred employees by the end of the 1920s. At the same time, Stalin's personal secretariat seems to have developed from a handful of assistants to a large staff of highly qualified specialists in the main fields of state administration who decided, in practice, many important questions before they were presented to the official decision-making organs of the party. Stalin himself did not have to deal with all information on his own.

This development of the internal apparat took place in step with a further centralization of the entire communication system. Thus, by means of a thorough reorganization of the party administration in 1930, the party Secretariat became able to carry out a far more direct steering of economic policies. Within the party apparat itself the move was also toward more centralization. Whereas previously each Central Committee department had its own chancellery, a large general Chancellery was now created to cover the entire Central Committee staff. From then onwards, according to a contemporary writer, the head of this chancellery could keep Stalin fully informed on all that was taking place in the central administration of the party.[12]

All in all, it would thus seem justifiable to claim that by the end of the 1920s Stalin's relative superiority in the field of communication was indisputable. But we must still try to avoid the pitfall of assuming that this meant his knowledge was optimal, his breadth of view complete, and his freedom of action unlimited.

The increase in administrative centralization that took place during this period undoubtedly brought with it an added strain on the vertical communication channels, with the result that much relevant information was stopped or delayed on its way from sender to recipient. For this reason alone, the decision-making process often must have borne the stamp of haphazardness. But Stalin's own political thinking also harbored a certain disrespect for expert advice and information. His policies were ultimately based on a "voluntaristic" action philosophy, an ideology of struggle. He lived according to the maxim of both Napoleon and Lenin: "On s'engage, et puis on voit." He believed that by hard pressure, brutal coercion and militant mobilization methods, indecision and recalcitrance could be overcome — and political miracles, such as the "experts" had not dreamt of, could be accomplished.[13] He was undoubtedly not alone in thinking this, but due to the central position he had by now acquired in the Soviet communication system, the decisive point in this context is that the ideas were his.

Stalin's militant philosophy came much to the fore during the industrialization and collectivization campaign around 1930. The very fact that he was able to carry through this epoch-making "revolution from above," demonstrated clearly Stalin's firm control of the communication channels and his sure ability to counteract important gatekeeper blockages close to the center of the political system, aided and abetted as he was by activist groups which provided pressure "from below." However, the drastic methods used in the Stalinist revolution also resulted in extreme strain being placed on the entire communication network. And this, in turn, not only led to general confusion in the administrative process, but also to the creation of numerous new gatekeeper groupings that could limit Stalin's freedom of action.

The only way to ensure that Stalin's revolutionary policies were carried out throughout the country had been to place considerable power in the hands of the local party bosses, and also to impose on the leading cadres in general a greater personal responsibility for the fulfillment of party directives. At the same time, however, leading cadres both in Moscow and the provinces were pressed extremely hard from the top to perform according to Stalin's expectations. They were given exceedingly difficult, sometimes almost impossible tasks to carry out. The directives they received simply could not all be fulfilled simultaneously, either because administrative or economic resources were insufficient or because the directives themselves were more or less incompatible in practice. The leading party and state officials at the various levels of the hierarchy were thus forced to make many precarious political choices on their own, which in one way of course helped to increase their personal influence and maneuverability, but which also made them extremely vulnerable to criticism from the party top.

On the whole, they were constantly under threat of severe sanctions if they failed, or if Stalin deliberately chose to channel away from himself, and towards various groups of scapegoats among the officials in the field, people's dissatisfaction with party policies. This threat took on a specially dangerous character as a result of the fierce struggle between the party leadership and the Opposition at the end of the 1920s: local party officials who were unable to live up to Stalin's expectations could, on this basis, be charged with "Right deviationism," "rotten Liberalism" or other mortal political sins. On the other hand, they could expect great privileges and career openings if they were fortunate enough to steer clear of all these dangerous rocks.[14]

The combination of severe pressure and considerable power and privilege induced many local party bosses to react in a way that could be seen to offer a threat to the Stalinist system of communication. Regional leaders modelled their behavior on Stalin's: they acted like small dictators in their respective areas and — to use Merle Fainsod's classic expression — built up their own "satrapies" where they themselves were the uncontested leaders and all other important posts were filled from within the "family circle." The increased power vested in the party apparat at all levels and the close integration of the various communication channels resulted in the creation of close-knit power cliques which were able both to distort all sorts of communication on the way up and to dilute any Central Committee directive on the way down. Some of these gatekeepers at the intermediate levels of the hierarchy probably acted from purely personal power motives. Others offered resistance because they had been deeply shocked, disillusioned and bitter over the catastrophies brought on by Stalin's policies of brute force.[15]

From the point of view of the General Secretary, the gatekeeper problem must therefore have appeared to be just as acute as earlier on, although the premises had partially changed. At the same time, a number of other circumstances contributed to an increased focus on precisely this problem.

After the Left and Right Opposition had been eliminated from the top organs of the party in the late twenties, it had become less difficult to formulate the "correct" party line, i.e., to get the entire leadership to agree on the decisions Stalin wanted. This in itself helped to push interest still further in the direction of whether or not these central decisions were loyally carried out by the lower echelons of the system. The partially changed gatekeeper profile also helped to pinpoint the problem of control. The system no longer allowed for any open opposition to Stalin. All leading cadres and local officials overtly supported the party line without reservation although, in practice, many resisted Stalin's course and attempted to find their own solutions to the urgent political-economic problems. In Stalin's eyes they were therefore "double dealers" who deceived the party leadership and sabotaged the party line. They were hidden enemies who had to be unmasked. As Stalin had put it as early as the late twenties: it was necessary to remove anyone who came under the least suspicion.[16]

At the Seventeenth Party Congress in 1934 (officially designated as the "Congress of Victors" but where Stalin probably still had reason to doubt whether his victory was assured) plans were clearly afoot for a major offensive against the various gatekeepers. Stalin himself opened an attack on those "magnates" who believed that the Soviet laws did not apply to them but were solely directed at "fools," and who considered themselves sacrosanct by reason of their earlier services to the Bolshevik cause. According to the General Secretary, these people should be relieved of their leading posts without delay. Other speakers were equally direct.   Ia. Rudzutak, who reported on the Workers' and Peasants' Inspectorate and the Central Control Commission, stated that in many cases and places, party directives were fulfilled only in a formal, but not in a real sense. Such a formalistic attitude towards the fulfillment of party directives was simply the worst evil that the party had to contend with at that time. Hair-raising attempts to thwart party decisions were often given mild and conciliatory treatment by local party committees whose motto seemed to be: "The children may have done wrong, but you should not punish them too harshly." In spite of earlier purges, it had not been possible to rid the party of downright counter-revolutionary elements. There were even instances where responsible party leaders had incited lower organizations to hostile actions against party and state, or where class-alien elements within the party had threatened ordinary people with revenge should they expose them. Time and time again the party leadership had met up with a "conspiracy of silence."[17]

Thus, according to their own statements, the party leadership declared war on several categories of gatekeepers at one and the same time. There were the powerful local bosses who tried to run things their own way. There were the dyed-in-the-wool oppositionists. There were all those people who, for one reason or another, wanted to cover-up alleged traitors, enemies or just ordinary jaywalkers.

It is possible to catch a glimpse of several different motives behind the offensive. Of course, it was partly a question of getting rid of certain individuals who had been labelled as belonging to the Opposition, but it was probably just as much a question of instigating a general breakdown of all conceivable communication blockages between Stalin and the rest of society. The object was to destroy the last political-administrative defenses of the "magnates," to set all existing and potential gatekeepers one against the other, and thereby obviate the formation of new strong gatekeeper cliques at all levels of the hierarchy. In this offensive, information was both the goal and the means. Stalin needed, on the whole, to build up a more efficient system of communication, in particular as regards certain types of feedback. But the flow of information being channeled upwards to the top of the system was also to be used directly as a weapon in the struggle against the various gatekeepers: the "magnates" had to learn that Stalin would, at all times, be able to "expose" and compromise them by virtue of the supreme communication control he exercised.

In practice, no doubt, the various motives more or less merged into one. There is little to be gained by making a sharp distinction between political and administrative motives behind the attack Stalin aimed at his own apparat in the 1930s. At least there was one common denominator:

Stalin's deliberate and well-prepared attempt — his "plan" if you like — to eliminate once and for all the eternal gatekeeper problem.[18]

According to Stalin himself, keeping a check on the fulfillment of party directives was one of the two main organizational tasks for the party during the thirties. As Aleksandrov expressed it in his classic work *Kto upravliaet Rossiei*, the emphasis on this need for control served to "codify" purges in the apparat. It should therefore come as no surprise that the other main organizational task of the period was said to be the selection of personnel. Nor should it come as any surprise that Stalin's henchman Lazar Kaganovich found reason to state, in 1939, that keeping a check on the fulfillment of party directives was inextricably bound up with the ability to exercise "Bolshevik revolutionary vigilance" — the watchword of the Great Terror.[19]

There doubtless must have been a general need for administrative restoration after the shake-up of the Stalin revolution. From all accounts, chaos abounded throughout the local administration, but the constant intensification of the campaign for greater "vigilance" served, at the same time, to legitimize the setting up of an extra-ordinarily fine-meshed network of communication control. Obviously, it was much more difficult to expose secret enemies and potential traitors than to identify those in open opposition. For this reason, more and more subtlety in methods of control had to be applied. Enormous quantities of exceedingly detailed personal information had to be collected. Special procedures had to be thought up for the safe-keeping and distribution of party information to obviate the risk that any potential enemy might gain access to and expose classified material. The allegedly wide-spread "bungling" in the communication system could not but help class enemies to infiltrate the party. It also provided justification for investigating whether the bunglers themselves simply lacked an ability to keep their own desks tidy or whether they, too, were "enemies" who carried out deliberate sabotage.[20]

In brief, everything that happened on the organizational front during the 1930s served to make the security aspect of communication the center of attention.

Stalin's Own Communication System.

According to official Soviet sources, a network of so-called "special sectors" was formed as a result of the general reorganization of the Communist party apparat in 1934. It appears from the same sources that this network covered party committees down to and including the provincial level, but no information is given as to the specific functions of the special sectors.[21] All the evidence that has come to light since then gives good reason to assume that the official inauguration of the special sector system in 1934 represented a new phase in the development of the all-pervasive, security-motivated communication control desired by Stalin.[22]

It cannot be doubted that this system had a direct line to the General Secretary: the head of the central special sector in Moscow, Aleksandr Poskrebyshev, simultaneously acted as Stalin's leading personal assistant. It can also be clearly documented that the special sectors were responsible for the security of party communication. It was they who drew up the rigorous rules for safe-keeping and distributing secret material, and they who made sure that these rules were adhered to in practice.

Their activities, however, were not confined to security control. They also functioned as an important channel for the transmission of information. It may well be true — as one writer has maintained[23] — that all communications between Moscow and the local party committees were channelled through the special sectors. One thing is certain: they received, registered and dispatched material classified as secret. The filing of such material also involved the special sectors, whereas the transportation from place to place was carried out by the "field couriers" from the security service. By means of an ingenious system of record-keeping, officials at the upper levels of the special sector hierarchy were able to keep a tally on the movements of secret documents throughout the party's communication system. There was, for instance, a special journal for the registration of secret information on personnel, frequently of a compromising nature.

There can be little doubt that the secret communication in Soviet Russia was based on a strictly implemented need-to-know principle. The possibilities open to local authorities to follow a case in all its aspects were limited by many different means. For example, important secret letters to the provincial organizations had to be returned by the recipients to the original sender higher up the ladder after a short specified period, and without the local addressees being allowed to keep a copy in their own files.

The filtration of information by the special sector system continued right up to the top of the political pyramid. The leading special sector in Moscow, from all accounts, had absorbed the party's entire Secret Department and thus also its functions as a service organ for the Politburo, the Orgburo and the Party Secretariat. Poskrebyshev's office had become, as it were, the organizational basis for Khrushchev's later assertion: that all information was carefully selected, limited and weighed by Stalin before it was passed on to the Politburo.[24] Conversely, there is good reason to believe that classified information flowed without hindrance into Stalin's personal secretariat, which was by now at least as closely interwoven with the party's secret communication network as before.

According to an unpublished and hitherto unused emigré source which seems to be reliable,[25] the top special sector in Moscow was divided into the following subsections:

1. The chief of the special sector and his two deputies.
2. The Secretariat (part of which was in the Kremlin).
3. The *Komendatura*, i.e., the special guard.
4. The telephone office.
5. Control of the party apparat.
6. Control of the Commissariat/Ministry of Internal Affairs and the political police.
7. Control of military intelligence and the foreign department and counter-espionage department of the political police.
8. Control of the Commissariats/Ministries of Foreign Affairs and Foreign Trade as well as other state organs working abroad.
9. The guarding of Stalin and Molotov — and control of the guarding of other Soviet leaders.
10. Card index and archives.

The special sector worked independently of the normal Central Committee apparat. It carried out its own investigations of all items on the agenda of the Politburo and controlled and verified in this way all information in the reports from ministers and state officials to the highest decision-making body of the party. In addition, it functioned as a kind of "super police," subordinated only to Stalin and vested with full and complete authority to arrest any Soviet citizen under suspicion.[26]

In establishing the special sector hierarchy, Stalin had also equipped himself with a corps of efficient information agents which could be used to neutralize the gatekeeper role of the local "magnates." Special sector people in the provinces must have enjoyed considerable independence in relation to the party committee they were supervising. They were reportedly all appointed by Moscow. According to a former party official, they had no direct responsibility for the running of the local organizations. Their sole task was to control and communicate correctly. They would not, therefore, be particularly interested in concealing errors or omissions on the part of the provincial authorities.[27]

The security rating of the special sectors must have strengthened their freedom of action still further in that it made them more or less immune against outside interference. It must also have given them the right to investigate all nooks and crannies in the communication system and to draw heavily on material from the security service. The local special sector chiefs simultaneously functioned as personal assistants to the first secretaries of the various party organizations, so that they constantly had a check on all communication to and from these key political figures. Special sector officials were also present at all meetings of the local party organization: their job was to prepare the reports. As if this were not enough, they were said to have at their disposal a separate network of anonymous informers. All in all, there can have been little opportunity for the local magnates to utilize their gatekeeper role to hide material of any importance from Stalin's special agents.

Precisely when this entire system was established is not known. Although contemporary Soviet sources do not mention the special sector phenomenon until 1934, there is much to indicate that a special sector was set up in the Central Committee apparat as early as the end of the twenties, but only as a small office within the party's Secret Department which was then still going strong. There would seem to be an obvious connection between this initiative and the severe tightening of security control that found expression at that time in a number of measures: punishments for carelessness in dealing with classified documents were increased; more powers were given to the security service; plans for new control systems to prevent security leaks in the administration were put into operation; and a new framework for top-secret mobilization planning was created.[28] This development can be seen as a reflection of the fundamental dualism in all secret communication work. On the one hand, there is the actual administration of classified documents: this was the principal job of the old Secret Department. On the other, there is the control to ensure that people employed in the secret administration are reliable and that the various technical security requirements are fulfilled: this was probably one of the main tasks of the new special sector. The building up of this dual system to the point where Stalin was fully satisfied must certainly have taken some time. For instance, local party organizations did not have their own special sector right from the start. By 1934, however, everything was in place. A network of special sectors covering both Moscow and the provinces had been established, and this network had, in addition, absorbed the Central Committee's old Secret Department and its embryonic offshoots in the local organizations.

The special sector system covered the party alone and thus could not concern itself with communication leaks or gatekeeper problems in the state administration. Here, a network of "special departments" was created which was strongly evocative of Stalin's party-based control system, and not only in a terminological sense.

These special departments were attached to such bodies, ministries, educational institutions or large industrial enterprises. They handled security affairs and mobilization planning, but were not directly involved in the daily running of the various establishments. Their main function was to observe and control. They received copies of all the establishment's documents and collected all sorts of information on the people employed. They were closely tied in with the secret departments of the state administration — in some cases they probably replaced or absorbed these departments — and were therefore also involved in the filing and distribution of classified material.[29]

The special departments in the state apparat were one of the numerous ramifications of the Soviet security service and this, of course, could have involved a certain risk for the party leadership. In step with the growing stress being placed on the security aspects of the communication process, the security service chiefs might have become able to obtain for themselves a powerful gatekeeper role in relation to Stalin and his staff. However, as far back as the twenties it would seem that administrative steps were taken to counter precisely such an eventuality. The secret network in the state was placed under the supervision of a separate Special Department in Moscow which was headed by Stalin's close associate Gleb Bokii. Unlike all other departments in the security service, it reported directly to the party top, by-passing the official police leadership. Bokii's department also existed in the thirties, so there is every reason to assume that all the information collected by the numerous local special departments in the state administration continued to go through this channel directly to the party's top special sector under Poskrebyshev and through him to Stalin.[30]

In 1934, the other existing control organs were also placed more firmly in the hands of the General Secretary. The twin-organizations, the Central Control Commission and the Workers' and Peasants' Inspectorate, disappeared from the arena to be replaced by a Commission for Party Control and a Commission for Soviet Control. There were two immediate consequences of this reorganization. Firstly, the control apparat as a whole, which had previously enjoyed some (though dwindling) independence, came now entirely under the central party leadership — resulting, no doubt, in a more direct organizational contact with the special sector. Secondly, procedures were laid down to avoid any collusion between the local representatives of the new control organs and those organizations and institutions which were to be controlled.[31] Here, too, steps were being taken to meet a threatening gatekeeper problem. From Stalin's point of view, the control organs were now more than ever before in a position to take on the most important organizational task of the period — keeping a check on the fulfillment of party directives. The forces were lined up in battle order. Stalin once again stood ready to take on all comers.

Stalinism as a System of Communication.

It is not the intention here to review the political developments leading up to Stalin's Great Terror in the second half of the thirties. Nor is it the right place to discuss the degree to which the events taking place were the result of systematic advance planning by Stalin. There is good reason, however, to point out that the so-called "verification and exchange" of party documents which more or less dominated the party scene in 1935-1936 — that is, the years prior to the culmination of the terror during the *Ezhovshchina* — helped in many ways to legitimize the existence and activities of the special sector network.

The special sectors were doubtless involved in the safekeeping of party books and other party documents. The main purpose given for the verification campaign — to expose enemies and alien elements in the party — must also have been regarded by the party's security agents as a summons to take action. Nor can it have been without significance that responsibility for the purges that were part of the verification campaign had been put in the hands of the party organizations' own leaders, as opposed to the previous practice where special purge commissions took care of things. This inevitably must have given the special sector people from the respective party organizations a major share of the practical work in ferreting out enemies within the party. More specifically, the special sectors must have had plenty of scope in identifying those local party bosses who, in a fit of "opportunistic wantonness," neglected or even obstructed the verification campaign and in this way assisted "class enemies" to infiltrate the party.[31]

The numerous party press reports concerning errors and omissions in local administration should therefore not only be taken as evidence of widespread "bungling" in the party apparat. They also bear witness to the fact that the various control organs were now doing much more in exposing deficiencies and finding scapegoats, and they reflect Stalin's personal determination to use these exposures in his constant campaign against the system's more or less powerful gatekeepers.

Stalin may not have planned all his political actions in detail, but his political aims and methods seem at least to have had a certain fundamental consistency. This is the impression one gets not only by looking ahead towards the *Ezhovshchina* but also by retrospection.[32] The features that characterized "high Stalinism" as a communication system were clearly evident long before Stalin's final victory over the party. These features were:

1) a high degree of centralization, a strong emphasis on hierarchy, a permanent tendency towards an overloading of the vertical communication channels and the topmost decision center, and a constant striving to counter this overloading;

2) extreme secrecy in the administration, extensive use of the "need-to-know"-principle and unique opportunities for filtering information at the very top of the political system;

3) a constant stress on the need to control the fulfillment of directives from the top and thus on the necessity for a form of feedback information that concerned the implementation of decisions arrived at, more than the question of whether these decisions were correct in the first place;

4) a continuing trend towards the creation of still newer gatekeeper blockages in the communication process — as a result both of conditions inherent in the system itself and of the actual policies carried out, and in spite of the existence of numerous control mechanisms;

5) a marked proneness to treat gatekeeper problems and other communication breakdowns as a question of covert disloyalty and hidden political obstruction, and thus a constant emphasis on the security aspects of communication;

6) severe tensions between the tendency for new gatekeeper blockages to keep turning up and the increasingly drastic attempts by the supreme leadership to eliminate the gatekeeper problem once and for all through the attainment of maximum communication control.

Throughout all these areas, the special sector network played a most important role. For this reason it may be described both as a product of the Stalinist system and as a key to the Stalinist system. If we are to characterize Stalinism as a specific system of communication, we simply have to make the special sectors the center of attention. But if we are to explain why and how this system was developed, we must just as strongly focus on another burning question — the question of the General Secretary's personal motives and tactics. There is and can be no getting away from Stalin.

University of Copenhagen

NOTES

[1]Robert C. Tucker, ed., *Stalinism: Essays in Historical Interpretation*. New York: W.W. Norton and Company, 1977; Roger W. Pethybridge, *The Social Prelude to Stalinism*. London: Macmillan, 1974; Michal Reiman, *Die Geburt des Stalinismus: Die UdSSR am Vorabend der "zweiten Revolution"*. Frankfurt am Main: Europäische Verlagsanstalt, 1979; Sheila Fitzpatrick, ed., *Cultural Revolution in Russia, 1928-1931*. Bloomington and London: Indiana University Press, 1978.

[2]See, for example, the discussion in the *Slavic Review*, vol. XLII, no. 1 (Spring 1983), between J. Arch Getty, Robert C. Tucker and Niels Erik Rosenfeldt, especially Tucker's comment on Getty's article: "no interpretation that takes as little account of Stalin — his motives and his politics — as this one does can meet the needs of historiography..."(p.84). See also Letters to the Editor (from Hans-Henning Schröder, Niels Erik Rosenfeldt and Robert C. Tucker) in *Slavic Review*, vol. XLIII, no. 2 (Fall 1984), pp. 544-546.

[3]Jerry F. Hough, "The Cultural Revolution and Western Understanding of the Soviet System" in Fitzpatrick, *Cultural Revolution*, p. 245.

[4]Compare, for example, Sheila Fitzpatrick, "Ordzhonikidze's Takeover of Vesenkha: A Case Study in Soviet Bureaucratic Politics," *Soviet Studies*, vol. XXXVII, no. 2 (April 1985), pp. 153-172, especially p. 167.

[5]It is impossible to enumerate here the vast literature on organizational and political communication. Among the books and articles used for the following sketch of central problems of theory, special mention may be given to: Henry H. Albers, *Organized Executive Action: Decision-making, Communication, and Leadership*. New York: John Wiley & Sons, 1961; Preston P. Le Breton, *Administrative Intelligence-Information Systems*. Boston: Houghton, Mifflin, 1969; Karl W. Deutsch, *The Nerves of Government: Models of Political Communication and Control*. London: The Free Press of Glencoe, Collier-Macmillan, 1963; Anthony Downs, *Inside Bureaucracy*. Boston: Little, Brown, 1967; Robert C. Tucker, *Politics as Leadership*. Columbia: University of Missouri Press, 1981; John T. Dorsey, "A Communication Model for Administration," in *Administrative Science Quarterly*, vol. II (1957-1958), pp. 307-324; David Easton, *A Systems Analysis of Political Life*. New York: John Wiley & Sons, 1965; Erik P. Hoffmann, "Communication Theory and the Study of Soviet Politics," in *Communist Studies and the Social Sciences*, ed., Frederic J. Fleron. Chicago: Rand McNally and Company, 1971; Erik P. Hoffmann, "Ideological Administration under Khrushchev: A Study of Intra-Party Communication," in *Canadian Slavic Studies*, vol. IV, no. 4 (Winter 1970), pp. 736-766; Erik P. Hoffman, "Soviet Metapolicy: Information-Processing in the Communist Party of the Soviet Union," in *Journal of Comparative Administration*, vol. V, no. 2 (August 1973), pp.

200-232; Jerry F. Hough, *The Soviet Union and Social Science Theory*, Russian Research Center Studies, no. 77. Massachusetts and London: Harvard University Press, 1977; Harold L. Wilensky, *Organizational Intelligence: Knowledge and Policy in Government and Industry*. New York: Basic Books, 1967.

[6]See the numerous reports in *Izvestiia Tsentral'nogo komiteta rossiiskoi kommunisticheskoi partii (bol'shevikov)*, e.g., no. 2 (1925), pp. 3-4; nos. 13-14 (1925), p. 20; nos. 17-18 (1925), p. 8; nos. 22-23 (1925), p. 2; no. 39 (1925), pp. 2-3. See also I.V. Stalin, *Sochineniia*, vol. V(*1921-1923*). Moscow, 1950, p. 362; and Hoffmann, *Journal of Contemporary Administration*, p. 203; A. Beliakov and I. Shvets, *Partiinaia informatsiia*. Moscow, 1970, pp. 8-10; Jerry F. Hough, *The Soviet Prefects: The Local Party Organs in Industrial Decision-Making*. Cambridge, Mass.: Harvard University Press, 1969, pp. 99-100.

[7]Hoffmann, *Journal of Contemporary Administration*, p. 203; *Izvestiia Tsentral'nogo komiteta*, nos. 19-20 (1926), Prilozhenie, pp. 1-11;

[8]*Izvestiia Tsentral'nogo komiteta*, no. 39 (1925), p. 4; no. 41 (1925), p. 6; no. 10-11 (1926), pp. 1-5; nos. 16-17 (1926), pp. 1-4; nos. 19-20 (1926), p. 4 and Prilozhenie; nos. 24-25 (1926), pp. 2-5; nos. 27-28 (1926), p. 3; no. 52 (1926), p. 7; no. 4 (1927), pp. 4-5; no. 13 (1927), pp. 1-2; no. 16 (1927), p. 1; nos. 24-25 (1927), p.2.

[9]See, for example, *Izvestiia Tsentral'nogo komiteta*, nos. 19-20 (1926), Prilozhenie; no. 52 (1926), p. 7; no. 13 (1927), pp. 1-2; no. 16 (1927), p. 1.

[10]Compare, for example, *Izvestiia Tsentral'nogo komiteta*, nos. 7-8 (1927), p. 2. See also T.H. Rigby, "Stalinism and the Mono-Organizational System," in Tucker, *Stalinism*, pp. 53-73, especially p. 58; and Aleksandrov (A.S. Mikhel'son), *Kto upravliaet Rossiei: Bol'shevitskii partiino-pravitel'stvennyi apparat i stalinizm. Istoriko-dogmaticheskii analiz.* Berlin, 1933, p. 176.

[11]Niels Erik Rosenfeldt, *Knowledge and Power: The Role of Stalin's Secret Chancellery in the Soviet System of Government.* Copenhagen: Rosenkilde and Bagger, 1978; Niels Erik Rosenfeldt, *Stalinstyrets nervecenter. Nye studier i kilderne til det sovjetiske kommunistpartis hemmelige kancelli.* Copenhagen: Copenhagen University, Institute of Slavonic Studies, Rapporter 2, 1980; Niels Erik Rosenfeldt, "'The Consistory of the Communist Church': The Origins and Development of Stalin's Secret Chancellery," *Russian History/Histoire russe*, vol. IX; parts 2-3 (1982), 308-324; Niels Erik Rosenfeldt, *Stalin's Special Departments: A Comparative Analysis of Key Sources.* Copenhagen: Copenhagen University, Institute of Slavonic and East European Studies, Report no. 20, 1989; Leonard B. Schapiro, "The General Department of the CC of the CPSU," *Survey*, vol. XXI, no. 3 (1975), pp.53-66.

From at least the late twenties, secret (sub)departments were also in existence in certain local party organizations. This is confirmed not only by documents in the Smolensk Archives (see Rosenfeldt, *Stalinstyrets nervecenter*, pp. 48-49 and 99), but also by the Moscow telephone directory *Vsia Moskva!* The 1927 edition of this directory mentions a *sekretnaia chast'*, headed by A.F. Shuganova, in the Secretariat of the Moscow *guberniia* committee, and the 1928 edition refers to a *sekretnyi otdel* in the same committee, headed by E.A. Afanas'ev, with N.F. Shliapnikova as his deputy. It appears from this source that the chiefs of these secret (sub)departments were *not* identical with the personal assistants of the party leaders in the Moscow *guberniia*. Stalin's special system of personnel overlapping between his private secretariat and the top Secret Department had not yet been imitated at the local level (*Vsia Moskva*, 1927, p. 195; and 1928, p. 174). Soon, however, the situation changed. (see Rosenfeldt, *Stalinstyrets nervecenter*, p. 110).

It is interesting to note that the prominent Soviet intelligence agent Richard Sorge claims to have been a member of the Secret Department of the Soviet Communist Party Central Executive (*sic*) Committee from 1929. More specifically, he states that the Secret Department controlled his party membership card and his relations with the party and that, as a party member, he was responsible to this department and under obligation to report to it each time he returned to Moscow. Once a person had joined the party through the Secret Department, according to Sorge, he had to report to it for travel abroad (see Charles A. Willoughby, *Shanghai Conspiracy: The Sorge Spy Ring*. New York: E.P. Dutton, 1952, p. 166). Sorge's chart of the Soviet spy network in Japan indicates that he was responsible both to Military Intelligence and to what he called "the confidential affairs department of the Central Committee of the Soviet Communist Party" (*ibid.*, pp. 322-323).

Concerning the historical forerunners of this secret administration, see Daniel Tarschys, "Secret Institutions in Russian Government: A Note on Rosenfeldt's *Knowledge and Power*," in *Soviet Studies*, vol. XXXVII, no. 4 (October 1985), pp. 525-534.

[12]Rosenfeldt, *Knowledge and Power*, pp. 30-62, 129-160; and Rosenfeldt, *Russian History/Histoire russe*, pp. 308-316. See also Aleksandrov, *Kto upravliaet Rossiei*, pp. 263, 268-269, 316-320 and 358-359; and *Partiinoe stroitel'stvo*, no. 2 (1930), p. 70.

[13]See, for example, Robert C. Tucker, *Stalin as Revolutionary, 1879-1929: A Study in History and Personality*. London: Chatto and Windus, 1974, pp. 208-209 and 395-420; and Robert C. Tucker, "Stalinism as Revolution from Above," in Tucker, *Stalinism*, pp. 77-108, especially pp. 89-94.

[14]Compare, for example, Merle Fainsod, *Smolensk under Soviet Rule*. New York: Vintage Books, 1958, pp. 70, 74, 78, 80, 85, 240, 260-262 and 450; Hiroaki Kuromiya, "Edinonachalie and the Soviet Industrial Manager, 1928-1937," in *Soviet Studies*, vol. XXXVI, no. 2 (April 1984), pp. 185-204; David Christian, "The Supervising Function in Russian and Soviet History," in *Slavic Review*, vol. XLI, no. 1 (Spring 1982), pp. 73-90; John Arch Getty, "The 'Great Purges' Reconsidered: The Soviet Communist Party, 1933-1939." Unpublished Ph.D. dissertation, Boston College, 1979, p. 202; Niels Erik Rosenfeldt and Carsten Pape, *Sovjetstaten: Politikens Ruslandshistorie efter 1917*. Copenhagen: Politikens Forlag, 1983, pp. 82-88. Compare also *Izvestiia Tsentral'nogo komiteta*, nos. 45-46 (1926), p. 6; and *XVII s"ezd Vsesoiuznoi Kommunisticheskoi partii (b), 26 janvaria-10 fevralia 1934 g.: Stenograficheskii otchet*. Moscow, 1934 (reprint: Nendeln, 1975), pp. 33-34.

[15]See, for example, Fainsod, *Smolensk*, p. 85; and Rosenfeldt and Pape, *Sovjetstaten*, pp. 95-96.

[16]Compare, for example, *XVII s"ezd*, p. 33; Reiman, *Geburt des Stalinismus*, pp. 182 and 246; and Tucker, *Stalin as Revolutionary*, pp. 452-453.

[17]*XVII s"ezd*, pp. 34 and 289-290.

[18]See, for example, the discussion in *Slavic Review*, Spring 1983, between J. Arch Getty, Robert C. Tucker and Niels Erik Rosenfeldt.

[19]Aleksandrov, *Kto upravliaet Rossiei; XVIII s"ezd Vsesoiuznoi Kommunisticheskoi partii (b), 10-21 marta 1939 g.: Stenograficheskii otchet*. Moscow, 1939, pp. 265-266.

[20]See, for example, *Partiinoe stroitel'stvo*, no. 5 (1935), pp. 7-9; no. 15 (1935), p. 5; no. 17 (1935), p. 4; no. 24 (1935), pp. 12-18; no. 15 (1936), pp. 14-21 and 34; *Records of the All-Union (Russian) Communist Party, Smolensk District*, WKP 116/154e, p. 79; and WKP 499, p. 308; Roy Medvedev, *All Stalin's Men*.   Oxford: Basil Blackwell, 1983, p. 143.

[21]*XVII s"ezd*, pp. 561 and 672.

[22]Rosenfeldt, *Knowledge and Power*, pp. 63-97; Rosenfeldt, *Stalinstyrets nervecenter*, pp. 47-54; Rosenfeldt, *Russian History/Histoire russe*, pp. 317-323; Barton Whaley, *Soviet Clandestine Communication Nets*. Cambridge, Mass.: Center for International Studies, MIT, September 1969, pp. 64-67; Archie Brown, "The Power of the General Secretary of the CPSU," in T.H. Rigby, Archie Brown and Peter Reddaway, eds., *Authority, Power and Policy in the USSR: Essays dedicated to Leonard Schapiro*. London: Macmillan, 1980, pp. 135-157, especially pp. 138-139.

[23]Abdurakhman Avtorkhanov, *Stalin and the Soviet Communist Party: A Study in the Technology of Power*. Munich: Institute for the Study of the USSR. Series 1, no. 41 (September 1959), p. 107.

[24]*Khrushchev Remembers*. vol. 1. Harmondsworth: Penguin Books, 1971, p. 156.

[25]Compare this information with other evidence in Rosenfeldt, *Knowledge and Power*; and Rosenfeldt, *Stalinstyrets nervecenter*.

[26]"Organizatsiia i funktsiia Osobogo sektora TsK VKP/b."   A photocopy of this manuscript was received by the Library of Congress around 1950. The author has been identified by the library staff as V.V. Pozdniakov, but this is probably wrong. However, Pozdniakov seems to have collected and edited various émigré manuscripts, so he may have been the *editor* of the special sector article (see the other unpublished "Stat'i", attributed to V.V. Pozdniakov, in the Library of Congress). The description of the special sector system in the "Pozdniakov" manuscript is generally supported by hitherto unused statements in another émigré source, *viz.*, the Almazov manuscript from 1949 in the Boris Nicolaevsky Collection at the Hoover Institution on War, Revolution and Peace, Stanford. According to Almazov (former assistant to the chief of the Secret Police in the Belorussian Soviet Republic), the special sector collected information from a variety of different sources. External information came primarily from: a) foreign communist parties through the "special organs" of the Cominform or from "special residents" whose job it was to report on communist parties abroad; b) the foreign department and the counter-espionage department of the Ministry of State Security; and c) the Intelligence Bureau of the Soviet General Staff.   Internal information was transmitted to the special sector through all "operative departments" of the ministries of State Security and Internal Affairs, the organs of the Commission for Party Control and the organs of the USSR Procuracy. On the basis of this information, the special sector laid down the general policy and the specific tasks for all the above-mentioned institutions. Almazov also states that the special sector prepared drafts of directives to the Ministry of State Security in connection with criminal investigations and arrests and that it played a prominent role in the preparations for the trial of Marshal Tukhachevskii in 1937 (see Almazov manuscript,

31 August 1949, p. 1, and 30 March 1949, pp. 1-2, and compare also manuscript *Sistema sledstviia v MGB*, p. 2).

There are certain internal similarities between the "Pozdniakov" manuscript and the Ruslanov article, mentioned in note 30 (which also describes the special sector system). In some respects they may be mutually connected, perhaps with the late Boris Nicolaevsky as the middleman. On the other hand, the texts also differ on many important issues and cannot just be taken as offsprings of the same source. The Almazov manuscript, too, appears to contain original, independent information (see also Rosenfeldt, *Knowledge and Power*, pp. 63-71).

It is interesting to compare the structural-functional description of the special sector network, given in the above-mentioned sources, with the more general exposition of Stalin's methods by the former communist leader in the United States, Benjamin Gitlow. According to him, Stalin "instituted the 'dog-watch-dog' system in the Russian Communist party and later throughout the international Communist movement, by giving every important communist Party official an aide whether he wanted one or not. The aides, appointed by Stalin, spied on the officials, and the officials, also Stalin men, spied on their aides. The aides did much more than just spy on their chiefs. They insisted that their chiefs energetically carry out the Party line by making suggestions and introducing motions for the record. With insidious cunning records were built up, by the aides against their chiefs, of incompetence in office and failure to carry out the Party line. Thus Stalin has filed away in his archives a case against every Party official of importance. All he has to do when he wants to remove an official is to produce the record and call upon the aide to prefer charges against his chief before Stalin's hand-picked Control Commission." And further: "From 1924 to 1929 Stalin busied himself with building up a private army of his own within the OGPU.... Soon Stalin's private OGPU guard assumed functions that transformed it into a state within the state, which dominated the affairs of the Russian Communist party, the Soviet government and the OGPU of which it was a child.... Through this agency of the political underworld Stalin holds the reins of the world Communist movement firmly in his hands." (Benjamin Gitlow, "The Whole of Their Lives: Communism in America. A Personal History and Intimate Portrayal of its Leaders. New York: Charles Scribner's Sons, 1948, pp. 186-187; and compare Rosenfeldt, *Knowledge and Power*, p. 96, n. 122).

[27]Avtorkhanov, *Stalin*, pp. 106-107.

[28]Reiman, *Geburt des Stalinismus*, pp. 69-70, 86, 90, 144, 159, 182 and 242-246; Schapiro, *Survey*, pp. 54-55; Rosenfeldt, *Stalinstyrets nervecenter*, pp. 55-56; Rosenfeldt, *Russian History/Histoire russe*, p. 318; *Records...*Smolensk District, WKP 138, p. 1. The special sectors seem to have been far more involved in mobilization planning than hitherto assumed by Western Sovietologists (see Rosenfeldt, *Stalin's Special Departments*).

[29]Rosenfeldt, *Knowledge and Power*, pp. 71-85; Rosenfeldt, *Stalin's Special Departments* (a detailed study of the special departments' role in mobilization planning for wartime conditions).

[30]Compare P. Ruslanov, "Voskhozhdenie Malenkova," *Sotsialisticheskii vestnik*, nos. 7-8 (July-August 1953), pp. 128-129. In his book *Inside Stalin's Secret Police: NKVD Politics, 1936-1939* (London: MacMillan, 1985), Robert Conquest confuses the

civilian *Spetsial'nyi otdel*, headed by Bokii, with the military *Osobyi otdel*. On this point, therefore, his analysis of staff changes within the Soviet secret police is quite misleading (see, e.g., p. 203).

[31]*XVII s"ezd*, pp. 562 and 600. See also Jan S. Adams, *Citizen Inspectors in the Soviet Union: The People's Control Committee*. New York: Praeger, 1977, pp. 36-37. According to *Moskva chekistskaia* (another "Pozdniakov" manuscript in the Library of Congress), the Commission for Party Control had its own "special department," dealing with personnel matters in the Ministries of State Security and Internal Affairs (see especially p. 20).

[32]Compare, for example, *Partiinoe stroitel'stvo*, nos. 1-2 (1935), pp. 37-39; no. 13 (1935), p. 46; no. 15 (1935), pp. 1-5; no. 17 (1935), pp. 4 and 21; no. 24 (1935), p. 12; *Records*...Smolensk District, WKP 116/154e, p. 79; WKP 186, pp. 114-119; WKP 499, p. 308; Ruslanov, *Sotsialisticheskii vestnik*, p. 129; Schapiro, *Survey*, pp. 55-56. See also: the discussion in *Slavic Review*, Spring 1983, between J. Arch Getty, Robert C. Tucker and Niels Erik Rosenfeldt.

Mass Politics Under Stalinism:
Two Case Studies

Michael Gelb

One of the essential differences between Stalinism and earlier forms of authoritarianism lies in its combination of highly developed means of political and social control with a demagogic populism manifested by involving the masses in the political sphere. Stalinism was a form of dictatorship that rested on a foundation of mass politics, defined as all political campaigns and activities that required the participation of very large numbers of people. This somewhat simplified definition demands the qualification that the inclusion of the masses in political life was fused with a dialectically opposite exclusion from political and economic decision-making.

The purges and socialist competition provide case studies of the Stalinist synthesis of authoritarianism and populism. When the Central Committee Plenum of December 1935 met to discuss the young Stakhanovist movement and the verification of party documents, it was confirming the political usefulness of party purges and mass productivity campaigns. It not only approved recent experience, but indicated the centrality of the mass politics of industrial productivity and party purity in the Stalinist program for the second half of the 1930s.

This article seeks to shed light on political life under Stalinism by examining the verification of party documents and the Stakhanovist movement in the city of Leningrad in 1935. Leningrad provides a useful case study because of the leading role it has always played in both Soviet economics and politics, and because of the relative abundance of documentary evidence available on it in comparison with all other cities except the capital. While Leningrad may not have been typical of the country as a whole, it did represent the leading edge of Soviet development, and thus offers one of the best laboratories to study Stalinist political life. The resolution of the December Plenum described Stakhanovism as

> the organization of labor in a new fashion, the rationalization of technological processes, the liberation of skilled workers from secondary and preparatory tasks, the better organization of the workspace, the guaranteeing of the rapid

growth of productivity of labor, and the assurance of a significant growth in the pay of workers and staff.[1]

Raising output specifically through the reorganization of the process of production was the most important factor distinguishing Stakhanovism from earlier forms of socialist competition.[2] Stakhanovism also departed from the practice of the original socialist competition by relying relatively more heavily on material than moral incentives. One of the main purposes of the plenum resolution was to confirm an industry-by-industry plan for the promotion of the Stakhanovist movement and the inculcation in the workforce of the productive principles on which it rested. The strongest attack came against the older systems of output norms, based on technical levels rapidly being surpassed, managerial practices long abandoned, and labor qualifications characteristic of the First Five-Year Plan but inadequate for the needs of the Second and Third. The resolution directed all engineering and technical personnel to participate personally in the revision of norms, under the personal supervision of factory directors, rather than entrusting the matter to special norm setters. The productive capacities of all factories and shops were to be surveyed, taking into account the high rates of productivity demonstrated by Stakhanovists. Stakhanovist workers were to be involved in this review.

The plenum launched an attack on those persons — especially managers and specialists — seen as hindering the movement. The plenum resolution directed party organizations to struggle against the "conservative part" of the technical-managerial stratum, their satisfaction with the managerial practices of the past, and even their outright "class hostility." Perhaps managers and specialists did frequently oppose Stakhanovism, but this reflected sound technical objections, rather than the "class hostility" the plenum's participants posited.[3] In the official version, however, anyone who resisted, criticized, or doubted was a "saboteur of Stakhanovism." Though only managers and specialists were regularly attacked as "saboteurs," the lackluster performance of trade union organizations was also a frequent target. Neither factory party organizations nor the "backward elements" among the working class itself were left out. Andrei Zhdanov, head of the Leningrad regional party committee (obkom) complained that the recalcitrance and incompetence of the mass organizations showed in the "spontaneous" character of recruitment to the new movement, itself reflected in the vigorous development of Stakhanovism in some shops and its failure in others. Clearly such anarchy made Stakhanovism pointless: without consistent leadership the movement would founder.[4]

The "birth" of Stakhanovism in Leningrad, as elsewhere, was less the start of something new than the rebirth of socialist competition. Leningrad industry had all the necessary prerequisites for the success of Stakhanovism. It was the country's second largest industrial center, occupying first place in machine building and electrical equipment. It had a large, variegated, and skilled workforce; major enterprises of national significance whose influential administrators had the resources to invest in experimentation; the most powerful, active, and innovative party organization outside the capital; a dynamic Komsomol organization; and a large and multifaceted trade union apparatus. Socialist competition had enjoyed a vigorous development in Leningrad, and many of its specialized variants were pioneered in the city's enterprises.[5]

The first Stakhanovist superstar in Leningrad was N.S. Smetanin, a leather-worker employed on a nailing machine at the "Skorokhod" footwear factory, who on 21 September 1935 doubled the norm of 650 pairs. At the end of his shift the enterprise party committee (partkom) called meetings in all shops to announce the breakthrough and challenge others to follow Smetanin's example. In less than two weeks the factory counted some two thousand Stakhanovists, approximately twenty percent of its workforce. Many others surpassed Smetanin's record, and on 6 October Smetanin himself set a new record by turning out 1,860 pairs. Smetanin had been working at "Skorokhod" for some eighteen years at the time of his first record. He had already achieved national prominence through his leading role in the Izotovist movement, one of the predecessors of Stakhanovism. Smetanin minimized the importance of his long experience, however, maintaining that anyone could become a Stakhanovist. Besides a little forethought, some elbow grease, and the cooperation of management, all that was required was "knowledge of one's machine, the ability to squeeze out of it the maximum it can give, and a conscientious attitude to one's work." Not strength and not haste, but to work at a steady and even pace was Smetanin's secret of success:

> When I was making my record a timekeeper stood by my side. The stop watch showed that I had done 1,800 pairs — that is two and a half times the standard output — expending 13-13 1/2 seconds on each pair. There was not one pair on which I spent 11 seconds — that is rushed; and there was not one pair on which I spent 15 seconds — that is, slowed down.[6]

Stakhanovism caught on rapidly in Leningrad. Along with "Skorokhod," the "Kirov Factory" (heavy machine building), and "Electro-energy" were two other early centers of the movement. One survey of twenty-three Leningrad enterprises would soon claim a growth in numbers of

Stakhanovists from 484 on 10 October to 14,300 on the fifteenth, 23,014 on 1 November, and 39,758 two weeks later. This was 7.9 percent of the Leningrad industrial workforce. By the beginning of 1936 more than 100,000 workers had become Stakhanovists, twenty percent of the city's industrial workers.[7]

Such fantastic statistics suggest that workers were not simply hurrying to join the movement on their own initiative. Many shock and other socialist competition brigades must have simply redefined themselves as Stakhanovists. In other cases managers and trade union officials probably listed brigades and entire shops as Stakhanovist "on paper," that is, whether or not they were reorganizing their work according to Stakhanovist principles. Perhaps overeager leaders used coercive pressure in some cases to corral workers regardless of their real wishes. Periodic tirades of the Leningrad regional and city party committees (city committee = gorkom) against factory-level party and trade union officials who "underestimated" the importance of the new movement indicated their perception that without the constant hectoring of their leaders, workers would have dropped out in large numbers. In 1936 the Leningrad gorkom, for example, attacked primary party organizations (PPO) in light industry which had allowed the number of Stakhanovists to drop drastically (at one factory by seventy percent) in just a few months.[8]

Though official documents rarely acknowledge working class resistance to Stakhanovism, or dismiss it as coming from the "backward sector" of the class, attacks on Stakhanovists by their fellows and other manifestations of discontent were not unknown. In Leningrad such "sallies of the class enemy" included "slander" against Stakhanovists, threats, physical assault — even murder. Other forms of resistance included sabotage of machinery, tools, and Stakhanovists' output. Some workers tried to convince their fellows that Stakhanovism would lead to the exhaustion of the worker's strength, the lowering of his wages, and even a revival of unemployment.[9]

It was not only uncooperative workers who presented obstacles. The weakness, incompetence, and resistance of the trade unions also interfered. Though the party leadership commanded, threatened, and cajoled the trade unions to play a more active role, they consistently disappointed it. Possible explanations include a reluctance to take initiative, covert resistance to speedup, and good old-fashioned bungling. After the managerial "saboteurs of Stakhanovism," the trade unions were the regime's favorite whipping boy for its frustrations in cultivating the movement. The leadership complained that a "general characteristic of backwardness" typified the trade unions.[10] On 17 October the Leningrad Council of Trade Unions complained that its subordinate affiliates "underestimated" the importance of the Stakhanovist movement and had not propagandized the methods of Stakhanovist "innovators." Trade union committees at many Leningrad enterprises responded by making noises about putting the Stakhanovist movement at the center of their attention, a promise reiterated at a city-wide conference of trade union *aktiv* on 22 November.

The unions did make attempts to live up to such promises, playing a major role in mass technical education, providing better social services for Stakhanovist heroes, and even organizing competitions between trade union committees for the most active support of the movement, the widest application of its methods in production, and the best support for the "daily-life" and "cultural" needs of Stakhanovists and their families.[11] Nevertheless, despite five years of party instructions and at least two major reorganizations of its apparatus, official pronouncements would indicate that the trade union movement remained, on the eve of World War II, the ineffective bungler of Stakhanovism that the party had criticized in 1935.

Management was criticized not simply as a potentially hostile class force, but on purely technical grounds as well. Zhdanov touched on a number of these before an audience of Stakhanovists at Leningrad party headquarters on 21 October. He complained that many commanders of production did not believe in the "vanguard workers," and were "turning their backs" on the Stakhanovist movement. Some enterprise administrators, in direct contravention of party and state directives, used the exploits of Stakhanovists to unilaterally raise output norms for all the workers. Though this was in line with the regime's ultimate desires, the Central Committee and the commissariat of Heavy Industry had called a moratorium on raising norms until May 1936; most likely they wanted the first Stakhanovist wonder workers to be able to overfulfill norms by several times and give promotional propaganda the credibility it needed to attract people to Stakhanovism without alienating too many others before the movement got off the ground. In some places managers committed the opposite sin of lowering norms to exaggerate statistics of overfulfillment and to make it possible for everyone to become a Stakhanovist. This was wrong because Stakhanovism was specifically intended to create a new labor elite. Zhdanov repeated the charge that managers sometimes failed to create the necessary conditions for the introduction of Stakhanovist work methods, a facile accusation used to blame specialists for supply shortages and other problems that were beyond their control or to condemn those who refused to produce artificial successes in some shops by depriving others of equipment and supplies. Viktor Kravchenko, a metallurgical engineer who wrote about his life at two pipe rolling mills, felt that the regime's propaganda requirements for such hothouse heroes outweighed losses to overall production.[12] Ironically, and unfairly, some managers who resorted to this practice were themselves denounced for the sin of *rekordsmenstvo*. Zhdanov denounced the deceitful practice of other industrial administrators who, "in the race for naked numbers," listed as Stakhanovists workers and even entire brigades which had not in any way earned the title by changing their methods of work. In some cases, courageous managers and specialists procrastinated or denied outright that Stakhanovist methods were applicable in their shops and resisted attempts to apply them. Needless to say, Zhdanov regarded such administrators as saboteurs.[13]

The organizers of the Stakhanovist movement did see a role for the manager and the engineer, and indeed demanded their participation in the movement. An early instruction of the All-Union Central Council of Trade Unions insisted that it was the duty of every engineer and specialist to see to it that the sector he oversaw mastered Stakhanovist methods.[14] At Leningrad's first city-wide Stakhanovist conference Zhdanov said that any manager or specialist who did not further the development of Stakhanovism had no right to work in Soviet industry.[15] One of the tasks assigned to engineers at this early stage was to work with individual Stakhanovists on their projects for altering the way equipment and workspace were organized. At "Skorokhod" twenty-five Stakhanovists working on particularly promising experiments had engineers assigned to them.[16] The role of specialists in factory-based technical education grew, and for the remainder of the thirties the regime paid ever greater attention to schemes involving technical specialists in the Stakhanovist movement.

As emphasized in the resolution of the December Plenum, all specialists and managers were to participate in the revision of existing output norms, and in particular to make sure that the progressive piece rate system (under which remuneration for each additional unit of output rose at higher levels of productivity) was introduced wherever possible. As Zhdanov pointed out to a conference of Leningrad party *aktiv*, there were any number of enterprises at which pay systems not only failed to encourage high productivity, but penalized it. In the textile industry, for example, pay for each additional unit of output actually decreased after the worker reached 100 percent of his plan quota. Another "brake on Stakhanovism" in current pay systems was that while workers received piece rates, shop foremen, engineers, and specialists received annual salaries; this meant that they had no personal incentive to overfulfill plans.[17]

Throughout the fall of 1935 there was a flurry of party and trade union meetings at every level of Leningrad political life aimed at converting Stakhanovism from the domain of individual record-breakers into a genuine mass movement. In October many factories, following a resolution of the obkom *biuro*, held their first Stakhanovist conferences. On the twenty-fifth the gorkom convened the first Leningrad Stakhanovist conference. A city-wide meeting of engineers and technical specialists took place at the end of October, and major conferences took place in heavy industry and construction in November.

On 26 October a joint gorkom-obkom Plenum discussed the reports of factory directors, partkom secretaries, and trade union committee chairmen on work to promote Stakhanovism. This Plenum provided the occasion to reemphasize points already being made through the various avenues of propaganda, and to add new ideas suggested by the practical experience of the last two months. Special attention was to be devoted to developing the movement in "backward" factories and industries where the workers had not yet taken it up. There was a call for increased attention to quality, all too often abandoned in the mad rush to increase output, and leaders were advised to link Stakhanovism with the older "movement for excellence" (*otlichnichestvo*), one of the spinoffs from socialist competition. The plenum called for the "bolder and more decisive" advancement into management of those "commanders" who could effectively head the initiative of the Stakhanovists. While stressing the importance of the trade unions as a movement of the "widest masses," the plenum took one more swipe at their "formal-bureaucratic" approach, which "fettered" the masses' "creative initiative." The plenum underlined the importance of the press in familiarizing the masses with Stakhanovist heroes, explaining the reorganization of work at various factories, encouraging the best workers, prodding the slowest, and "exposing" the movement's "enemies." Management was to make the Stakhanovist movement into its pampered child by "surrounding the Stakhanovists with care and attention." Nor was the opportunity missed to reprimand managers and specialists who maintained a "narrow-minded" or "indifferent" attitude to Stakhanovism as a "class hostile and bureaucratic element" with which all mass organizations must conduct a "decisive and systematic struggle."[18] Party and trade union organizations were instructed to "reconstruct" their entire mass-political work, adapting workers' clubs, factory "red corners," and neighborhood culture centers (*doma kul'tury*) for this purpose. The plenum instructed district and factory party committees, trade union and Komsomol organizations, and enterprise management to convene conferences to consider means for the further development of the Stakhanovist movement.[19]

In Leningrad Stakhanovism saw out the year 1935 with a celebration of the movement's success. In the last two weeks of the year entire pages of *Leningradskaia Pravda* were covered by articles with such titles as, "Two to Three Times More," "We'll Go Further," and "The Kirovists Kept Their Word." They were splashed with futurist-style photographs of happy Stakhanovists posing behind machine-tools, arms around their buddies' shoulders, locks of hair hanging rakishly on their young foreheads. A series of "Stakhanovist shifts" and "Stakhanovist days" — a new gimmick imported from the Donbas — signified the beginning of the radiation of Stakhanovism into new spinoff movements. The press proclaimed that the next step would be the transition to Stakhanovist shops, Stakhanovist factories, and permanent Stakhanovist work. The last issue of *Leningradskaia Pravda* for 1935 reported the fulfillment of norms in various enterprises the day before by two, three, and four hundred percent. Workers who yesterday had barely met their quotas were written up today as models. One cannot lend too much credence to the miracles reported in special Stakhanovist issues of the papers, but one cannot ignore the reports either. They remind us not only of the sensationalist character of Stalinist mass politics, its desire for spectacles, the emphasis on gigantomania; but the young men and women grinning at us from the pages of *Leningradskaia Pravda* also remind us that there were real people performing these stunts, experimenting with new ways to exploit machinery, learning to falsify figures, grumbling at the slackers, grumbling at the norm-busters. These were the true believers, the sharps, the intimidated conformists, and the secret resisters who were the raw material of mass politics under Stalin.

How did the new movement reflect the authoritarian and populistic characteristics of Stalinist mass politics? The first thing that strikes one is the movement's predominantly top-down nature. The party leadership had seized on the initiatives of individual teams of worker-enthusiasts and political activists and converted them into a movement affecting the entire working class. It employed material incentives, a flood of propaganda, sanctions against party and trade union organizations that did not exert themselves to promote the campaign. The hectoring of party, trade union, and economic leaders drove the worker into the movement as often as did the desire for praise and recognition, the hope for monetary reward, and the ideological impulses of patriotism or party loyalty. In cases where the mass organizations relented for even a moment, the movement seemed to lose its inertia and foundered.

The movement helped the regime solidify its control over society.

Most importantly, it served to atomize the working class by setting it at odds with itself, primarily by fostering labor competition, above all through the use of piece rates. The antagonism between the upwardly mobile go-getters and those workers who resented the effort to increase their exploitation reinforced this effect. Official victimization of the slackers — through public humiliation, attacks in the factory press, condemnation in comrades courts — was also a way to break workers' will to resist Stalinist industrial policy. The facilitation of the upward mobility of the Stakhanovists, on the other hand, bred a kind of Stalinist *meshchanstvo*, or "petty bourgeois philistinism," helping to solidify the dictatorship's conservative social base.

Stakhanovism also provided an avenue of attack against the technical-managerial intelligentsia, checking its desire to stake out a more secure position, and counterbalancing the regime's dependence on its skills and knowledge. Ideally this would result from the development of such a high level of technical skills among the workers that professional engineers and specialists would no longer be needed. This goal would ultimately prove impossible, but a more immediate form of attack came in the charges of "sabotage" levelled against managers and specialists at every Stakhanovist conference and at every party or trade union meeting. Implications of "sabotage" of the Stakhanovist movement were more explicit in the popular press than in the more restrained words of the December plenum resolution; presumably the tone of verbal attacks at shop-level mass meetings was even more hostile. By keeping the notion of the class alien *spets* fresh in the public memory, the party created a stock of scapegoats whom it could blame for the failures of its own economic policies, thereby diverting the lightning of public discontent from itself onto a defenseless, but highly visible victim. In 1937 the Ezhovshchina would convert the Stakhanovist attack on the prerogatives of management and specialists into a far more menacing force.

However, we must not overlook the movement's genuinely popular side. Even if the success of the campaign depended on constant direction from the party, in the final analysis it could not succeed without real mass enthusiasm for the building of the brave new world. The same wells of support that fueled the shock work movement made Stakhanovism possible. Though premiums, privileges, and increased wages played a more important role than in the past, moral incentives still contributed their share. Getting one's picture in the factory paper, the pleasure many must have felt when their factory earned a "Red Banner" in a nationwide competition, and the flattery showered on the Stakhanovists by the entire propaganda apparatus must have attached a certain amount of pride to the name "Stakhanovist." One should not ignore the patriotic impulses that made many dream of the day when backward Russia would overtake the decadent West.

Aside from its reliance on mass enthusiasm, Stakhanovism was a popular phenomenon in the sense that it provided a channel for mass upward mobility for anyone willing to invest some elbow grease and scratch his head over the textbooks for a technical course or two. The movement did not discriminate between Russian and Kazakh, male and female, young and old. The innovative and energetic could hope to achieve not only honors, premiums, and higher wages, but schooling, job promotion, or a springboard into politics. Stakhanovism was a central part of the regime's promotion of technical education, fostering a whole array of factory-based courses that allowed workers to study without leaving their jobs. For people whose parents had been illiterate, and whose grandparents serfs, the value of this cannot be overstated. Mass technical education, along with the upward mobility it made possible, was one of the most important social bases of Stalin's popularity.

On a more general level, Stakhanovism embodied the utopian notion that one day workers would have the skills to run industry without the tutelage of managers and engineers. Stalin had said that the goal of Stakhanovism was to break down the differences between mental and manual labor, and to raise the "cultural-technical level" of ordinary workers to that of engineering-technical specialists. This project was in part a reflection of the regime's desire to prevent the crystallization of the technical intelligentsia into a class that might one day exert its independence of state and party control. The new proletarian cohorts who had advanced through the Stalinist industrialization program were politically more reliable. Despite the manipulative aspect of Stakhanovism, the movement was based on certain utopian presumptions rooted in the revolutionary tradition. Though experience would show it impossible to eliminate the division between engineer and worker, Stakhanovism would reduce the separation of conception and execution fostered in capitalist countries under the influence of Taylorism and "scientific management." While managerial science in the capitalist world aimed at the conversion of the worker into the brute adjunct of the machine, Stakhanovism was an effort to liberate the creative potential in each individual. It was an industrial policy that encouraged the worker's self-respect and recognized society's indebtedness to his efforts. Though Stalinist reality sullied this ideal, and though it was a form of exploitation, many if not most workers saw Stakhanovism in a positive light.

The factors of authoritarianism and populism can be identified even within the party purges. The verification of party documents was one of a long series of party-cleaning operations that began shortly after the revolution and continued through the Ezhovshchina of 1937 and 1938. The verification began in May 1935 and dragged on in some places until February 1936, after several postponements of its completion date. Its historical significance derives primarily from its transitional role between the older, more limited type of membership screening and the more politically-oriented, arbitrary, and violent Ezhovshchina. For this reason, it is interesting to examine the official evaluation of the Central Committee at its Plenum in December 1935.

As the plenum resolution states:

> the most important result of the verification of party documents is that party organizations, at the same time as they exposed alien people who had crept into the party, eliminated to a significant degree the elements of that organizational disorder, brought into order the system of recordkeeping on members of the party, better studied communists, and on this basis advanced many new, talented workers into leading party, soviet, and economic work.[20]

In other words, the verification had three purposes: to purify the party by driving out elements unacceptable to its Stalinist leaders; to strengthen it as an instrument of public administration by establishing strict principles of accounting and recordkeeping; and to solidify Stalinism's social base through the populisitic program of drawing larger numbers of rank-and-file communists into the lower and middle levels of party leadership.

In the secret circular that initiated the verification, the Central Committee attacked the chaos that reigned in the records of most party organizations. One of the problems discovered during the purge of 1933, and which played a role in the decision to initiate the verification, was the fact that tens of thousands of party cards had been given out without any record of the people to whom they had been given. During the First Five-Year Plan party organizations had stumbled over themselves to recruit as many workers as they could, paying little attention to recordkeeping, the party statutes, and the approval of the appropriate higher agencies. Many unaccounted-for cards had fallen into the hands of people who were not genuine members, allowing them to take part in party life and even obtain leadership positions. Other factors complicated matters. Party organizations often included in their membership lists many who had moved to other parts, where they joined other party organizations and acquired a second *bilet*. Some lost or claimed to have lost their party cards, and routinely obtained new ones.

There was a virtual black market in stolen, forged, and duplicate party documents.   At a time when membership opened the doors of opportunity, a party card was a valuable commodity to those who could not join party licitly.

There was a genuine need for a general document check. But out of fear for its own dictatorship, and in order to create a permanent state of alarm among party members, the Stalinist leadership spread the idea that the absence of reliable records had made it possible for all sorts of "hostile elements" to join the party. The verification was not to be simply a technical housekeeping operation, but an effort to hunt down those whom the leadership identified as the enemies of socialism: "class aliens" who had hidden their social background (or who were hounded simply for the fact of their background, rather than for having hidden it); every stripe of past, present, and potential oppositionist; and "crooks and swindlers" whose corruption diminished the resources required by socialist construction.

The resolution of the December Plenum stated that the verification had "successfully decided the basic task laid out in the letter of the Central Committee of 13 May 1935 — to establish Bolshevik order in our own party house — and raised the level of all party life, heightening the Bolshevik fighting ability of party organizations." The last point deserves special emphasis. The verification, as a review of each communist and the PPO to which he belonged, was an opportunity to evaluate the effectiveness of the party's "mass work." In addition to its other tasks, the verification was a large-scale criticism/self-criticism campaign designed to strengthen the party as the "leading force" in society.

But the Central Committee's expression of satisfaction was somewhat *pro forma*.   For one thing, the verification had not yet brought recordkeeping into satisfactory order in all localities; the problem of *uchetnost'* (accountability) remained. In some places second verifications had to be conducted, either at the behest of the Central Committee or of regional committees. The purge took much longer to complete than originally anticipated, and was not yet finished when the December Plenum met.   In addition, the verification had shown that many communists' party cards contained inaccuracies or incomplete information.   This was also the situation with members' record files (*uchetnaia kartochka*), dossiers kept at the raikom (district committee) or, in major industrial establishments, by the enterprise partkom.   The Central Committee still felt insecure enough about the state of recordkeeping that it ordered a companion membership regulation to the verification, the exchange of party documents, to be conducted in 1936. As a purge, the exchange of party documents was supposed to eliminate "passive" communists — those who "did not justify the lofty title of party member" — by refusing to renew their party documents. The "passives" were those who did not take seriously the statutory obligations to "raise their ideological level," to carry out party assignments, to pay membership dues, and so forth. There was some controversy about this, and the central and regional committees repeatedly attacked lower party organizations for going too hard on basically loyal, if incompetent rank and filers. Some passives began to be eliminated after the December Plenum but before the end of the verification. They were attacked in the opening months of the exchange. But in the summer of 1936, the Central Committee switched the emphasis away from the passives.

The fact that the leadership wanted a second purge indicated a dissatisfaction with more than the state of grassroots leaders' clerical skills, or whether rank-and-filers paid their dues on time. Another problem was that the verification had not succeeded in uncovering all of the enemies who, so the leaders believed, or wanted the membership to believe, remained. "The main lesson," according to the plenum resolution, "is that members... and party organizations still have only poorly mastered the many Central Committee instructions about the need for an all-around heightening of Bolshevik vigilance..."[21]. Reiterating the Stalinist line that the enemy would struggle more desperately the greater the successes of socialist construction, the Central Committee warned that "the enemy uses the opportunist kind-heartedness and absent-mindedness [of communists} for this purpose." It was the failure of class vigilance that explained, for example, why it had been possible for people expelled as enemies to retain their party cards, re-join in another place, and even gain entrance to the party apparatus, where "exploiting their unsupervised position and the neglect of leading party workers to the technical side of party work, they gave out party documents or sold them to fellow participants in their subversive work."[22] The purport of such warnings was that the verification had been a measure to put pressure on both rank-and-file and the lower-level leadership to intensify efforts to "expose" the class enemy wherever he could be found.

The claim that the verification had strengthened the party by uncovering new reserves of energy and talent among the "party masses" is more than empty talk. In times of trouble the party had more than once resorted to mass enrollments, especially from the industrial working class. Though new enrollments had ceased after the initiation of the 1933 purge and would not reopen until the conclusion of the exchange of party documents in late 1936, this period had seen intensified pressure to improve the party's ability to educate, train, and promote new leadership cadres from the rank-and-file. In Leningrad the verification led to the appointment of 82 new partkom secretaries, 78 party organizers, and 478 other leading workers. Raikomy had discovered 1,620 new *rezervisty*, while primary party organizations had acquired over 2,000.[23]

To what degree the regime wished to turn the verification into a campaign of denunciations is not clear. There is no doubt that suspected oppositionists were being hounded with a new fury. Victor Kravchenko, who underwent all the party-cleaning operations of the thirties, reported that in 1935 expulsion from the party often meant immediate arrest.[24] On the other hand there were periodic attacks against the practice of lower-level party leaders who "repressed" rank-and-filers suspected as class enemies or oppositionists, or who merely did not fulfill the duties of party membership. The most famous reprimand was Andrei Zhdanov's speech on the errors of the Saratov party apparatus, in which he condemned the firing of communists from their jobs upon expulsion from the party, and the employment of reprimands and expulsions in situations which required "patient explanatory work" instead.[25] There were extensive rights of appeal to higher agencies for party members unfairly expelled. Nevertheless, the signals for moderation received by lower party committees were overwhelmed in a torrent of demands for class vigilance. The Central Committee's calls for leniency may have been purely hypocritical attempts to appear as the defender of the little man and to make middle and lower-level officials bear the opprobrium for abuses. Or they may have reflected a genuine concern to protect loyal, though lazy or incompetent, party members. The former seems closer to the truth, but in any case, the verification did degenerate into something of a witch hunt; its companion operation, the exchange of party documents of 1936, after a brief period of moderation, continued the hunt.

Materials from the Leningrad press illustrate the issues raised at the December Plenum. The chaos in party records was more than just an excuse for a purge. A plenum of the Vyborgskii raion committee heard many reports on the problem of lost and unaccounted-for party cards. At the Industrial Institute 29 communists had lost their cards. At the "Red Yarn" spinning mill 25 persons no longer belonging to the party still retained theirs. One hundred and seventy candidates' cards, as well as nine membership files, were currently untraceable. *Leningradskaia Pravda* described as "criminal" the negligence that reigned in many of the raion's PPO, and darkly hinted at "connivance" in allowing cards to fall into the hands of the party's enemies.[26]

Despite the inflammatory propaganda, the evidence suggests that it was neither the machinations of the class enemy, nor any lack of class vigilance that caused the problem, but rather the fallibility of petty bureaucrats and rank-and-file party members. The typical lower-level party leader often had only a few years of formal education, the rank-and-file communist even less. It is unlikely that such persons would have had a real understanding of the need for accurate recordkeeping. Thus, at the "October" textile factory the partkom stored important documents, including secret correspondence, in complete disarray in a dirty bast sack; the partkom secretary felt that by having thus gathered the documents, she had "put party housekeeping in order." The protocols of party meetings at a government agency in Volodarskii raion had somehow found their way into the workers' co-operative store, where salespersons used them to wrap food for the customers. This was not such a great loss, however, because the protocols that survived were so slovenly that they gave no idea of what had happened at meetings.[27] Half of the archive of the party organization of the Oktiabrskii raion's Education Department had been destroyed by rats, and the same fate threatened the other half. It was difficult to find the protocols of party meetings, and when located, they often had no date or signature. It was impossible to find any materials relating to the 1933 purge. The desk of the partkom secretary, where documents of current importance were kept, bore the character of "a pig sty in a bad kolkhoz."[28]

If the need to review the membership and membership records justified the verification, it nevertheless was also a genuine purge, designed to rid the party of the enemies and potential enemies of the regime. The verification continued earlier efforts to eliminate dissidents, and signified an intensification of the enemy hunting of the 1933 purge.[29] As *Leningradskaia Pravda* warned, the verification had shown that many apparently loyal party members had turned out to be "most evil enemies of the party — white guards, Trotskiists, crooks and swindlers." Their exposure and expulsion was the verification's most important task.[30]

The line was that former oppositionists, who had recanted their views, were secretly continuing their oppositional work. They were joined by "class aliens," party members whose social origins lay among the propertied classes of the pre-revolutionary and NEP years. Technically, the charge against the aliens was that they had hidden their pasts when they joined the party. The real charge was that they had joined specifically with the purpose of undermining socialist construction. To be sure, there must have been many who hid bourgeois class backgrounds or the dekulakization of their families, but one is not convinced that these were the bitterly scheming counter-revolutionaries painted in Stalinist propaganda. To judge by unofficial accounts,[31] and even by reading between the lines in the official sources, they appear to have been falsely accused scapegoats, the frightened losers in a social revolution, trying to adapt to the brave new world as best they could, hounded by the merciless inheritors of their social standing.   The verification also went after the "crooks and swindlers" who no doubt joined the party in large numbers to take advantage of whatever opportunities it offered for material gain.   Grafters, the members of local influence rackets, embezzlers, and bribe-takers were uncovered, expelled, and arrested in large numbers.   Except for cases in which "oppositionists" and "class aliens" were tainted for purposes of propaganda with a false accusation of corruption, most of the stories about official malfeasance have the ring of truth about them.   This was one more legitimate basis for the verification.

Since only a minority of Russia's population had been born into the proletariat or poor peasantry, a large portion of the party membership was at least theoretically vulnerable to a charge of class alien background. It is no surprise that "class aliens" are the largest category − in Leningrad perhaps half or two-thirds − of those driven from the party during the verification.   One can read of the devastation of entire party committees on this basis.[32]   The expulsions reported in the press included a machinist from Leningrad's largest enterprise, the Kirov Factory, who had complained too loudly at a health resort about the property he and his family had lost during the revolution;[33]   the chairman of the trade union committee of Leningrad's "Marti" shipbuilding yard, denounced as an "alien and rogue" because his father had once employed wage labor and owned a large house, cattle, and five hundred *desiatiny* of land;[34] and an employee of the Nogin spinning mill who came under investigation when it was discovered that she had received a spare*bilet* by joining the party twice, and whose father had allegedly owned his own shipping company.[35]

One particularly noteworthy case reported the personal campaign of exposure waged by a worker Stalinist who appealed to a succession of party agencies at the factory, raion, and oblast' levels in order to obtain the elimination of the sons and grandsons of a former manufacturer from the party, their dismissal from their jobs, expulsion from institutes, and deportation from Leningrad.   *Leningradskaia Pravda* eventually intervened and attacked party leaders at the "Red Dawn" telephone equipment factory and the Vyborgskii raikom for their complacency when originally approached on the matter.[36]   The case boded ill for raikom secretary Smorodin. During the exchange of party documents in 1936 the charges against him were increased from a mere lack of class vigilance to knowingly abetting the enemy.   The case illustrates a number of important aspects of the verification. None of the victims of the Stalinist snitch was accused of specific wrongdoings: they were just from the wrong class. It was not they who were important, but the fact that their case provided the obkom the opportunity to make an example of a partkom and raikom that did not take the Central Committee's strictures on class vigilance seriously enough. On a more general level, the story shows how the party leadership encouraged personal vendettas among the rank-and-file as a way to maintain a climate of antagonism and mistrust which would render impossible solidarity against the higher apparatus. The whole affair epitomizes the fanaticism that demanded the extirpation off the "class alien" element root and branch, and which was increasingly dominating party propaganda and membership policy.

If the class aliens were the most numerous group of expellees, propaganda made the most fuss about uncovering oppositionists. Most oppositionists were Zinov'evists and Trotskiists who had long ago given up resistance to the Stalin juggernaut and been forced to confess their errors as a condition for remaining in the party. Now the claim was that their admission of guilt had been insincere and that they had continued their "subversive work."

The Zinov'evists were public enemy number one in 1935, perhaps because Kirov's assassin allegedly belonged to their number.[37]   In any case, the attack was intense. The press labelled Zinov'evists "white bandits" and "double dealers"; if one was unearthed somewhere, the press trumpeted that he had "sneaked" into the organization. The presence of more than one Zinov'evist became "a large-scale infiltration of enemies."[38] People associated too closely with any of the victims of the Zinov'evist trials following the Kirov assassination were automatically expelled from the party, as at the "Dzerzhinskii" textile factory, whose partkom secretary was the wife of one of those executed.[39]   Often, Zinov'evists holding responsible positions were charged with abuse of authority. The Zinov'evist trade union committee chairman at the "Kuibyshev Carburetor Factory," for instance, was accused of having arbitrarily removed ten shop floor workers from the committee in order to replace them with his own appointees.[40]

Among the Trotskiists expelled were the partkom secretary of an industrial construction agency who had corresponded with Trotskii in the 1920s, an engineer from the "Kazitskii" radio factory who had supported the Trotskiist opposition in 1923 and voted against the expulsion of Trotskii and Zinov'ev in 1927, and a partkom secretary at a metallurgical institute who was accused of having supported a number of "Trotskiist positions" in the institute's wall newspaper.[41] Reports about other kinds of oppositionists were rare. One former Menshevik was typed as a criminal because he had spent time in a tsarist labor camp for forgery.[42]

In another case the entire party organization of a metallurgical institute was denounced for the fact that it had not hounded out the assistant director of the institute, a former Menshevik who had served an eight-year term for "counter-revolutionary activity."[43] Curiously enough, this study found no references to expulsions of adherents of the right opposition or former members of other political parties.

Not all victims of the verification were necessarily driven from the party on such unfair grounds. As an effort to uncover persons engaged in various forms of economic malfeasance, it led also to the expulsion of individuals who would have been intolerable in public organizations in any country. Press reports on expulsions for economic crime are more reliable than those about class aliens and oppositionists, primarily because we know to what a great degree the system of "influence," or *blat*, really did flourish in the thirties.

One illustrative case involved a nest of graft surrounding Khrisanfov, the director of a recycling center in Leningrad's Kirovskii raion. Khrisanfov allegedly was a former monk who had been expelled from the party in 1929, only to surreptitiously join it a second time. The verification found him working at the recycling center, where he allegedly exploited all possibilities for personal gain. In 1934 he appealed to his superiors for funds "to send two shock workers to a resort," using the money (1,395 rubles) to go there with his wife. In 1935 he used the same trick, this time receiving 3,270 rubles. In seven months of 1935 the oblast' social security administration gave him 960 rubles, and his trade union gave him 510 for "supplementary food allocations." Khrisanfov covered his actions through bribery rather than secrecy. Among those taking graft from him were the chairman of the trade union committee, the manager of one of the workshops, and the partkom secretary. The latter suggested to one of the raikom party instructors that he might also participate in these handouts, but the latter refused, failing, however, to inform the authorities about these "strange managerial gifts."

The raikom instructor's lack of concern was not atypical. *Leningradskaia Pravda* attacked the oblast' social security administration, to which the reprocessing center belonged, for the chaos that reigned in its accounting section. The newspaper charged that it knew of many cases of embezzlement, sometimes running into thousands of rubles, but fought against the problem half-heartedly. The paper also attacked the center's mass organizations, which were "out of touch with the worker masses," and in which "a total lack of self-criticism" reigned. When Kirovskii raikom brought the trade union committee chairman's corruption to the attention of the chairman of the trade union's oblast' committee, the latter maintained a lenient attitude, purportedly remarking that "one should take into account the fact that Zheznevskii has three children, which is why he took bribes ...." *Leningradskaia Pravda* condemned Novikov's indifferent, if pragmatic, conclusion: "since [Zheznevskii's] authority has been undermined [i.e., not because he was an enemy of socialism], he will have to be removed."[44] This case provides a good example of how the verification was used to accomplish tasks other than political repression.

By focusing on the verification's role as purge, Western scholarship has ignored a populistic aspect of the operation. The most serious failure in the party's mass work that came under systematic attack during the verification was that the lower-level leadership did not concern itself with the interests of the rank-and-file, see to their political education, or include them in party affairs. Most importantly, it did not devote enough attention to the *rezerv*, the grassroots activists who were suitable for advancement into leadership roles. The press touted the verification as a means to correct this shortcoming by acquainting leaders with the rank-and-file. This made it possible, in the words of one raikom secretary, to "place ten newly matured, solid proletarian-Bolsheviks [into] the place of every crook and class enemy we expel...."[45]

Kirovskii raikom was one of the least enthusiastic in its mass work. The verification had supposedly led to the promotion of some eighty comrades to the raikom *rezerv*; seventy others had been advanced shortly before. However, by October the raikom still had no information, not even the last names, on the reservists discovered during September, and was still unfamiliar with those who had been advanced earlier. That it was directly involved in the political training of only thirteen out of 150 new *rezervisty* indicated its lack of concern.

Not all new reservists were ignored this way, and some were being taught important leadership skills. Among the tasks to which they were assigned were the preparation of information for raikom *biuro* discussions, the planning of monthly raikom work schedules, and attending important conferences and meetings. One group of reservists, guided by a raikom instructor, was investigating preparations for the verification at the "Zhdanov Shipbuilding Works," while another was reviewing PPO work with party candidates. Nevertheless, the raikom's work with the reserve was still unsatisfactory. To use the language of the time, most reservists were included "only formally."[46]

An official of the Department of Party Cadres discussed the problem at several raion enterprises. At the timber export agency "Eksportles" the partkom gave candidates the impression that they had no right to vote or even speak at meetings. One of them complained that his only party assignment since 1933 had been the collection of membership dues for the International Organization for Assistance to Fighters for the Revolution. "This work has stultified me," he said, "but they don't give me any other. In general, here at the harbor nobody pays any attention to candidates." At another enterprise several comrades working with the para-military organization "Osoaviakhim" had collected dues for a year in advance and had no current assignments at all.[47]

One PPO that reported genuine success in recent work with its *rezerv* was at the "Dzerzhinskii Textile Factory," where the verification had recently eliminated a large part of the leadership, including the partkom secretary, the wife of one of the Zinov'evists shot after the assassination of Kirov. The elimination of so many leaders meant that the partkom could offer its new activists an adequate selection of meaningful assignments. Over the last months a new *rezerv* had been created, and nineteen women had been advanced into leading work. As *Leningradskaia Pravda* blandly put it, "new people came into the leadership at the factory."

Among the promotees was the weaver Smirnova, ignored and "mistrusted" by the old leadership, who was elected party organizer of the weaving shop when "it became necessary" to remove her predecessor. Reportedly, the shop was now "boiling with mass political work." Another promotee was the assistant partkom secretary, the weaver Zascherinskaia. Six of the newly advanced women worked (apparently freed from production) in leading positions at the all-factory level, while another thirteen were working as shop organizers and group organizers but were not freed from their production jobs.

The organization currently had a *rezerv* of twenty communists and intended to expand it in the future. There were only two propagandists, so eight reservists were being trained to lead study circles and "political schools" in the near future. The new secretary claimed that the partkom involved the reserve in its affairs, allowing them, for example, to participate in the formulation of its monthly work plans. Other outlets for their energies included studying and improving the distribution of party assignments and preparing material for the next partkom meeting on work with the engineering technical section of the trade union.[48]

Raikomy, prodded by the Central Committee and the obkom, drew upon this resource, though left to their own devices, they would not have made a very impressive contribution to this form of party remodelling. "Mass work" remained a highly formalized affair and offered few opportunities for real decision-making or political initiative. Many PPOs had difficulty finding enough party assignments for their members. This resulted from the fact that the PPO had only limited responsibilities: mainly propagandizing the latest campaigns and encouraging workers to improve productivity. Raikomy and partkomy often resorted to make work in order to occupy their *aktiv*, especially when the pressure was on to do so, as during the verification.

The impression one gets from the volume of such reports is that the Central Committee saw PPOs as spawning grounds for new leadership cadres. It is easy enough to understand the need to expand the numbers of grassroots leaders. The pressure to "raise" new cadres was actually part of a broader social policy aimed at the creation of a new, specifically Soviet intelligentsia and white-collar workforce. More specifically, with the cessation of new enrollments in 1933, the party lost an important source of organizational labor power. It, however, still had to replace leaders eliminated by the purges and to meet growing manpower needs resulting from the establishment of new enterprises and the growth of administrative agencies. The party was learning rapidly to replace leaders not merely on an individual basis, but in batch runs, even by entire committees. This suggests (but does not prove) that those in command were planning a massive replacement of personnel within the party and state apparatus.

Despite its optimistic wording, one detects a certain dissatisfaction with the progress of the verification in the December Plenum resolution. If it had been a complete success, it should not have been necessary to undertake a follow-up party cleaning, the exchange of party documents. But plans for this operation accounted for the major part of the resolution. The necessity for a second membership review indicated that party organizations had still not mastered the organizational practices the Central Committee required of them. As an opportunity for grassroots party leaders to become better acquainted with the rank-and-file, the verification made possible the discovery of new sources of leadership talent. There remained many problems in this area; too many raikom officials were still unfamiliar not only with the rank-and-file, but even with PPO leaders. Finally, the resolution noted that the job of ridding the party of internal enemies was still far from complete.

Though the verification had no doubt justified itself in the eyes of the leaders, Stalin, Ezhov, and others were planning to continue the purge into 1936 and probably beyond. The verification certainly seems an effort to inflame the public imagination with the notion that hidden enemies were at work everywhere, impeding the efforts of the Central Committee and undermining socialist construction. The rising volume of anti-oppositional rhetoric in the last weeks of the verification seems deliberately calculated to justify further purges.

Since only those of proletarian or poor peasant parentage were totally immune from accusation as class aliens; since the simple fact of having voted for an oppositional candidate in a party election, even more than ten years ago, might attract investigation and expulsion; and since a large part of the population, party members no less than anyone else, engaged in illegal economic acts from time to time; for all these reasons, a majority of the party's members were liable to expulsion on one basis or another. The hunt for enemies was probably intended as a means to instill in every communist the fear of denunciation and to guarantee that he would conform to whatever values and goals the leadership advocated. The more a person had to hide, the more eagerly he would espouse the party line.

The verification reconfirmed old precedents and established new ones that eased the path to the superpurge of 1936-1938. Character assassination, holding people responsible for the actions of their fellows, encouraging talebearers and informers, and penalizing party members for actions committed before they had been defined as crimes — these were some of the tools that had proven of continuing value in the effort to cow all resistance to the Stalinist machine. *Leningradskaia Pravda* carried more than one report about a party member attacked for defending those who he felt had been unjustly expelled. The press promoted the idea that turning one's back on a relative or comrade under attack was the highest morality: some were denounced for maintaining contact with "Zinov'evist" spouses, others for helping a brother or cousin hide from the political police. Remaining legal and moral limits to the arbitrary exercise of power were being further eroded.

It was now an official axiom that the party was infested with masked opponents of the regime and the social order. In political discourse "oppositionist," "class enemy," and "crook" had become virtually interchangeable terms. The leaders had perfected the use of political intimidation to silence dissent, atomize the party masses, and further strengthen their own grip on the party.

On the other hand, the recruitment, training, and promotion of new leaders minimized the negative impact of party-cleaning operations and reinforced an image of Stalin and the "little Stalins" surrounding him as populists on the side of the rank-and-filer against the heartless party bureaucrat. The mechanisms for the rapid creation of new cadres had proven their value: now the party could replace any number of "leading personnel" without inordinate fear of the resulting organizational chaos.

The verification had other populistic aspects. It was conducted by commissions appointed by the raikomy, putting control in the hands of people closer to the rank-and-file than in the purge of 1933, which had been run by commissions appointed from above and supervised by a Central Purge Commission of the Central Committee. This made the verification seem a local affair, a kind of organizational self-review. One of the means to accomplish this was for the PPO to organize participatory campaigns to "prepare for the verification," which included all sorts of pep talks, crash political education courses, propaganda displays, and a critical review of the recent activities of PPOs and their leaders.

Verification commissions encouraged rank-and-file communists to report on each other and to attack their immediate leaders. In many organizations during the second half of the summer, the Central Committee and regional committees ordered those raikomy which had conducted the verification in an incompetent, dilatory, and "go easy" manner to start the operation over.[49] Evidence from the Smolensk archive shows that these repeat verifications turned into an open season on raikom leaders, with higher authorities encouraging the rank-and-file to air all grievances against their bosses.[50] Under such circumstances denunciation was a form of popular participation (albeit manipulated from above) in the party-cleaning process.

Initiated and guided from Moscow, the verification was a mechanism of "revolution from above." An effort to cauterize every possible source of opposition, it can be seen as a measure aimed at consolidating a totalitarian regime in the party. By decreasing the distance between the bureaucracy and the rank-and-file, rallying the mass of party members against a minority of scapegoats, and drawing more people into political life, especially in grassroots leadership roles, the verification reflected the populist face of Stalinism. Since millions of party members, candidates, and sympathizers were affected by the verification — whether as victims or as beneficiaries — the operation was an important aspect of Stalinism's mass politics.

Reporting on the December Plenum to a meeting of Leningrad party *aktiv*, Andrei Zhdanov explained that the coming exchange of party documents and the renewal of enrollment, along with the development of the Stakhanovist movement, required a "still greater mastery of the art of leadership." Stalin and his allies saw party purges and socialist competition as instruments of political leadership. They were means by which they could increase the strength of the state, solidify party domination over society, and secure their own dictatorship within the party. Stakhanovism was envisaged as more than just a productivity campaign: as a movement of the entire population, it was to become an instrument of global social management. Although the verification of party documents was an internal party affair, it also had implications for the manner in which the party would dominate society: the perfection of internal party discipline meant the perfection of the party's command over society. The verification, like other purges, was a form of mass politics not merely because the party was itself a mass organization, but because it influenced the party's relationship to society as a whole. From the point of view of Stalin's Politburo, this is why the politics of party purity were so essential.

Though separate and differing campaigns, the verification and Stakhanovism each reflected in its own way the Stalinist synthesis of authoritarianism and populism. They were both attempts to mold the industrial working class and the mass membership of the party in the interests of the regime. Both reflected the strategy of eliciting mass participation in political life. To be sure, the mix of authoritarianism and populism differed in each case: Stakhanovism clearly reflected more popular initiative; the verification, the political obsessions of the regime. Though Stakhanovism, a non-party movement, involved much greater numbers than the verification, the latter, consisting of the evaluation and manipulation of millions of party members and fellow travellers, was no lightweight in the arena of 1930s mass politics. Both movements tried to rally loyalty and repress dissent by directing the masses' suspicion and anger at defenseless scapegoats: the "saboteurs of the Stakhanovist movement" in one case, and the "class aliens" and oppositionist "counter-revolutionaries" in the other. Finally, both Stakhanovism and the verification of party documents sought to open the doors of opportunity to rank-and-file workers. In the case of Stakhanovism, this was through technical training and job promotion; in the verification, it was through advancement into political leadership. Most importantly, both Stakhanovism and the verification helped Stalinism establish a base of support among the industrial working class.

Franklin and Marshall College

NOTES

[1]*KPSS v rezoliutsiiakh i resheniiakh s"ezdov, konferentsii, i plenumov TsK*, vol. V: *1931-1941*. Moscow, 1971, p. 232.

[2]The four basic areas of Stakhanovist innovation were the division of labor processes; the rationalization of the physical movements of workers in the production process; the alteration of technical processes and the way machinery was employed; and the alteration or replacement of the machinery itself. V. Seletskii, "Nachalo stakhanovskigo dvizheniia v Leningrade (Sentiabria-Noiabria 1935 g.)," *Voprosy istorii*, no. 11. (November 1951), pp. 50-52.

[3]Victor Kravchenko, *I Chose Freedom*. New York: Charles Scribner's Sons, 1946, pp. 187-198, 298-302; John Scott, *Behind the Urals*. Cambridge: Houghton Mifflin Co., 1942, pp. 163-170.

[4]*Leningradskaia pravda* (hereafter *LP*), 18 January 1936, p. 2.

[5]On the preconditions for the success of Stakhanovism in Leningrad, see Seletskii, *Voprosy istorii*, pp. 30-34, 36-37.

[6]*Labour in the Land of Socialism: Stakhanovites in Conference.* Moscow, 1936, pp. 211-213. The chairman of the factory's trade union committee recounts the first five weeks of the Stakhanovist movement in *LP*, 29 October 1935, p. 3. On Smetanin's biography, see Seletskii, *Voprosy istorii*, p. 49.

[7]R. Ia. Khabibulina, *Leningradskie kommunisty — organizatory stakhanovskogo dvizheniia (1935-1937).* Leningrad, 1961, p. 54; Seletskii, *Voprosy istorii*, pp. 45, 55; the figures are broken down by factory on p. 46; a listing of some of the first Stakhanovist records in Leningrad is on pp. 39-41.

[8]Khabibulina, *Leningradskie kommunisty*, pp. 150-151.

[9]Seletskii, *Voprosy istorii*, p. 43; Kravchenko records the angry outburst of a worker at an official meeting announcing the reduction of piece rates, pp. 189-190.

[10]See, for example, the comments of P. Alekseev, head of the Leningrad Council of Trade Unions, at the First Leningrad Stakhanovist Conference, *LP*, 26 October 1935, p. 2.

[11]*LP*, 11 October 1935, p. 1.

[12]Kravchenko, *I Chose Freedom*, pp. 298-302.

[13]*Pokolenie udarnikov; sbornik dokumentov i materialov o sotsialisticheskom sorevnovanii na predpriiatiiakh Leningrada v 1928-1961 gg.* Leningrad, 1963, p. 93.

[14]*LP*, 11 October 1935, p. 1.

[15]*LP*, 27 October 1935, p. 1.

[16]Seletskii, *Voprosy istorii*, p. 45.

[17]*LP*, 18 January 1936, p. 3.

[18]In the Don basin the obkom passed a resolution in September to expel anyone condemned as a "saboteur of Stakhanovism." Seletskii, *Voprosy istorii*, p. 39.

[19]Khabilbulina, *Leningradskie kommunisty*, pp. 63-64; *Pokolenie udarnikov*, pp. 90-96, *LP*, 29 October 1935, p. 1; *LP* 30 October 1935, 1; Seletskii, *Voprosy istorii*, pp. 43-44.

[20]*KPSS v rez.*, vol. V, pp. 243-244.

[21]*Ibid.*, p. 244.

[22]*Ibid.*, p. 245.

[23]*LP*, 27 February 1936, p. 1.

[24]Kravchenko, *I Chose Freedom*, p. 172.

[25]*LP*, 12 July 1935, pp. 1, 2, 5.

[26]*LP*, 29 May 1935, p. 3.

[27]*LP*, 2 July 1935, p. 1.

[28]*LP*, 14 June 1935, p. 3.

[29]Scattered evidence suggests that the number of expellees falling into the category "class alien" rose in Leningrad urban raions from approximately one-fifth in the 1933

purge to anywhere between one-half and two-thirds in the verification. *LP*, 18 January 1936, p. 4; 9 February 1936, p. 3; 17 February 1936, p. 3.

[30]*LP*, 28 July 1935, p. 1.

[31]For an account of the purge of a "class alien" in 1933, see Kravchenko, *I Chose Freedom*, pp. 136-137.

[32]*LP*, 6 September 1935, p. 3.

[33]*LP*, 23 December 1935, p. 3.

[34]*LP*, 11 September 1935, p. 3.

[35]*LP*, 11 October 1935, p. 3.

[36]*LP*, 9 October 1935, p. 3.

[37]Elizabeth Lermolo, who knew Nikolaev, was arrested in connection with his case, and spent time in jail with his mother and sister, denies this, maintaining instead that Nikolaev was an eccentric party loyalist, disenchanted with Kirov precisely because he tolerated ex-Zinov'evists in the Leningrad apparatus.   Elizabeth Lermolo, *Face of a Victim*. New York: Harper and Brothers, 1955, pp. 67, 72-73.

[38]The absurd lengths to which the official line went is seen in an editorial which referred to a "small but active group of Zinov'evists and churchgoers" at the "Red Triangle" footwear factory. *LP*, 28 September 1935, p. 1.

[39]*LP*, 2 July 1935, p. 3.

[40]*LP*, 6 September 1935, p. 3.

[41]*LP*, 6 September 1935, p. 3; 14 July 1935, p. 3.

[42]*LP*, 29 July 1935, p. 3.

[43]*LP*, 14 July 1935, p. 3.

[44]*LP*, 9 August 1935, p. 4.

[45]*LP*, 25 August 1935, p. 3.   The same secretary comments on his own work with two of the raion's factory committees in *LP*, 23 August 1935, p. 3.

[46]*LP*, 4 October 1935, p. 3.

[47]*LP*, 18 September 1935, p. 3; on the textile factory "Red Banner," see *LP*, 30 September 1935, p. 3.

[48]*LP*, 2 July 1935, p. 3.

[49]For examples from the Leningrad region, see *LP*, 26 July 1935, p. 2; 28 July 1935, p. 1; *LP*, 8 September 1935, p. 1. For complaints by the Central Committee about various other regional organizations, see *LP*, 28 June 1935, p. 2; 14 August 1935, p. 2.

[50]See Arch Getty, *Origins of the Great Purges: The Soviet Communist Party Reconsidered, 1933-1938*. Cambridge: Cambridge University Press, 1985, pp. 104-121 (page numbers based on manuscript version of book).

The Soviet Bureaucracy in 1935:
A Socio-Political Profile

William Chase and J. Arch Getty

One of the most significant and unfortunate gaps in Western historiography of the Soviet Union during the 1930s is in the area of bureaucratic history. Thanks to the pioneering work of Merle Fainsod, Western scholars understand the structure of the party and state bureaucracies and the functions which many agencies performed. Although recent works have raised serious questions about how those bureaucracies did or did not function and political conflicts within those bureaucracies, our knowledge of bureaucratic structures remains sound.[1] But as the debate over the political behavior within the bureaucracy deepens, new questions have arisen.

Among the most important, but unfortunately least asked questions are: what types of people staffed the bureaucracy? from what social backgrounds did they come? how much and what types of education did they have? how many were Communist Party members and, of those, how many were "Old Bolsheviks" and how many were the "new men"? what were their revolutionary credentials and formative political experiences? in short, what were the social and political characteristics of those who ran the USSR in the 1930s?

Although these questions may seem simple, finding satisfactory answers to them is very difficult. Yet being able to answer them is essential if we are to understand the Soviet bureaucracy not merely as a structure (or set of structures), but as an institution staffed by human beings. Understanding the social and political composition of the Soviet bureaucracy can provide us with insight into how these institutions functioned and why they functioned as they did. But if one were to search for answers to these very basic questions in the Western literature, the results with few exceptions would be very disappointing. Nor would one find much solace in a Soviet secondary literature which is replete with statistics on certain groups of party members, but much less on the socio-political composition of the bureaucracy.[2]

One of the consequences of this historiographic gap is that, consciously or unconsciously, we have accepted the implicit assumption of the totalitarian model: the structure of the bureaucracy in the 1930s is more important than those who staffed it. Although few today give much credence to the totalitarian model, our inability to answer the questions posed above means that we have simply sought new models to define and describe the bureaucracy. The task of historians is to provide the evidence on which models are based. Unfortunately, historians have abdicated their role for too long.

This article's modest purpose is to provide a partial socio-political profile of the USSR's bureaucrats in the mid-1930s. For analytical purposes, we chose to examine the composition of the Soviet bureaucracy in 1935. This year was chosen for two reasons: 1) the chaotic First Five-Year Plan had ended and some order and stability existed within the bureaucracy's ranks;[3] 2) the chaos and mass bureaucratic turnover occasioned by the *Ezhovshchina* had not begun. The analytical method employed here is prosopography, or collective biography based on rigorous social science methodologies. In conducting this research, no assumptions were made that biographical past, social origins or any other factors were determinants of behavior or predictors of later activities. Rather, this research was undertaken to begin to answer the questions posed above in the hopes that it might provide insight into the composition and possibly the behavior of the Soviet bureaucracy in the mid-1930s.

The data for this analysis came from the Soviet Data Bank, a project under the authors' direction which contains biographical and office holding information on Soviet state and party officials in the pre-World War II period. Because the Soviet Data Bank was not complete at the time this analysis was undertaken, the findings presented here are of necessity tentative and preliminary.

The Selection Set

Our selection set consists of 283 officials who worked in the Soviet state and/or Communist Party bureaucracies in 1935. The criteria by which the 283 were chosen were two: they had to have held a bureaucratic position in 1935, and biographical data on them had to be in the data bank.[4] Hence those chosen do not represent a random sample. To overcome this deficiency and bias, we weighted the selection. (See the Appendix for a discussion of the weighting procedures.)

The officials chosen ranged from Politburo members to sub-department administrative personnel in the state apparatus. Of the 283, 83 were chairmen of agencies (i.e., commissariats, state committees, trade unions, trusts), 98 were members of all-Union or republic-level party Central Committees, 100 were members or candidate members of presidiums or collegiums within agencies, 95 were chairmen of departments or commissions within agencies, 12 were chairmen of sub-departments within agencies, and 55 were lower-level personnel in departments or sub-departments.

Clearly, many people held more than one position simultaneously. In 1935, one-fifth of the sample held four or more positions, 10 percent held three positions, another 20 percent held two positions and the remaining 50 percent held only one position. Almost three-quarters (72.3 percent) of the offices held were in the national (USSR) bureaucracy, another 17.3 percent were in republic-level bureaucracies, and one in eleven (8.9 percent) were in city-level or lower bureaucracies. For analytical purposes, we divided the selection's members into three major agency groups based on their specialization in 1935: state (includes the military), economic (includes trade union and transport), and party. Of the 283, almost half (46.3 percent) specialized in work within the state sector, one-third (33.9 percent) within the economic sector, and one-fifth (20.1 percent) within the party sector. Of the total sample, about 90 percent (88.5 percent) were Communist Party members and two-thirds (65.6 percent) of them were "Old Bolsheviks," having joined the party before 1917.

The 1935 Bureaucracy: A Social Profile

Before presenting a detailed social profile of our selection, it should be asked whether the 1935 bureaucracy was representative or unrepresentative of Soviet society at large. In terms of gender, it was certainly not representative — only 3.5 percent were females.[5] However, the age structure of the selection was quite representative of the population at risk (as measured by age) to hold bureaucratic positions. The mean year of birth was normally distributed around 1886, and the mean age in 1935 was fifty years (49.7) old (see Table 1). The "old man" of the group was A. P. Karpinskii, who was born in 1847; the "baby" was G. M. Popov, who was born in 1906.

An examination of the selection set's province of birth reveals that the 1935 bureaucracy was generally representative of the nation's 1939 ethnic composition.[6] Slightly more than half (52.2 percent) were born in provinces within the RSFSR's 1939 borders; another 17 percent were born in the Ukraine. These figures are comparable to the proportions of Russians (58 percent) and Ukrainians (16.4 percent) in 1939. Within the Slavic lands, provinces of birth were widely dispersed geographically. The only significant concentrations worthy of note were those of Moscow (5.7 percent) and St. Petersburg (5.7 percent) *gubernii* which together comprised one-ninth of the total. People born in Georgia were over-represented; 9.4 percent of the selection were Georgians compared with only 1.3 percent nationwide in 1939. But with the exception of the latter group, the provinces of birth are more or less representative of the late imperial and 1939 population distribution.

These same figures can be viewed from a different perspective. Precisely because of the party's urban bias, it is surprising that almost 60 percent (57.5 percent) of the sample came from provincial towns and villages (see Table 2). Viewed in this way, it is fair to describe the sample as a group of provincials. The juxtaposition of these perspectives is not merely an exercise to prove that statistics can be manipulated to support different viewpoints, but rather to suggest that quick and facile conclusions have their pitfalls. Nowhere is this more clearly demonstrated than by examining the sample's social origins.

Although one's birth environment provides some idea of the milieu in which one was raised, it is not a predictor of one's social origins. As Table 3 indicates, one-third (32.7 percent) of the group came from peasant families, one-fifth (22.6) came from working class families, and slightly less than one-fifth (18.5 percent) were born into families of professionals or *intelligenty*.[8] Comparative analysis of social origins and birth environment provides insight into the changing and complex nature of late imperial society. Of those born in villages, almost one-third (30.6 percent) were the children of industrial workers. Put another way, more than half (51.7 percent) of the children of industrial workers were born in villages. Equally striking is the fact that 15.4 percent of those with peasant parents were urban-born.[9] By contrast, three-quarters of those with professionals or *intelligenty* for parents were urban born (see Table 4).

Although birth environment is no predictor of social origins, social origin is a better predictor of one's future occupation (see Table 5). For this paper, we classified the selection on the basis of the last occupation before the revolution. Almost two-thirds (62.1 percent) of the children of workers became workers themselves. But very few (13.8 percent) of the children of peasants remained in agricultural occupations and none were landowning peasants themselves. In fact, half (48.3 percent) of the children of peasants became workers. To social and labor historians of the pre-revolutionary period, the blurred distinction between town and country or between worker and peasant is axiomatic. But to those who study Soviet government and politics in the 1930s, these finding should serve as a warning not to ignore the complexities of late imperial society in which future Soviet leaders passed their formative years. Precisely what the impact of pre-revolutionary experiences had on Soviet leaders is an area of research which begs exploration.

The only other social group in the sample deserving of mention here are the children of parents who worked in "white collar" jobs. Slightly more than one-quarter of our group fell into this category; about one-fifth (18.5 percent) were from families of professionals or *intelligenty*. Three-quarters of them were urban-born and 70 percent followed in their parents' footsteps. In contrast, virtually none (4.9 percent) of the children of workers and peasants became professionals or *intelligenty*.

The evidence clearly indicates that those who governed the USSR in 1935 were the social products of the rapid and tumultuous changes which accompanied pre-revolutionary Russian industrialization. Most Soviet leaders in 1935 were not the children of or themselves professionals or *intelligenty*, but rather were toilers from the bottom of imperial Russian society both by social origins and occupation. In fact, at the time of the revolution, almost 60 percent were workers or soldiers — two of the social groups which most directly suffered from the hardships of industrial life and the horrors of war. Nor were the 1935 leaders the products of any imperial-period upward social mobility. Their mobility was limited to movement into and within the working class, and is better described as being lateral rather than upward.

Some people may take issue with our description of the movement from peasant to worker as lateral mobility. We do not wish to rekindle an old debate, but rather to offer some new evidence and a perspective. Those people in our selection whose parents were making the transition from peasant to proletariat, that is the village-born children of workers and the urban-born children of peasants, had the lowest educational levels of the offspring of any other social group, lower even than the village-born children of peasants and the urban-born children of workers.

There may be several reasons why this is so. It may well be that village-born children of workers were denied educational opportunities because the need for labor in the absence of one's father precluded school. Or it may be that the periodic movement between town and country made it impossible for them to attend school regularly.[10] There may be other reasons. More interesting to ponder is what effect the denial of educational opportunities had on those youth who experienced first-hand the realities and hardships of both peasant and proletarian life, and who were deprived of the expanding educational opportunities of which their rural and urban peers availed themselves. One is tempted to suggest that their variegated social experiences created in them heightened expectations, frustrations and anger. But until more research into the educational and social costs of the movement from peasant to proletarian is conducted, we must content ourselves with private speculations.

As a group, however, members of the selection were more educated than the population of both the late imperial period and the 1930s.[11] One-half had completed university studies and almost two-thirds of the remainder had finished secondary school. Only 10 percent had no formal education as of 1935 (see Table 6). Of those with some education, 80 percent had received it before the revolution. Although the number of people in the selection who received Soviet educations is small (N=18), and therefore necessitates the presentation of preliminary conclusions only, the data deserve mention.

Of those who completed or had some university education before the revolution (N=74), one-half studied law or medicine and 6.5 percent studied economics. No other faculty of study attracted significant numbers of people. More than one-third (37 percent) of this group studied in one of the two capitals. Twelve people studied at Moscow University, but the only notable cluster of people there simultaneously consisted of three people: N. A. Bukharin, N. E. Khrisfanov and N. A. Izgaryshev were there between 1907 and 1910. Of the six who studied at St. Petersburg University, four (G. L. Piatikov, N. N. Kristinskii, G. I. Lomov, and S. Z. Eliava) were there in 1907. The only other identifiable cluster of people who attended school together consisted of O. I. Shmidt, A. I. Vyshinskii, and V. P. Zatonskii who attended Kiev University in 1912 and 1913. The remainder of those educated in pre-revolutionary times attended institutions which were widely dispersed geographically. We can note again that our group of provincial-born officials were educated in the provinces.

Those who completed their education in the Soviet period had a dramatically different educational profile. Virtually all received their education in Soviet-era institutions: the Higher Military Academy, the Institute of Red Professors, the Industrial Academy in Moscow, the Communist Academy in Moscow, the Artem Communist Academy and higher technical institutes. Not surprisingly, this group eschewed law and medicine opting instead to study Marxism-Leninism, history, military subjects, machine-building and agriculture.

If the data accurately reflect the trends within the bureaucracy, the upper levels of the 1935 bureaucracy, especially the economic agencies, had not yet been permeated by the Soviet-educated economic and technical specialists who flocked to the classrooms in the aftermath of the 1928 Shakhty trial and the concomitant rapid expansion of educational opportunities.[12] In 1935, those educated before the revolution dominated the country's bureaucratic elite. In fact, one in nine (11 percent) of those in our sample are non-party, pre-revolutionary educated *intelligenty*, or to use the parlance of the period "bourgeois specialists." Surprising as this may seem in the aftermath of the Shakhty trial and the Cultural

Revolution, more surprising is the fact that the vast majority of these "bourgeois specialists" survived the *Ezhovshchina.*

Two other groups had markedly different educational profiles: "Old Bolsheviks" who joined the party before 1917, and the "new Bolsheviks" who joined during or after that year. Amazingly, "Old Bolsheviks" as a group were less educated (by a quantitative factor of 10 percent) than their new comrades. Given Soviet educational opportunities and priorities, it is not surprising that newer party members who completed their education after 1917 had more formal education. Nonetheless, this remained largely a pre-revolutionary educated leadership which "Old Bolsheviks" dominated.

Let us conclude this social profile of the 1935 bureaucracy by returning to the issue of how representative it was of the society which it governed. In some respects, it was very representative; in others, much less so. Males vastly outnumbered females, and the levels of education completed were much higher than those of either late imperial society or those of the 1930s. A disproportionately large number of people came from major cities and the families of professionals and *intelligenty.* On the other hand, the age structure of the bureaucracy was comparable to that of the population at risk to hold office, most were not urbanites but provincials whose provinces of birth represented a cross-section of the nation, and most were the children of peasants and workers. If we assume (and it seems fair to do so) that during the 1930s the social profile of no country's bureaucracy mirrored that of its society, then we can state that the Soviet bureaucracy was as socially representative of the country it governed as that of any other country. Although this is not the appropriate place to do so, there is much evidence to suggest that the 1935 Soviet bureaucracy was socially more representative of its society than, for example, that of Great Britain or France.

The 1935 Bureaucracy: A Political Profile

Predictably, the vast majority (88.5 percent) of our selection were Communist Party members. Of those, two-thirds (65.5 percent) were "Old Bolsheviks," 16.2 percent joined during 1917, and the remaining 18.2 percent joined after 1917. Within the 1935 bureaucratic leadership, "Old Bolsheviks" outnumbered the "new Bolsheviks" by two to one. But within the party, the proportion of "Old Bolsheviks" was much smaller and had been shrinking steadily since 1924. Although precise figures on *partstazh* for 1935 are lacking, it is known that the year before only 22.6 percent of the voting delegates to the Seventeenth Party Congress were "Old Bolsheviks." Their minority status in the party stands in stark contrast to their majority status within the bureaucratic elite and underscores their dominance of the organs of political power.

For those who joined the party before 1917, a clearly discernible pattern exists. As Table 7 indicates, the two pre-revolutionary periods that witnessed the greatest influx of new members — 1903-1905 (13.7 percent) and 1912-1916 (15 percent) — coincided with periods of intense social conflict and radical political upsurges.[14] The largest cohort of party members in our group were those who joined in 1917. Clearly, the party's ability to attract new members in the years before it became the governing party was dependent on the shifting political climate.

More than one-third of the selection set joined the party in either St. Petersburg/Petrograd/Leningrad (18.4 percent) or in Moscow (17.3 percent). The remaining members joined the party in widely scattered provinces. Because the two capitals housed the largest and most politically active party committees, were the country's largest industrial centers, and, in the case of Petrograd in 1917, contained large numbers of troops, they were natural magnets for revolutionaries and one expects them to have seen the enrollment of disproportionately large numbers of new members. Nonetheless, two-thirds of our selection joined the party in other locales. Taken together with the above evidence on province of birth and place of education, there seems to be little doubt that provincials dominated the 1935 bureaucracy.

Of our selection's party members, one in eight (13.4 percent) had belonged to another political party before joining the Bolsheviks. One-third (31.6 percent) of that group of 38 had been Mensheviks; one-half had been members of other Social Democratic parties. Another 15.8 percent had belonged to parties (mostly Social Democratic ones) in foreign countries, the Baltic lands or Poland.[15] More than half (57.2 percent) of those who had belonged to a previous political party joined the Bolsheviks during or after 1917.

Because the data on our selection's pre-revolutionary activities are somewhat incomplete, we shall confine our comments to a few observations. Based on the available data, more than half (53.4 percent) engaged in notable pre-revolutionary political activities. The median number of activities was three, but the range was wide: one-quarter had one activity, one-half had three or fewer, and 18 percent had ten or more (see Table 8). One of the most active members of our selection during the pre-1917 period was F. I. Goloshchekin, who spent the years 1903-1906 in the St. Petersburg area where he engaged in a variety of party committee activities in the capital, Kronstadt and Sestroretsk. During the 1905 revolution, he devoted much of his energy to agitprop work among the soldiers and sailors. Between 1906 and 1909, Goloshchekin was in and out of prison. Then in 1909 he went into exile and served on the editorial board of *Proletarii* in France. He returned to Russia late that year, this time going to Moscow where he resumed his underground party work. Goloshchekin's skills won him election to the party's Central Committee at the 1912 Prague Conference. His new stature and responsibilities cast him in the role of itinerant revolutionary who moved frequently between the two capitals and the Urals. In 1913, he was arrested twice and eventually exiled to Siberia where he remained until the revolution.

As Goloshchekin's activities suggest, "party committee work" was the most frequent of the pre-1917 political activities. Excluding such work, the most common activity was newspaper work which comprised almost half (46.1 percent) of all activities. Historians are familiar with the importance which the Bolsheviks and Lenin in particular placed on party newspapers. Here we have evidence of precisely how important newspaper work was in the political lives of underground revolutionaries. More than one-quarter (27.8 percent) of the activities centered on organizing workers, another Bolshevik priority. Trailing far behind these two activities were organizing students (9.7 percent, mostly during 1903-1905) and soldiers (7.2 percent) during the Russo-Japanese War and the World War. Analysis of where these activities were conducted reveals that almost one-third (31.9 percent) occurred in the two capitals and that the remainder were widely scattered across the provinces.

Because the vast majority of our selection's pre-revolutionary political activities were illegal and underground, they ran a great risk of running afoul of the Okhrana. Forty percent (39.3 percent) of our selection had been arrested by the tsarist police. Of those, 43.6 percent has one arrest record; three-quarters had three or fewer arrests. (The median number of arrests was two.) A few people (5.7 percent) had been arrested ten or more times. Some people passed virtually all of the pre-revolutionary twentieth century in prison or internal exile. Such was the fate of A. P. Smirnov, who, save for 1905-1906 and the World War, spent the rest of the period under one form or another of police detention. For A. I. Rykov, the only continuous time after 1900 when he was not incarcerated or in exile was 1902-1905.

One-half of those with prison records had been arrested in St. Petersburg or Moscow; the other half in widely scattered provinces. The figures re-confirm the importance of the two capitals as revolutionary centers. But one should be careful no to inflate the importance of these figures which may be as much an indictment of the ineffectiveness of the provincial police as they are an indicator of the capitals' preeminence.[16] For those unfortunate enough to have been arrested, half found themselves exiled and one-third imprisoned. The rest were either released under surveillance, deported or conscripted.   Half of those exiled were sent to Siberia and one-fifth to the far northern regions of European Russia. Some like Kalinin were luckier. At the time of his first arrest in St. Petersburg in 1899, Kalinin worked as a lathe-operator at the Putilov Works. After spending ten months in jail there, he was exiled to Tbilisi where he secured a job as a lathe-operator and immediately joined the Tbilisi RSDRP organization. Within five months, he was arrested and exiled to Revel' where he resumed his former occupation and revolutionary activities.   In 1903, he was arrested again and spent six months in St. Petersburg's Kresty prison. Then in its infinite wisdom, the Okhrana released Kalinin and exiled him to, of all places, Revel' where, to no one's surprise, he resumed his underground activities. Such tales give one pause to wonder about the judgment which some Okhrana officials possessed.

When the 1917 revolution erupted, our selection set was literally spread all over the globe — from eastern Siberia to the United States — and involved in a spectrum of political activities and occupations (see Table 9). Despite this diaspora, most of the group immediately began to participate in revolutionary activities. Almost two-thirds (63.3 percent) participated in political activities in 1917 and two-thirds of them began doing so in March 1917. As Table 10 indicates, 15 percent did not engage in revolutionary activities until the eve of the Bolshevik seizure of power.

As was the case with pre-revolutionary activities, the number of 1917 political activities varied widely (see Table 11). The median number of such activities was three, but this figure masks somewhat the distribution. Sixty percent of the selection had three or fewer activities (excluding participation at congresses or conferences), but 4.5 percent had ten or more activities.   N.V. Krylenko had eighteen separate activities.   He devoted most of his energy in 1917 to revolutionary work among the troops, first in the Ukraine where he was the chairman of a divisional soldiers' committee and later in Petrograd where he worked as an organizer among the troops, was an organizer and delegate to the All-Russian Congress of Bolshevik Frontline and Rear Military Organizations, a member of the Petrograd Military Revolutionary Committee and a regular contributor to *Soldatskaia Pravda*. He was also a delegate to the first two Congresses of Soviets.

During 1917 as before, the most common political activity was party committee work, but the relative importance of such work declined significantly. Only one-quarter of the activities were so described. The next most frequent activity consisted of being a deputy of, or working in, a Soviet (22.6 percent). Military Revolutionary Committee and Red Guard membership accounted for one-sixth (16.2 percent) of all activities. Taken together the latter three activities accounted for almost 40 percent (38.8 percent) of all 1917 political activities. Newspaper work, so prominent an activity before 1917, dwindled to a meager 7.7 percent of that year's activities. Nor did union or factory committee activities (6.7 percent) occupy much of the group's energies.[17] Once again, an analysis of where the activities occurred showed that half of all the selection's 1917 activities took place in the provinces.[18]

This division of revolutionary activities provides another insight into the political profile of those who governed the USSR by demonstrating that the Bolshevik revolution was not simply a *coup d'etat*, but rather a logical extension of political developments in 1917. Several have convincingly argued that the dramatic increase in Bolshevik popularity in that year resulted from a confluence of worsening economic, political and social conditions and active grassroots Bolshevik political agitation and organization, particularly in factory committees and other local worker organizations.[19]

Based on our preliminary findings, it appears that those who staffed the bureaucracy in 1935 were not actively engaged in the latter grassroots activities. Rather they concentrated their energies on those institutions which expressed and legitimized grassroots demands — the Soviets and political parties. Given that upwards of one-fifth of the group's 1917 activities consisted of participation in various congresses and conferences and that many were prominent members of their party committees and Soviets, it appears that we can refine our earlier characterization of the 1935 bureaucracy as one dominated by "Old Bolsheviks." Not only were the "Old Bolsheviks" the governing elite in 1935, they were also members of the revolutionary elite in 1917.

More than a decade ago, Marc Ferro argued that to understand the early Soviet bureaucracy one had to examine the origins, structures and demands of the emerging revolutionary bureaucracy in 1917.[20] Although our findings are preliminary, the evidence suggests that not only is Ferro correct, but also that those who dominated the state and party bureaucracies in 1917 continued to do so until the *Ezhovshchina*, despite the continuous and rapid turnover within these bureaucracies,[21] and the assumed political transfers and purges associated with Stalin's ascension to power. The political cohort which rode the revolutionary wave to victory in 1917, regardless of their subsequent horizontal and vertical movements within the bureaucracy, continued to dominate it in the mid-1930s.

Some Observations on 1935 Officeholding

Let us return briefly to our selection's bureaucratic activities in 1935.

The purpose of this article is not to analyze the bureaucracy or why those who staffed it did so, but rather to present a socio-political profile of Soviet bureaucrats in 1935.   While not concerned with ascertaining whether there were political or bureaucratic determinants of why the 1935 bureaucrats held the offices which they did, we were curious as to whether or not one's biographical profile had any bearing on where one worked.   Toward this end, we divided the selection into three bureaucratic agency groups based on their area of specialization in 1935. The three groups were state (includes military), party, and economic (includes transport and trade unions).

Analysis revealed that age, social origins, *partstazh*, and pre-revolutionary and 1917 revolutionary activities had nothing to do with one's bureaucratic specialization in 1935. When one was educated was relevant.   Those in party agencies were most likely to have been educated after 1917, whereas no one who worked in economic agencies had been Soviet-educated.   When we analyzed the educational levels of those in the three agency groups, we found that, although party agencies had more Soviet-educated personnel (and such people were likely to have had higher educational levels than those educated before the revolution), only one-quarter (26.6 percent) of those in party agencies had completed higher education and almost one-fifth (17.4 percent) had no formal education.   By comparison, about 60 percent of the personnel in both the state (58.3 percent) and economic (58.2 percent) agency groups had attended or completed university.   Although most people in economic agencies in 1935 had higher educations, one in eleven (8.8 percent) had no formal education.   Clearly, amount of education was not a determining factor in who worked in party and economic agencies.

Despite their relative educational deficiencies, party people held the most number of offices per person (mean = 3.5).   In fact, they held more than twice as many as those in economic agencies (mean = 1.8) and almost twice as many as those in state agencies (mean = 2.0).   (The overall mean = 2.3)   Although "Old" and "new" Bolsheviks held about the same number of offices per person, whether or not one participated in 1917 revolutionary activities affected significantly how many offices they held in 1935.   The average number of offices held by 1917 activists was 2.5 compared to 1.8 for those who had not participated in the revolution.

Participation in the revolution also significantly affected one's 1935 rank.   Those active in 1917 had slightly higher ranks than those who were not.   The amount of education also affected one's rank.   Surprisingly, educational level was negatively correlated with rank, that is those with less education were more likely to have had higher ranks.[22]   Although educational level and revolutionary activities were the only significant factors directly affecting rank in 1935, there was no correlation between them (see Figure 1).

Although these findings are of necessity preliminary, they do suggest possible avenues for future research. Given that educational levels were negatively correlated with rank, one obvious question is whether or not there were significant and discernible political factors which explain why those who staffed the bureaucracy's upper ranks worked where they did. For example, to what extent did practical experience or personal connections determine who worked where?   How extensive were personal networks?   Only future analysis will help to refine and answer such questions.

The Fate of the 1935 Bureaucrats

No study of the Soviet bureaucracy in the mid-1930s would be complete without a discussion of its members' fates during the *Ezhovshchina*. Because this is a study of the bureaucracy on the eve of that horrible event, the topic is especially relevant. Of those in our selection set whose cause of death is known (N=213), more than half (56.1 percent) died during the *Ezhovshchina*; only one-fifth (18 percent) outlived Stalin (see Table 12)

One interpretation of the *Ezhovshchina* holds that Stalin used the NKVD to eliminate several clearly identifiable groups: "Old Bolsheviks," especially those who were the heroes of the pre-revolutionary party and of 1917; former oppositionists; Stalin's political rivals; and those who knew too much about the General Secretary's past[23]   Although 64 percent of our selection's "Old Bolsheviks" died as a result of the *Ezhovshchina*, "Old Bolshevik" status was not a statistically significant determinant of why people were purged. Nor did one's pre-revolutionary and 1917 political activities or stature, social origins, or the timing and quantity of education have any bearing on whether or not they fell victim to the Great Purge.

Only four factors proved to be statistically significant characteristics of purge victims (see Table 13). Former oppositional membership was one. Of the thirty-six people within the selection who had belonged to an oppositional group, 85.7 percent perished during the *Ezhovshchina*, whereas only 52.2 percent of non-oppositionists shared their comrades' tragic fate.   That 11.4 percent of the selection had oppositional backgrounds and yet retained powerful positions a year after Kirov's assassination seems high in light of the long-standing argument that the assassination sparked a "heresy hunt" for oppositionists that culminated in the *Ezhovshchina*[24] This fact alone should make us ponder the validity of that aspect of the traditional view. Those with higher ranks, that is the top echelon of the bureaucracy, were also more likely to be purged.[25] Party membership also proved to be significant. More than 60 percent (61 percent) of the selection's party members died during the *Ezhovshchina* as opposed to only one-fifth (22 percent) of non-party people. Finally, age was a significant factor, but not in the way which one might expect. Younger people were at greater risk of being purged. The mean age of the victims was 48 years as opposed to a mean age of 52 years of the survivors.[26]

So those at greatest risk to be purged were former oppositionists, high-ranking officials, party members, and younger officials. It is important to stress that these were the significant aggregate characteristics of victims of the *Ezhovshchina*, but they were not connected in the same people. That is, the NKVD did not decide that these four criteria were those by which they selected their victims. Those who possessed one or more of the characteristics were at greater risk to be arrested.

Our data are not yet complete enough to establish causality. These four are relative characteristics, but we cannot say that they caused one to be arrested. More research on larger samples and the use of more sophisticated statistical tests will be required before causality can be determined. Preliminary though they are, the finding do not support the common assumption that the *Ezhovshchina* was aimed at the "Old Bolsheviks," the heroes of the pre-revolutionary movement or of 1917, the older generation or the remnants of the *ancien regime's* intelligentsia. The only verifiable aspect of the standard view which seems to hold true is that former oppositionists were likely to die during the *Ezhovshchina*. From these data, it is impossible to state that the *Ezhovshchina* was "aimed" at any identifiable social or political group other than former oppositionists

Figure 1 expresses the statistically significant relationships among the only variables related to one's fate in the purges of the 1930s. Of the four variables known to affect purge status, age was the strongest, followed by 1935 rank and party membership, with oppositional membership a distant fourth.[27] One's revolutionary past, educational level, *partstazh* influenced one's rank, but none of these three (or any other variable) had a significant effect on purge status. These relationships suggest two conclusions.

First, it seems that one's fate in the purges was determined by factors rooted in the 1930s rather than the past. The model suggests that categorizations based on one's background (education, underground or revolutionary activity, "Old Bolshevik" status, social origins, etc.) did not determine one's fate during the *Ezhovshchina*. Rather one's rank, party status, and apparently age *in the 1930s* seemed to be crucial. One's contemporary position or immediate situation in the mid-thirties was more important than one's past. Second, the R^2 figure indicates that this model explains almost half of the determination of purge fate. While this figure suggests a statistically respectable explanatory model, more work needs to be done to clarify the situation. Personal links and networks, as well as one's exact location in the bureaucracy on the eve of the Great Purges, seem promising factors for future investigation using the recently developed and more sophisticated techniques of path analysis and linear models.

Conclusion

The purpose of this article has been to present a socio-political profile of the 1935 bureaucracy, something which is essential to any investigation of that apparatus but which has yet to be done systematically. In some respects, these bureaucrats were representative of the people whom they governed; in others, they were less so. However, those who staff bureaucracies are rarely chosen on the basis of whether or not they are representative of their fellow citizens, but according to other, often political, criteria. The 1935 bureaucracy was one in which high rank was not a function of age or education or social origin or any other biographical factor. Rather high rank was a function of *partstazh* and revolutionary service. In short, "Old Bolsheviks" dominated the 1935 bureaucracy. These remained the proven and trusted officials who, by virtue of their powerful positions and ability to select personnel, were able to perpetuate their political cohort. That "Old Bolsheviks" so clearly dominated the 1935 bureaucracy in spite of their decidedly minority status within the party and the presence of vast numbers of recently and better educated personnel suggests that, in the bureaucracy as in the factories, "Old Bolsheviks" used their power to hold at bay a new and better educated generation of younger rivals.[28] None of those in leading positions in economic agencies were Soviet-educated. In the bureaucracy as in the factories, that generation, despite being better educated and more numerous, had not yet penetrated the bureaucracy's commanding heights. Eager though they may have been to do so, they were forced to wait in the wings.

In light of this, it is tempting to hypothesize that the *Ezhovshchina* was at least in part an effort to advance and reward those with proletarian backgrounds, more education, fewer political credentials and more recent *partstazh* — the "new men."[29] However, our data do not support such a view. Were this to have been the case, we would expect to find statistically significant correlations between death during the *Ezhovshchina* and "Old Bolshevism, education, and revolutionary credentials. No such correlations exist. This is not to say that future research based on larger samples and more variegated sources will not yield evidence to support this hypothesis. But at a minimum, this analysis casts doubt on that hypothesis and demonstrates the importance of testing hypotheses and assumptions.

We have all become accustomed to using terms such as "Old Bolshevik" and "the proletariat" as shorthand to describe political and social groups and to characterize their behaviors and fates. While we all suspect that such terms are stereotypes which over-simplify complex social formations, we have continued to use them. Implicit in our thoughts about "Old Bolsheviks," for example, is a view of a homogeneous community of bespectacled *intelligenty* who were professional revolutionaries. Yet our data show[30] that "Old Bolsheviks" in fact included a number of heterogeneous social groups. Those who joined the Bolsheviks before 1917 had widely diverse social origins, educational levels, occupations, and ages. Half of them were the children of workers or peasants, but more were the children of peasants than of workers. At least 40 percent of the "Old Bolsheviks" at the time of the revolution were industrial workers; none were peasants. Only a third were the children of *intelligenty*, professionals, state servants and employees. One in five "Old Bolsheviks" never went beyond primary school and fewer than one-third completed higher education. Indeed, as a group, they were less educated than those who joined the party after the revolution and, based on their provinces of birth, where they were educated, and where they engaged in political activities, it is fair to describe them more as a group of provincials than cosmopolitans. In 1917, the ages of our "Old Bolsheviks" ranged from 19 to 52 years. Clearly, there was no typical "Old Bolshevik."

While invalidating the stereotypic "Old Bolshevik," our data also allow us to refine generalizations about the social origins of party members. For example, to assume that Bolsheviks of working class origin shared common social backgrounds is misleading. Some were urban-born; others were village-born. But these hereditary proletarians were not the only workers within the Bolshevik ranks. First-generation workers, most of whom came from the peasantry, also joined the party. Which "generation" of workers dominated the ranks of proletarians who joined the Bolsheviks before 1917 is a question which continues to fascinate Western historians of the late imperial period. For some the influx of members of the hereditary proletariat in the party is of greatest significance, while others stress the importance of first-generation workers.[31]   The findings presented here suggest that both views have merit and are not mutually exclusive.

If we are to advance our understanding of Bolshevism and the social milieu from which Bolsheviks came, we must combine political and social history in new ways. Historians of Bolshevism could profit by the findings and methods of students of pre-1917 Russian society. So too can students of the pre-war Soviet bureaucracy benefit from this growing body of historical literature.   We believe that social science methodologies can help historians to untangle the complexities of Soviet social and political history.   We hope that the application of statistical and quantitative methods applied to collective biography represents a fruitful approach to unraveling problems in certain areas of research.

University of Pittsburgh
University of California, Riverside

NOTES

[1]Merle Fainsod, *How Russia is Ruled*. Cambridge, Mass: Harvard University Press, 1965; *Smolensk under Soviet Rule*. New York: Vinatge, 1963; J. Arch Getty, *Origins of the Great Purges: The Soviet Party Reconsidered*, 1933-1938. Cambridge: Cambridge University Press, 1985; Roberta T. Manning, "Government in the Soviet Countryside in the Stalinist Thirties: The Case of Belyi *Raion* in 1937", *The Carl Beck Papers in Russian and East European Studies, no. 301 (1983/84);* Gabor Rittersporn, "The State against Itself: Socialist Tensions and Political Conflict in the USSR, 1936-1938," *Telos*, no. 41 (1979), pp. 87-104.

[2] In the case of party statistics, the obvious exception to this is T.H. Rigby, *Communist party Membership in the USSR, 1917-1967*. Princeton: Princeton University Press, 1968. Even in the Soviet literature, data on the composition of the party between 1933 and 1939 are very rare because the party stopped releasing such data.

[3]For a discussion of the high turnover rates within the bureaucracy during the First Five-Year Plan, see J. Arch Getty and William Chase, "Patterns of State and Party Officeholding in the Soviet Bureaucracy, 1929-1931," Paper presented to the Third Annual Conference of the National Seminar on Russian Social History in the Twentieth Century, University of Pennsylvania, January 1983.

[4]The sources of data used in this analysis were the 1923, 1925-1931 and 1936 editions of *Vsia Moskva, adresnaia i spravochnaia kniga...*.; Edward L. Crowley, *et al.,* eds., *Party and Government Officials of the Soviet Union, 1917-1967*. Metuchen, NJ: Scarecrow Press, 1969; Georges Haupt and Jean-Jacque Marie, ed., *Makers of the Russian Revolution*. Ithaca, NY: Cornell University Press, 1974; Borys Levytsky, *The Stalinist Terror in the Thirties: Documentation from the Soviet Press*. Stanford, Hoover Institution Press, 1974; *Velikaia oktiabr'skaia sotsialisticheskaia revoliutsiia: entsiklopediia*. Moscow, 1977; *Geroi oktiab'ria: Kniga ob uchastnikakh Velikoi*

Oktiabr'skoi sotsialisticheskoi revoliutsii v Moskve. Moscow, 1967; *Who Was Who in the USSR*. Metuchen, NJ: Scarecrow Press, 1972. "Deiateli Soiuza Sovetskikh Sotsialisticheskikh Respublik i Oktiabr'skoi Revoliutsii," *Entsiklopedicheskii slovar' Russkogo Bibliograficheskogo Instituta Granat*. Moscow, 1925-1928, vol. 41, chast' I-III; Borys Levytsky, *The Soviet Political Elite*. Munich and Stanford: Stanford Universsity Press, 1969; *Geroi grazhdanskoi voiny: Kniga o moskvichakh-uchastnikakh boevykh srazhenii*. Moscow, 1974; *Protokoly s"ezdov i konferentsii Vsesoiuznoi Kommunisticheskii Partii (b): Shestoi s"ezd RSDRP(b) (Avgust 1917)*. Moscow, 1934. Data were also taken from the rich personal research files of Professor Sheila Fitzpatrick; the sources of her data are far too numerous to list here. We are especially grateful to Professor Fitzpatrick for making her files available to us for inclusion in the data base.

Western historians of the Soviet period rarely use proposopography as an investigative method. However, a study of the Social Democratic movement before 1917 does. See David Lane, *The Roots of Russian Communism: A Social and Historical Study of Russian Social Democracy, 1898-1907*. University Park: The Pennsylvania State University Press, 1968. Given that this paper and Lane's study examine very different groups, no attempt will be made to correlate the findings.

[5]The proportion of women in the sample is not only small vis-a-vis Soviet society, but also vis-a-vis the Communist Party which dominated the bureaucracy. In July 1932, 16.5 percent of the party's members were females. "O rabote partiinykh organizatsii sredi zhenshchin," *Bolshevik*, no. 1 (January 1951), p. 11. However, the proportion of voting delegates at the Seventeenth Party Congress in 1934 who were females was even smaller than the all-party statistic – 7.2 percent. *XVII s"ezd Vsesoiuznoi Kommunisticheskoi Partii (b), 27 ianvaria-10 fevralia 1934g.: stenograficheskii otchet*. Moscow, 1934, p. 149.

[6]Data on the ethnic composition of the 1939 USSR population come from Frank Lorimer, *The Population of the Soviet Union: History and Prospects*. Geneva: League of Nations, 1946, pp. 112-172, especially 138-139.

[7]An examination of the selection set's known ethnic composition yields rather different results. Although Slavs accounted for more than three-quarters of the USSR's 1939 population, within our selection they accounted for only slightly more than half (54.4 percent). Russians were particularly under-represented, comprising only 41 percent of the selection but 58 percent of the 1939 population. Baltic peoples, Jews, and people from the Caucasus were over-represented within the selection. In 1939, less than 1 percent of the Soviet population were Balts, but within the selection they accounted for 15.1 percent; Latvians accounted for 10 percent of the selection. Jews, who accounted for about 2 percent of the 1939 population, also accounted for 10 percent of the selection. People's from the Caucasus – Armenians, Azerbaidzhanis, and Georgians – comprised 12 percent of the selection, a proportion three times larger than that in the national population. The figures for Georgians were 6 percent and 1.3 percent respectively.

Because the number of those whose nationality we knew for certain is small (N=66), we caution the reader not to over-estimate the significance of this unrepresentative ethnic composition. The reason for the small sample size is that we only recorded nationality when we knew it to be true and not based on the place of birth. Given the considerable geographic mobility of people, especially Slavs, during the late imperial period and the mixture of different nationalities in certain areas (e.g., the mixture of Ukrainians, Poles, Russians, Belorussians and Jews in the western Ukraine or Belorussia), we chose to err on the side of caution.

[8]As of July 1932, the "social position" of Communist Party members was: workers − 65.2 percent; peasants − 26.9 percent; employees and others − 7.9 percent. Rigby, *Communist Party Membership*, p. 325. Based on this data, one might be tempted to label our sample as unrepresentative, but it is important to keep several factors in mind. First, ours is a sample of the 1935 bureaucracy, not of the party. Second, from the 1924 Lenin levy, the proportion of workers in the party rose sharply. Finally, the 1933 *chistka* resulted in the expulsion of disproportionately high numbers of workers and peasants. For a discussion of the post-1924 social composition of the party, see Rigby, *Communist Party Membership*, pp. 88-235. On the 1933 *chistka*, see Getty, *Origins*, chapter 2.

[9]For a discussion of this phenomenon, see: Petr I. Liashchenko, *History of the National Economy of Russia to the 1917*. Translated by L.M. Herman. New York: Octagon, 1970, pp. 542-545; P.M. Shestakov, *Rabochie na manufakture tovarishchestva "Emil' Tsindel'" v Moskve: statisticheskoe issledovanie*. Moscow, 1900. See also Robert E. Johnson, *Peasant and Proletarian: The Working Class of Moscow in the Late Nineteenth Century*. New Brunswick: Rutgers University Press, 1979.

[10]For an example of a family which owned land in a village and the head of which worked in a Moscow factory, a situation which meant that the children periodically travelled between the village and city, see E.O. Kabo, *Ocherki rabochego byta*. Moscow, 1928, pp. 103-107.

[11]For a discussion of the educational levels of the population at large, see Nicholas DeWitt, *Education and Professional Employment in the USSR*. Washington: National Science Foundation, 1961; Sheila Fitzpatrick, *Education and Social Mobility in the Soviet Union, 1921-1934*. Cambridge: Cambridge University Press, 1979. Our selection was also more educated than the party leadership at the time. According to Ezhov's report to the Seventeenth Congress, 31 percent of the delegates to that convocation had finished secondary school and only 10 percent had completed their higher education. *XVII s"ezd Vsesoiuznoi Partii (b), p. 303*.

[12]For a discussion, see Fitzpatrick, *Education*; Kendall E. Bailes, *Technology and Society under Lenin and Stalin: Origins of the Soviet Technical Intelligentsia, 1917-1941*. Princeton: Princeton University Press, 1978.

[13]According to Ezhov's report to the 1934 Party Congress, 10 percent of the party's members had joined the party during or before 1920. *XVII s"ezd Vsesoiuznoi Kommunisticheskoi Partii (b)*, p. 303.

[14]On the two periods as ones of rising social conflict and revolutionary activities, see Sidney S. Harcave, *First Blood: The Russian Revolution of 1905*. New York: Collier, 1964; Laura Engelstein, *Moscow, 1905: Working Class Organization and Political Conflict*. Stanford: Stanford University Press, 1982; Leopold Haimson, "The Problem of Social Stability in Urban Russia, 1905-1917," *Slavic Review, vol. XXIII, no. 4 (1964) pp. 619-642; vol. XXIV, no. 1 (1965), pp. 1-22; History of the Communist Party of the Soviet Union*. Moscow, 1960, pp. 3-4.

[15]The following sample members had belonged to a political party before joining the Bolsheviks: A.M. Anikst, V.A. Antonov-Ovseenko, S.I. Aralov, G.I. Broido, A.I. Egorov, M.S. Epshtein, A.G. Goikhbarg, K.K. Iurenev, M.I. Kalmanovich, S.I. Kaplun, L.M. Khinchuk, I.I. Khodorovskii, F. Khodzhaev, V.G. Knorin, A.M. Kollontai, F. Feliks, D.Z. Lebed', V.L. Leder, A.M. Lezhava, L.A. Liberman, P.P. Liubchenko, A. Lozovskii, G.N. Mel'nichanskii, N.L. Meshcheriakov, V.P. Mililutin, G.L. Piatakov, N.N. Popov, B.P. Pozern, A.F. Radchenko, Kh.G. Rakovskii, Ia.E. Rudzutak, M.L. Rukhimovich, A.G. Shikhter, Ia.Z. Surits, I.S. Unshlikht, A.Ia. Vyshinskii, V.P. Zatonskii.

[16]On the inefficiency of the provincial police, see Neil Weissmann, "Regular Police in Tsarist Russia, 1900-1914," Paper presented to the Third Annual Conference of the National Seminar on Russian Social History in the Twentieth Century, University of Pennsylvania, January 1983.

[17]For a comparison of these activities with those of the Moscow Bolshevik cadres in 1917, see William Chase and J. Arch Getty, "The Moscow Bolshevik Cadres of 1917: A Prosopographic Analysis," *Russian History/Histoire Russe*, vol. V, no. 1 (1978), pp. 103-105.

[18]Because virtually all congresses and conferences, organized by either political parties, trade unions, factory committees or the Provisional Government, were held in one of the two capitals, the proportion of activities which occurred in Moscow and Petrograd is somewhat inflated.

[19]For examples, see Alexander Rabinowitch, *The Bolsheviks Come to Power*. New York: Norton, 1976; Diane Koenker, *Moscow Workers and the 1917 Revolution*. Princeton: Princeton University Press, 1981; S.A. Smith, *Red Petrograd: Revolution in the Factories, 1917-1918*. Cambridge: Cambrige University Press, 1983.

[20]Marc Ferro, "The Birth of the Soviet Bureaucratic System" in *Reconsiderations of the Russian Revolution*, Ralph Carter Elwood, ed., Cambridge, Mass: Slavica, 1976, pp. 100-132.

[21]See Getty and Chase, "Patterns of State and Party Officeholding."

[22]Spearman's r = -.3899, which is statistically significant at the .05 level.

[23]For example, see Robert Conquest, *The Great Terror: Stalin's Purges of the 1930s*. New York: Collier, 1973.

[24]For examples of this view, see *ibid*, pp. 51-133 *passim*; Fainsod, *Smolensk*, pp 35-92, especially 57.

[25]That higher ranking people were at greater risk to die during the *Ezhovshchina* should not be surprising in light of Khrushchev's claim that 70 percent of the Central Committee members elected in 1934 were purged. N.S. Khrushchev, *The Secret Speech Delivered to the Closed Session of the 20th Congress of the CPSU* (introduction by Zhores and Roy Medvedev), London, 1956, p. 33. Khrushchev's figures may be slightly high. According to Getty, 62.5 percent of that Central Committee's members were purged. J. Arch Getty, "The Great Purges Reconsidered: The Soviet Communist Party, 1933-1939" (unpublished Ph.D. dissertation, Boston College, 1979), p. 503.

[26]It is important to note that age is an independent variable. No statistical

relationship existed between age and *partstazh* or between age and rank. And given that oppositionists were generally older, obviously oppositional membership was not a function of age.

[27]Oppositional membership explains so little because only 11 percent of the selection were in former oppositions.

[28]On generational tensions in Soviet factories in the 1930s, see David Granick, *Management of the Soviet Industrial Firm in the USSR*. New York: Columbia University Press, 1954. See also, Shelia Fitzpatrick, "Stalin and the Making of the New Elite, 1929-1939," *Slavic Review*, vol. XXXVIII,no. 3 (1979), pp. 377-402.

[29]Fitzpatrick, *Slavic Review*, pp. 377-402.

[30]Chase and Getty, *Russian History/Histoire Russe*, pp. 103-105.

[31]For example, see Haimson, *Slavic Review*; Victoria E. Bonnell, *The Roots of Rebellion: Workers' Politica and Organizations in St. Petersburg and Moscow, 1900-1914*. Berkeley: University of California Press, 1983.

Table 1

Age in 1935 (%)

n = 281

30-34	1.4
35-39	6.1
40-44	22.0
45-49	21.4
50-54	25.0
55-59	12.5
60-64	6.5
65-69	3.0
over 69	2.2

mean age = 49.7

Table 2

Birth Environment (%)

n = 101

Village	40.0
Town	17.5
City	42.4

Table 3

Social Origins (Father's Class) (%)

n = 140

Peasant	32.7
Worker	22.6
Professional	18.5
Employee	9.8
Artisan	6.6
State Service/Mil.	3.6
Merchant	3.4
Noble	1.9
Meshchanin	.8

Table 4

Father's Class by Birth Environment (%)

n = 76

Father's Class	*Rural-born*	*Urban-born*	*Total*
Worker	51.7	48.3	100.0
Peasant	84.6	15.4	100.0
Professional/Intel.	23.5	76.5	100.0

Table 5

Father's Class by Subject's Occupation (%)

n = 76

	Occupations			
Father's Class	*Workers*	*Peasants*	*Prof./Intel.*	*Soldiers*
Sons of Workers	62.1	2.5	0	35.4
Sons of Peasants	48.3	13.8	4.9	32.9
Sons of Prof./Intel.	4.2	0	69.0	26.8

Note: Subject's occupation was calculated on the basis of the last known occupation before the 1917 revolutions. Thus, for many, the last occupation occurred during World War I.

Table 6

Highest Educational Level Completed (%)

n = 124

No Formal	9.4
Primary completed	5.7
Secondary Completed	31.6
Higher Completed	50.4
Postgrad. Completed	2.9

Table 7

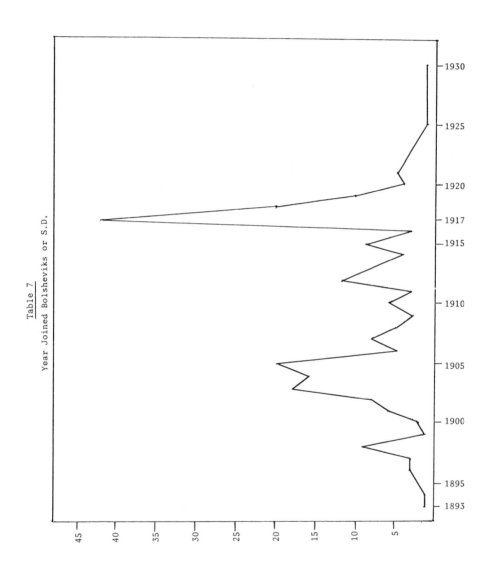

Table 7
Year Joined Bolsheviks or S.D.

Table 8

Number of Prerevolutionary Political Activities

n = 151

Number of Political Activities	Percent of Bolsheviks with pol. activities
1	23.2
2	14.8
3	15.0
4	8.4
5	4.2
6	6.1
7	3.5
8	3.9
9	2.6
10	3.2
11	2.5
12	1.6
13+	10.8

mean number of activities = 3.0
median number of activities = 2.0

Table 9

Occupation as of March, 1917 (%)

	n = 92
Worker	32.5
Soldier	24.6
Prof./Intel.	22.2
Employee	7.6
Peasant	4.1
Other	9.0

Table 10

Month Began 1917 Revolutionary Activity (%)

	n = 146
March	63.2
April	4.4
May	3.7
June	.5
July	3.5
August	6.0
September	3.8
October-November	14.9

Table 11

Number of Revolutionary Political Activities

n = 151

Number of 1917 Activities	*Percent of Bolsheviks with revolutionary acts*
1	21.4
2	22.3
3	17.1
4	11.0
5	7.5
6	7.2
7	4.5
8	2.0
9	2.3
10	.9
11	1.1
12+	2.5

mean number of activities   = 3.7
median number of activities = 3.0

Table 12

Cause of Death (%)

	n = 209
Died in Prison	51.2
Natural	39.9
Executed	4.9
Suicide	2.6
World War II	1.5

Table 13

Characteristics of Those Purged in 1930s (%)

	Purged	Not Purged
Total (%) (n=283)	56.1	43.9
Mean Age in 1935* (n=283)	48.2	51.9
Oppositionists* (n=25)	85.7	14.2
Non-Oppositionists* (n=18)	52.2	47.8
Party Member (n=180)	60.9	39.1
Non-Party Members* (n=26)	22.2	77.8

*Correlation statistically significant at .05 level.

Figure 1

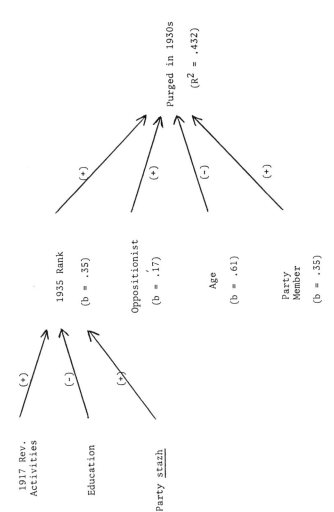

Figure 1

Multiple Classification Results of Purge Variables

Notes: b = beta score from multiple classification analysis. Betas are relative scores which measure the comparative effect of each of the four independent variables on "Purged in 1930s".

Appendix

The group of 283 Soviet leaders under study here was drawn from the Soviet Data Bank, a project under the direction of the authors which is aimed at assembling, verifying, and disseminating a machine-readable data bank of biographical information on the Soviet state and party leadership from the pre-World War II period. The data bank contains information from a wide variety of published and unpublished sources (see below) and is the largest collection of biographical data now in use by non-governmental scholars. It is now complete and available for purchase from the authors.

The present group consists of those party and state officials from all levels and agencies who are known to have held office in 1935, and for whom the data bank currently contains reasonably complete and verified biographies. It is therefore not, strictly speaking, a "random sample" since inclusion in the group is based on such factors as availability of a complete biography and the current levels of verification and inclusion in the data bank. On the other hand, a group of 283 senior leaders does represent a reasonable section of the top and middle levels of the 1935 bureaucracy. Persons interested in obtaining the list of 283 people should contact one of the authors.

Because high-ranking persons were more likely to have biographies written about them (then or now), our target group is "biased" toward the higher ranks of the 1935 bureaucracy; middle and lower levels are thus underrepresented in a statistical sense. To correct for this sampling bias, we have weighted the group by rank so that our calculations better reflect the aggregate characteristics of the bureaucracy as a whole. We assume that in terms of rank, the Soviet bureaucracy (like all others) is roughly pyramid-shaped with relatively few representatives at the apex and a great many more nearer the low-ranking base of the structure. The apex of the pyramid is heavily represented by members of our basic group of 283 officials, the base much less so. Hence, in accordance with accepted sociological techniques, we conservatively weighted the group such that middle and lower ranking officials were given somewhat higher weight in statistical calculations. Correcting in this way allows us to make observations, generalizations, and conclusions which apply to the middle (and to some extent lower) as well as upper levels of the Soviet bureaucracy in 1935.

In this and other calculations, it is difficult to determine precise rank given the plethora of job titles at various levels; ranking is one of the major problems in the "hard" social sciences. To calculate an official's rank for analytical purposes, we used a two-judge procedure with a subtractive factor. That is, the two authors assigned each of the several hundred stated ranks into one of eighteen hierarchical categories. Then, points were subtracted from each rank category, according to the level of the position, to arrive at the final rank. Thus, although their stated job titles were the same, a Central Committee secretary in a national republic had a lower rank than one at USSR level; a party secretary at raion level ranked lower than one at oblast level; the editor of a provincial newspaper ranked lower than the editor of *Pravda*.

Finally, a technical note on statistics. In assessing the relationship between two factors, or variables, we used a variety of tests: cross tabulation, Kolomogorov-Smirnov Test, Kruskal-Wallis Test, and one and two-way analyses of variance. We chose .05 as our criterion threshold for statistical significance.

Peasants And The Party: Rural Administration In The Soviet Countryside On The Eve Of World War II

Roberta T. Manning

In recent years, Western scholars have come to assess the political position of the Russian peasantry after the collectivization of agriculture in increasingly harsh terms. Some have gone so far as to compare the permanent impact of collectivization to the restoration of serfdom and to deny absolutely that Soviet peasants enjoyed the rights and status of other Soviet citizens.[1]

These assessments rest heavily upon episodic accounts of the experiences of the collectivization period and isolated decrees of the central government, either taken out of context[2] or else issued repeatedly in such a manner that leads one to assume that the decrees in question were never really implemented in the localities to any significant degree.[3] Local administration in the pre-war Stalin period, after the upheavals of collectivization and the cultural revolution had subsided, has received amazingly little attention from scholars. Least of all is known about how government functioned in the depths of the countryside, where two-thirds of the Soviet populace still resided on the eve of World War II.[4]

Sources on which such studies could rest have long been available to scholars in the form of the Smolensk Archive, particularly the materials from Belyi raion, where archival files for the late thirties are especially rich.[5] The Belyi files indicate that recent views of the permanent impact of collectivization on the peasantry have tended to be exaggerated. To be sure, the rights of peasants to dispose freely of their produce were limited after collectivization as was indeed true of other Soviet citizens; and the burden of procurements remained onerous throughout the pre-war years.[6] But peasants enjoyed numerous rights in other spheres of Soviet life in comparison with pre-revolutionary times.

The Revolution opened up the political system to peasants as was not at all the case under the *ancien regime*.[7] By 1937, 61 percent of the members of the Belyi raion party organization, which staffed the topmost local administrative positions, were persons of peasant origin[8], recruited predominantly in local villages[9] since the onset of collectivization.[10] The peasantization of the Belyi party organization proceeded rapidly after the

NEP came to a close, although opportunities for social mobility open to peasants in the 1930s left the party with few members who were rank-and-file collective farm or sovkhoz members[11]

Not surprisingly, most peasant party members occupied low level administrative positions in the countryside, as chairmen of rural soviets, collective farms and rural consumer cooperatives. Only 12.2 percent were rank-and-file collective farmers.[12] But as the thirties progressed, increasing numbers of party members of peasant origin came to occupy official posts in the towns, as Table 1 indicates. Some of them also assumed key positions in the raion administration, providing Belyi raion in the mid- to late 1930s with at least two of its three raion executive committee chairmen (E.P. Stogov and F.M. Shitov) and at least one, possibly more, of the three first secretaries of the local party raikom as well (A.F. Karpovskii).[13] To be sure, the peasantization of the party only reached the national leadership in the post-Stalin period, when persons of peasant origin and/or experience of working on family or collective farms came to provide 45 percent of the membership of the Party Central Committee and four of the five men occupying the party first secretaryship after the death of Stalin.[14] But this process was well under way on the raion level by the eve of the war and obviously affected the aspirations of collective farm youths, who by the mid- to late thirties harbored ambitions never before entertained by Russian peasants[15], while rising rural educational levels rendered the achievement of such ambitions increasingly feasible.[16]

Table 1. Urban-Rural Balance within the Belyi Raion Party Organization, 1925-1937 (in percentages of total party membership).

YEAR	% party membership of peasant origin	where local communists resided	
		Town	Countryside
1925	33.8%	26.9%	73.1%
1934	76.9%	5.7%	54.3%
1937	61.1%	55.6%	44.4%

Source: The Smolensk Archive, WKP 321, pp. 135-139; Fainsod, *Smolensk Under Soviet Rule*, pp. 122-123; WKP 313, pp. 33, 47, 100, 125 and 147.

Paradoxically, however, as political and occupational opportunities for peasants expanded, the party's political base in the countryside eroded, as Tables 1 and 2 indicate. The impact of upwardly mobile peasant party members who left the countryside for the town was enhanced by the 1933-1936 freeze on the admission of new party members[17] and the repeated membership screenings of the mid-thirties. These "screenings" or "purges" fell most heavily upon low-level rural party members, who were expelled from the party en masse for "passivity" and chronic alcoholism, or were held responsible before the courts for the endemic mismanagement, corruption, and disorganization of the collective farm economy in these years.[18]

Table 2. Erosion of the Party's Rural Base in Belyi Raion, 1934-1937.

Location	No. of ppos August 1934	No. of ppos 1937
I. Town	15	16
II. Countryside		
Shamilovo sovkhoz	2	1
ppos on collective farms	9	3
Party-candidate groups on collective farms	11	1
Party-Komsomol groups on collective farms	6	2
ppos in rural soviets	4	1
Party-candidate groups in rural soviets	0	8

Source: WKP 313, pp. 313, pp. 72-76; WKP 321, p. 138; WKP 385, pp. 352-368.

The party consequently was absent from much of the countryside as the nation entered its third decade of Soviet rule. In 1937, only five of the twenty-one primary party organizations (ppo) in Belyi raion were located outside the town of Belyi, including 3 ppos on the raion's 210 collective farms.[19]

The Komsomol in Belyi raion proved incapable of offering the party much political support in the countryside[20]. Only a quarter of the raion's collective farms possessed Komsomol ppos in 1937.[21] The raion Komsomol secretary himself admitted that the communist youth organization was "falling apart," with its membership declining and its raikom rarely even bothering to convene meetings.[22]

The party consequently had little choice but to govern the countryside "campaign style," as the Belyi raikom secretary disparagingly dubbed the local style of government.[23] Several times a year, members of the twenty-six-man "town aktiv" and the sixteen-man "rural aktiv"[24] descended on the raion's 34 rural soviets, 210 collective farms and more than 800 villages (25) to oversee the progress of spring sowing and the collection of vital agricultural and forest procurements.[26] In the process, the other business of government in the raion, including meetings of the party's raikom bureau, the raion's highest executive authority, ground to a halt, as the topmost raion leaders were dispersed along with other members of the aktiv as plenipoteniaries to the rural soviets and collective farms.[27]

Even then, rural-based communists complained that such emissaries did little more than issue orders, criticize local officials in a high-handed fashion and then depart, without gaining much insight into local problems and conditions[28] The emissaries themselves questioned the effectiveness of such whirlwind visits, complaining that they felt more like "jockies" than "political organizers."[29] Such efforts were rendered more difficult by the lack of paved roads, compounded by the local terrain, with its numerous tiny villages and *khutora*, and the proliferation of impassable forests and bogs.[30] Raion authorities, with few automobiles at their disposal and even fewer adequate highways, traveled to the countryside by bicycle or horseback and were at times hindered in their ability to visit rural localities by a lack of adequate funding for fodder.[31]

Six months or more could easily pass without any raikom representative appearing in any given rural soviet;[32] and some villages in the raion failed to receive any visitors from the raion center (much less an official emissary) for up to a year and a half.[33] Yet the presence of such emissaries was essential for the routine operation of rural administration, as the rural soviets were said to function only "when a comrade is sent them by the raion."[34]

By the late thirties, the raion center was nominally connected with 32 of the 34 rural soviets by telephone. But telephone lines to four rural soviets never functioned. Service to the others was often "down" for months on end, due to the chronic shortage of spare parts for needed repairs. No telephone service at all existed on the collective farms.[35]

Under these conditions, it is not surprising that the party managed to accomplish little outside of towns other than the operation of the military draft[36] and the collection of procurements. But the government's ability to collect procurements, even during the bumper harvest of 1937, the highest yet on record, [37] faltered, as Table 3 indicates, with the dwindling of the party's rural base between 1934 and 1937.[38]

Table 3.   Fulfillment of Agricultural Procurements in Belyi raion
(percentage of agricultural procurements fulfilled), 1934-1937.

Product	1934	1935	1936	1937
grain	92.5%	91.8%	67.3%	89.7%
potatoes	95.0%	68.6%	67.3%	84.0%
hay	72.0%	70.4%	76.0%	77.0%
flax seed	93.6%	100.0%	108.8%*	n.d.
flax fiber	76.0%	116.0%	95.0%*	n.d.

Source: WKP 321, p. 232; and WKP 111, p. 221.
*Subsequently these figures were said to have been falsified, but no
revised figures could be found in the Smolensk Archive. WKP
321, p. 195.

Local political leaders even found it difficult to collect vital
information on country life.   As late as 1937, raion leaders lacked
accurate data on the numbers of livestock, the amount of available
fodder, and the amount of arable land in the raion, which rendered all
efforts at economic planning ineffective.[39] A significant portion of the
economic data collected appears to have been deliberately falsified or
collected by barely literate brigade leaders with weakly developed record
keeping skills.[40]

As far back as 1934, raion and oblast leaders were aware that the
ambitious sowing plans, formulated at higher levels of government based
on such inaccurate data, existed only "on paper," and that no system of
crop rotation whatsoever prevailed on the collective farms.   Yet they
were powerless to influence the internal operation of the collective farms
to remedy this situation, a deficiency that would result in charges of
"wrecking" being leveled against local leaders during the Great Purges.[41]
Local leaders also were unable to enforce national legislation limiting the
size of private plots[42] or to secure "proper distribution of collective farm
income as stipulated by law, i.e., according to the number of labor days
earned, rather than according to the number of workers or "eaters" in
collective farm families or the amount of capital each family had
contributed to the collective farm upon its establishment.[43] As late as
1935, 40 percent of all collective farms nationwide lacked definite
boundaries.[44]

Peasants, with impunity and with the knowledge of the local raikom
secretary, took advantage of the party's weakness in the countryside to

find ingenious ways to "beat" the collective farm system.   Collective farmers were able to raise their incomes substantially by speculating in meat in Moscow, as dwindling livestock herds drove meat prices up to record levels.   Entire collective farms, at times led by their chairmen, neglected their collective labors at the peak of the work season to travel to the Moscow markets with their livestock, often in violation of Soviet laws seeking to preserve existing livestock herds.[45] Peasants also increasingly joined collective farms merely to obtain a private plot and lower taxation rates and refused to perform more than the minimum amount of labor necessary to remain a collective farm member.   Such practices allowed individual peasants, who accounted for 14.4 percent of the peasant households in Belyi raion in 1937, to live better than most collective farmers, by reducing the amount of land cultivated to a small garden plot to avoid taxes and hiring themselves out as day laborers to desperate, labor-short collective farms at harvest season at exorbitant wages.[46]

The most that raion and oblast leaders could do to combat such practices was to place political, administrative, and judicial pressures on low level rural officials.   In the mid-thirties, such officials were removed from office, expelled from the party, berated as "sheep", "fools," "addlepates," and "beachbums," or were hauled before the courts in significant numbers for a variety of offenses.[47] The party's rural base was further eroded by such prosecutions.   Efforts to transfer pressure to peasants by confiscating peasant property to cover arrears in taxes and procurements provoked traditional peasant resentment of government and often resulted in the physical resistance on the part of peasants to confiscating authorities, thereby rendering rural administration more difficult still.[48]

By 1936-1937, higher authorities and the courts, desirous of correcting the illegalities of the collectivization period and mitigating peasant resentment, began to resist the violations of the legal rights of peasants and low-level officials alike.   Legal authorities became more demanding in terms of the amounts and kinds of evidence required to prosecute and convict low level officials.[49] Legal limits were placed on the ability of officials to collect arrears by seizing peasant property by administrative procedure.   Officials now had to obtain court orders for the seizure of such property, thereby warning peasants that such seizures were imminent and giving them ample time to conceal such property from the authorities.[50]

The new model charter of collective farms, introduced in 1955, enhanced the power of the collective farm *vis à vis* outside authorities, inhibiting the ability of the government to appoint and to remove collective farm chairmen at will.[51] Although initially this provision was ignored by raion authorities[52], local officials who persisted in such practices increasingly found themselves censured[53], expelled from the party[54], or hauled before the courts in a series of public show trials of offending officials in the spring and summer of 1937.[55]

The government also proved willing, within limits, to adjust its agricultural policies to peasant desires.[56] Repeatedly throughout the mid- to late thirties, taxation, procurements and food loan arrears were cancelled[57] and procurement prices were raised.[58] Substantial food loans also became common government practice, as orders went out that no collective farmers were to be allowed to go hungry in event of short harvests, as had frequently occurred in the past.[59] Sowing plans for crops, like flax, originally pushed by the government but unpopular with peasants[60], were progressively reduced as a result of peasant petitions, as Table 4 indicates. Further reductions were scheduled for the 1938 agricultural year with the introduction of the Vil'iams grasslands system of crop rotation, which significantly increased the amount of land devoted to fodder crops and pasture.[61]

Table 4. Reductions in the amount of Land Planted in Flax in Belyi Raion, 1935-1937

Year	Amount of arable land (in hectares)	Amount of land planted in flax (in hectares)	% arable planted in flax
1935	63,910	19,930	26.5%
1936	46,836.1*	10,789.5	23%**
1937	50,212	10,505	20.9%

SOURCE: WKP 321, p. 126; WKP 235, pp. 19-20; WKP 237, pp. 96-98; and WKP 238, p. 23.

*The reduction of the amount of arable land in the raion between 1935 and 1936 was due to the loss of eight of the raion's 42 rural soviets in an administrative reorganization at the end of 1935.

**Had matters been solely up to raion authorities, however, the amount of land planted in flax would have been even greater. The Belyi raikom secretary boasted in 1935 that 38.6% of the arable land in the raion would be planted in flax the following year! WKP 313, p. 147.

Possessing limited means to influence rural life, the party proved surprisingly responsive to the complaints of ordinary peasants in Belyi raion in 1937, the only year and place for which peasant complaints and official responses to such complaints have been preserved in the Smolensk Archive.[62] The Belyi raion party committee (raikom) files for that year contained 106 complaints from peasants: 74 from collective farmers, 10 from individual peasants and 22 from local peasants currently serving in the Red Army.[63]

Although the signatories of these 106 collective and individual complaints represented at most 200 to 300 of the raion's 60,950 rural inhabitants[64], the letters came from 88 percent of the rural soviets and 30 percent of the collective farms in the raion. Moreover, when the social origins of the soldier complainants are considered, collective farmers and individual peasants are found among the complainants in proportions almost identical to their representation among the raion's population at large, as Table 5 indicates.[65] Consequently, the problems and grievances outlined in these complaints were probably characteristic of those plaguing the raion's peasant population at this time.

Table 5. Representation of Collective Farmers and Individual Peasants among the Authors of Peasant Complaints in the Belyi Raikom Complaint Files and Among the Peasant Population of the Raion in 1937.

	Representation among complaints	representation among the raion's peasant population
collective farmers	87.7%	85.6%
individual peasants	12.3%	14.4%

Source: WKP 203, pp. 1-463; WKP 362, pp. 1-571 and WKP 321, pp. 138-139.

Overwhelmingly, as Table 6 indicates, the target of peasant complaints were low-level officials, in the main collective farm chairmen, chairmen of rural soviets and other rural officials with whom the peasants came into frequent contact. Higher, more remote authorities above the rural soviet level only rarely figured in these complaints, either because such officials rarely impinged directly upon peasant life or because complaints against raion-level institutions were generally handled by authorities outside the raion and thus would not normally appear in raikom files.[66]

Table 6. The Target of Peasant Complaints In Belyi Raion in 1937(a).

number of complaints	against whom or what were the complaints directed

I. Complaints against collective farm leaders and officials

25	collective farm chairmen
15	collective farm administration (chairman and board)
24	collective farm in general (usually for failure to render welfare payments due)
1	chairman of the collective farm revision commission
10	collective farm brigade leaders
1	collective farm storekeeper

II. Complaints against rural soviet-level officials

12	rural soviet chairmen
9	rural soviet in general (usually tax or welfare-related)
1	rural soviet member
1	rural court
2	members of rural election commission for the elections to the Supreme Soviet
2	party members (without designating the offices they held
1	local teacher

III. Complaints against higher authorities

1	forestry official
3	raizo (raion land department, the local branch of the Commissariat of Agriculture
2	MTS (one of these was pension-related)
1	a local Komsomol currently studying in the town of Belyi
1	SOBES (social security office)
1	Communist Party raikom

SOURCE: WKP 203 and WKP 362 NOTE: These complaints add up to more than the total number of collective farmer, individual peasant and soldier complaints because often more than one institution was named.

The tone of the complaints was outspoken, uninhibited and informal, in sharp contrast to the fawning, self-abnegating deference that permeated peasant petitions in the pre-revolutionary past.[67] The Soviet government after all was a political regime whose officials were addressed as "Comrade," rather than "Your Excellency." Government representatives, even on the raion level, were recruited from the peasant population and possessed little more education than the population at large, unlike the *ancien régime*.[68] Belyi peasants consequently addressed raion leaders as equals, insisting on their rights as Soviet citizens, displaying an acute awareness of the law, and even threatening on occasion to go over the head of the party raikom to higher authorities should their complaints go unheeded.[69]

The substance of the complaints, as Table 7 indicates, centered around two main issues, violations of Soviet democracy and chronic mismanagement and corruption.[70] Peasant concern about their democratic rights, however, was intimately related to their own well being, since such charges were only leveled against officials who were simultaneously accused of mismanagement and/or corruption. Charges of mismanagement and/or corruption also usually accompanied the other charges listed in Table 7, except for charges of failure to render welfare payments due. This linkage indicates that Belyi peasants in 1937 were mainly concerned with official misdeeds that adversely affected local peasants economically, as one might well expect in a year following a short harvest when food and fodder were in short supply even though actual cases of hunger were uncommon.[71]

Table 7:   The Substance of the Complaints Registered by Rural Residents in Belyi Raion in 1937 (a)

number of institutions or individuals against which complaints were made	charges made against them
42 cases	violations of Soviet democracy
36 cases	gross mismanagement
22 cases	corruption or embezzlement of public property

15 cases	"systematic drunkenness" on the part of officials
24 cases	"alien elements" or "class enemies" in positions of authority
12 cases	"wrecking"
1 case	"Trotskyists" in positions of authority
24 cases	nonpayment of welfare payments due
9 cases	complaints against the mistreatment of individual farmers
9 cases	improper fines, dismissals from work and expulsions from collective farms

SOURCE: WKP 203 AND WKP 362

(a) NOTE: The total number of cases adds up to more than 138, since some complainants made multiple charges, sometimes against the same person or institution.

Such concern was not misplaced, for the letters indicate that mismanagement, disorganization and economic inefficiency of an extreme, even startling, nature plagued at least 16.7 percent of the raion's collective farms. Crops were not sown or harvested on time. Arable land failed to be planted for lack of seed. Crops perished in the ground unharvested or rotted in the open air for want of adequate storage facilities. The declining livestock herds were poorly housed and grossly neglected. Accounts were not properly kept and at times were not kept at all, due to the short supply of trained bookkeepers; and work schedules and work assignments were often non-existent.[72] Most of these problems stemmed from a lack of organizational and accounting skills on the part of farm leaders, compounded by the reluctance of many peasants to work under such conditions.

The party raikom proved most willing to meet peasant complaints in Belyi raion in 1937. Over 70 percent of all peasant complaints were resolved in favor of the complainant, as Table 8 indicates.[73] The complaints of peasants fared far better than complaints made by rural specialists and officials, most of which were simply ignored since less than half (48 percent) were resolved favorably while 52 percent remained unresolved, with the outcome unclear or still pending at the end of 1937. Only 16 percent of the peasant complaints shared such a fate. The average amount of time required for the raikom to process peasant complaints was also significantly shorter than the amount required to process the complaints of specialists and officials, as Table 9 demonstrates.[74]

Table 8. How Complaints Were Resolved in Belyi Raion in 1937 by Social Groups.

Categories of Complainants	resolved favorably		complaint denied		outcome un-clear, no action, or pending		TOTAL
	Nos.	%	Nos.	%	Nos.	%	
Collective farmers	55	74.3%	6	8.1%	13	17.6%	74
Soldiers	17	77.3%	3	16.6%	2	9.1%	22
Individual peasants	3	30.0%	5	50.0%		20.0%	10
TOTAL PEASANTS	75	71%	14	13.0%	17	16.0%	106
Rural specialists and officials	12	48.0%	0	0.0%	13	52.0%	25
Others	5	71.4%	1	14.3%	1	14.3%	7
TOTAL	92	66.6%	15	10.9%	31	22.5%	138

SOURCE: WKP 203 and WKP 362

Table 9: Time Required to Process Rural Citizens' Complaints in Belyi
Raion in 1937 by Social Groups

social category	# complaints resolved	# complaints pending	average time to resolve (in days)	median time to resolve (in days)
Collective farmers	61	13	45	36
soldiers	20	2	46	42
individual peasants	8	2	79.5	73
specialists and officials	10	13	133.3	140.5

SOURCE: WKP 203 and WKP 362

As a result of peasant complaints, nineteen collective farm chairmen
and five rural soviet chairmen were removed from office in Belyi raion in
1937, along with one collective farm bookkeeper, one collective farm
accountant, one brigade leader and several members of collective farm
boards.[75] Criminal charges (usually corruption or embezzlement) were
filed against ten of these collective farm chairmen[76] and four of the rural
soviet chairmen,[77] while two rural soviet chairmen were expelled from the
Communist Party in response to peasant complaints.[78]

The weakness of local administration in the countryside, the
willingness of the Soviet government to continue to amend its agricultural
policies to accommodate peasant desires, and the surprising
responsiveness of the party raikom to peasant complaints contradicts our
traditional image of party-peasant relations in the 1930s. Indeed, the
weakness of the party's administrative network in the countryside should
lead us to question our traditional image of collectivization as a
development universally opposed by the entire peasant population,[79]
although it is clear that hardcore opposition to collectivization did persist
and the actual functioning of the collective farms left much to be desired.

Some peasant support for collectivization must have surely existed.
Otherwise why did Russian collaborators (interviewed by the Harvard
émigré project) feel compelled to carry "firearms and grenades" and to
sleep "only where German troops were stationed" on their travels about

the countryside to decollectivize agriculture for the Germans in the Smolensk region in early 1942?[80] Or why did 40 percent of the peasants interviewed by the Harvard project fail to list the collective farms as an aspect of Soviet society that they would like to change?[81]

Materials in the Smolensk Archive suggest that collectivization may well have changed peasant life less than we realize, since brigades in Belyi raion were based on villages, and links consisted of family members; however much higher authorities tended to deplore such practices.[82] High prices on the collective farm markets, bred of endemic food shortages, may well have compensated peasants to a significant degree for low procurement prices. Certainly peasants were able to purchase increasing amounts of industrial goods throughout the 1930s. Although peasant demand for such products continued to far outrun the supply of such goods, peasants in the 1930s began to demand products like manufactured shoes for their children which never before were found in significant quantities in the villages.[83] Moreover, the practice of recruiting an increasing number of local officials from the local peasantry may well have helped peasants "beat" the system through the collection of statistical data that deliberately underestimated the size of harvests and existing livestock herds in order to reduce the toll of government exactions upon peasants.[84]

Certainly considerably more research on the Soviet countryside in the 1930s on the micro-level and a more nuanced view of the party-peasant relations is warranted.

Boston College

NOTES

[1]See, for example, Karl-Eugena Wadekin, *The Private Sector in Soviet Agriculture*. Berkeley: University of California Press, 1973, and Moshe Lewin, *The Making of the Soviet System: Essays in the Social History of Interwar Russia*. New York: Pantheon Books, 1985, pp. 176, 183-185, 227-231, 266 and 270-272.

[2]The best example of a decree taken out of context was the re-introduction of the passport system in 1932, which is usually interpreted by Western scholars as an attempt to limit the geographic mobility of peasants, since peasants were not automatically issued passports as were other categories of Soviet citizens. Yet three and a half million peasants left the Soviet countryside to establish residence in towns between 1935 and 1937 alone. See M.A. Vyltsan, *Zavershaiushchii etap sozdaniia kolkhoznogo stroi (1935-1937) g.g.)*. Moscow, 1978, p. 91. Moreover, the mobility of other categories of Soviet citizens was also limited in 1932, since the right of workers and employees to leave their jobs was restricted by law. This legislation, too, appears not to have been enforced for much of the pre-war period, leading a recent study to conclude that this decree, like the reintroduction of passports, was an attempt to

facilitate the rationing of food products in a famine-stricken, underdeveloped nation administered by officials with excessively underdeveloped record-keeping skills. Robert Beattie, "'A Great Turn' that Never Happened: a Reconsideration of the Soviet Labor Decree on Labor Discipline of November 1932," *Russian History*, forthcoming.

[3]See, for example, the repeated Soviet efforts to limit the size of the private plots of collective farmers through the model *ustav* of 1935 and government instructions reissued in 1937 and 1939. Vyltsan, *Zavershaiushchii etap*, pp. 31, 37, 41-42, and 47-48, and Lazar Volin, *A Century of Russian Agriculture: From Alexander II to Khrushchev*. Cambridge, Mass.: Harvard University Press, 1970, p. 268.

[4]The exceptions to this general rule are Alex Inkeles and Raymond Bauer, *The Soviet Citizen*. Cambridge, Mass.: Harvard University Press, 1968, and Merle Fainsod, *Smolensk Under Soviet Rule*. Cambridge, Mass.: Harvard University Press, 1958. But neither work singles out the interrelationship of the rural population and government for an in-depth study.

[5]Archival files from Belyi raion include the stenographic proceedings of all the raion party conferences and meetings of the raion party committee (raikom) and raikom bureau for 1937, two files of citizen complaints and official reactions to these complaints, and minutes of rural primary party organizations from the same period, among other materials. WKP 321, WKP 111, WKP 440, WKP 101, WKP 241, WKP 242, WKP 385, WKP 239, WKP 266, WKP 313, WKP 439 AND WKP 277.

[6]Vyltsan, *Zavershaiushchii etap*, pp. 157-172.

[7]Peasants were barred by law from entering state service before 1906, and even then, the posts that they could occupy were limited. S.I. Sidel'nikov, *Agrarnaia reforms Stolypina (uchebnoe posobie)*. Moscow, 1973, p. 16.

[8]WKP 321, p. 139. The social categories in use by the party at this time tended to underestimate the representation of peasants, since *batraka* (agricultural wage laborers) and sovkhoz workers were categorized as "workers," as were peasants with the most rudimentary industrial experience. WKP 321, p. 115.

[9]See the biographical data on Belyi raion party members in WKP 321, pp. 1-304, and WKP 111, pp. 1-233. These data indicate that by the end of the thirties local offices, save the first (and occasionally the second) raikom party secretaryship tended to be filled by local people rather than from outside the raion. Such practices were by no means unique to Belyi raion, according to the raw interview data of the Harvard Emigre Interview Project of 1950-1951. *Project on the Soviet Social System. Interview Records Schedule B* (bound transcripts found in the library of the Harvard Russian Research Center), interview no. 470, p. 9.

[10]68.6 percent of the members and candidates of the Belyi raion party organization in 1937 had joined the party between 1928 and 1932. WKP 321, p. 139.

[11]In 1932, 26.9 percent of Communist party members nationwide were peasants by origin, but only 20 percent of these were actually employed as peasants. T.H. Rigby, *Communist Party Membership in the USSR*, Princeton: Princeton University Press, 1968, p. 199.

[12]Data are only available on the occupations of isolated rural communists, those

unable to belong to primary party organizations due to a dearth of fellow communists in their locality. Such communists, however, accounted for 64 percent of all rural party members in Belyi raion in the mid-thirties. WKP 313, pp. 70-74. However, 19.9 percent of such communists in the Western oblast as a whole were rank-and-file collective farm members in 1937 while 37.4 percent were in nearby Ivanovo oblast.

[13]WKP 111, pp. 193-196, and WKP 321, pp. 193-198. Biographical data are simply not available for long-time Belyi raikom secretary Kovelev, raikom secretary P.I. Galkin and raion ispolkom chairman E.G. Gerasimov.

[14]Mark R. Beissinger, "Politics," *The Soviet Union Today*. Chicago: University of Chicago Press, 1983, p. 41.

[15]For example of such studies, *Sotsialisticheskoe sel'skoe khoziaistvo Soiuza SSSR*. Moscow, 1939, p. 105; *Komsomol'skii rabotnik*, 1939, nos. 20-21, p. 21; *Sotsial'nyi oblik kolkhoznoi molodezhi po materialam sotsiologicheskikh obsledovanii 1938 i 1969 g.g.* Moscow, 1976, pp. 80-88, 259-260; Vyltsan, *Zavershaiushchii etap*, pp. 215-218; *Molodaia gvardiia*, July 1935; *Pravda*, 30 August 1935, *Pravda* subsequently did a follow-up story on the youths in the Voronezh oblast village of Novozhivotinnii, who wrote compositions for the writer Maxim Gorkii in 1935 on what they wanted to be when they grew up. Many of these children did achieve their youthful ambitions. *Pravda*, 4 November 1968. Memoirs of Soviet defectors who were peasant youths in the 1930s confirm the picture of unprecedented opportunities for social mobility for peasant youths. See, for example, Peter Pirogov, *Why I Escaped*. London: Harvill Press, 1950 pp. 122-143, and Vladimir and Evdokiia Petrov, *Empire of Fear*, Garden City, N.Y.: Doubleday, 1954.

[16]Vyltsan, *Zavershaiushchii etap*, pp. 215-218.

[17]Rigby, *Communist Party Membership*, p. 215.

[18]J. Arch Getty, *The Origins of the Great Purges: The Soviet Communist Party Reconsidered, 1933-1938*. Cambridge: Cambridge University Press, 1985, pp. 38-91 and 107-111; WKP 385, pp. 63-73, 129, 145, 154-164, 176-177, 180-181, 216, 289, 292, 336-337, 346, and 351-354; and Rigby, *Communist Party Membership*, pp. 200-209.

[19]WKP 440, pp. 1-174. However, primary party organizations existed in 1937 on 13 percent of the collective farms in Melitopolsk raion, Tauride oblast, a model raion selected for a major study of its collective farms. In 1939, after two years of intensive attempts by the party to fortify its rural base, 43.7 percent of the collective farms in Moscow oblast possessed ppos and nationwide 12 percent of all collective farms had ppos on the eve of the war. But as late as the end of 1939 ppos existed on only 1.7 percent of the collective farms in Leningrad oblast, a figure not much greater than that which prevailed in Belyi raion in 1937. WKP 321, p. 138; WKP 313, p. 100; Rigby, *Communist Party Membership*, p. 235; V.A. Selenev and A.N. Gutarov, *Sovetskaia derevnia v predvoennye gody, 1938-1941 (iz istorii kolkhoznogo stroitel'stva v osnovykh raionov severo-zapada RSFSR Leningradskaia oblast). Kratkii istoricheskii ocherk*. Leningrad, 1976, p. 182; Vyltsan, *Zavershaiushchii etap*, p. 112; and A.E. Arina, G.G. Kotov, and K.V. Loseva, *Sotsial'no-ekonomicheskie izmeneniia v derevne: Melitopol'skii raion (1885-1938 g.g.)*. Moscow, 1939, pp. 85-89.

[20]WKP 313, pp. 53 and 88.

[21]WKP 416, p. 12. In the Western oblast, the larger territorial unit to which Belyi

raion belonged, only 21 percent of the collective farms possessed Komsomol ppos in 1937, compared to 42 percent of collective farms nationally. *Ibid*, 175 and Vyltsan, *Zavershaiushchii etap*, p. 233.

[22]WKP 321, p. 142, 133, 170, 177, 234; WKP 111, pp. 33, 46, 57, 77 and 97; and WKP 416, pp. 12-175.

[23]WKP 321, p. 134.

[24]WKP 198, p. 47.

[25]WKP 321, pp. 207-214, and WKP 313, p. 89.

[26]In December 1937 the party raikom dispatched eighty local communists to the countryside to ensure the collection of the seed fund for the planting of the next year's crop, since only 40 percent of the seeds needed had been collected so far. But this was an extreme response to an extreme situation and was not typical of local party practices in the mid to late thirties. WKP 321, p. 293.

[27]In 1937, such work occupied raion bureau members for a total of 126 days. Even purging activities at the height of the Great Purges ceased locally at these times! WKP 321, pp. 44, 113-117, 146, 170-177 and 257-267; WKP 111, pp. 10-14, 17-18, 143; and WKP 234, p. 393.

[28]WKP 111, pp. 19, 26, 37-38, 44, 46, 48, 74, and 97.

[29]*Ibid*., pp. 14 and 17.

[30]Roberta T. Manning. "Government in the Soviet Countryside in the Stalinist Thirties: the Case of Belyi Raion in 1937," *The Carl Beck Papers in Russian and East European Studies*, Paper No. 301, pp. 7-8.

[31]WKP 362, pp. 231-232; WKP 234, p. 398; and WKP 313, pp. 8 and 77.

[32]WKP 111, pp. 48-49.

[33]*Ibid*, p. 216.

[34]WKP 321, p. 96 and WKP 111, p. 128. Weakness of the rural soviets appears to have been a national problem. WKP 236, pp. 63-148, and Vyltsan, *Zavershaiushchii etap*, p. 237.

[35]WKP 198, p. 57; WKP 362, p. 12; and WKP 111, p. 97. The postal service was equally inefficient, since it took one to one and a half months for reports of raikom plenum meetings to reach rural party members. WKP 111, p. 65.

[36]Although no problems were encountered in the drafting of soldiers in Belyi raion in 1937, difficulties materialized during the horse draft and in collecting the defense loan. Moreover, civilian para-military organizations, like OSO and MORP, simply did not exist on the collective farms of the raion. WKP 362, pp. 586-590; WKP 111, pp. 37, 180, and 204; and WKP 321 pp. 293-295.

[37]Manning, *Carl Beck Papers*, pp. 4-5.

[38]The raion also encountered unprecedented resistance among peasants to the collection of forest procurements and the collection of seed funds for the following agricultural year. WKP 321, pp. 95, 263, 267, 275 and 293; WKP 111, p. 227; WKP 237, p. 624.

[39]WKP 111, pp. 72 and 170; WKP 235 p. 137; WKP 238 pp. 80-81 and 143; and

Izvestiia, 6 April 1937.

[40]WKP 111, pp. 13, 26-28, 47, 53, 82, 98, 102-103, 107-108, 128, 152, 169-170, 186-189, 201; WKP 321, pp. 93, 195, 204, 228-229, 253-254; and WKP 266, pp. 7-8.

[41]WKP 313, p. 89; WKP 238, pp. 33-37, 80-81, 261-263, 280, 297-298; WKP 386, p. 371; WKP 111, pp. 18, 20, 26, 257-258; WKP 321, pp. 252-254; WKP 290, pp. 327-350; and *Kollektivizatsiia sel'skogo khoziaistvo v zapadnom raione RSFSR (1927-1937 g.g.)*. Smolensk, 1968, pp. 444, 473, 499, 500-502, and 506-507.

[42]WKP 235, p. 98, and Vyltsan, *Zavershaiushchii etap*, pp. 31, 37, and 41-42.

[43]WKP 321, pp. 47-48, 196 and 276-277; WKP 111, p. 179; Vyltsan, *Zavershaiushchii etap*, p. 40; Selenev and Gutarov, *Sovetskaia derevnia*, pp. 76 and 91; Arina, Kotov and Loseva, *Sotsial'no-ekonomicheskie izmeneniia v derevnia*, p. 327.

[44]Vyltsan, *Zavershaiushchii etap*, pp. 46-48.

[45]WKP 111, pp. 50 and 170; and WKP 321, p. 262.

[46]WKP 321, pp. 127-129, 196, 231; and WKP 111, pp. 106-108; *Kollektivizatsiia sel'skogo khoziaistvo v zapadnom raione RSFSR*, pp. 518-525. For the ability of individual peasants to avoid taxes, see WKP 111, pp. 106-108.

[47]WKP 111, pp. 3, 6, 22, 29-30, 33-34, 37, 44-45, 48-49, 66, 97, 179 and 182, and Vyltsan, *Zavershaiushchii etap*, pp. 114-115, and 119-120. In Belyi raion in 1934 alone, 53 rural officials were sentenced to prison terms for various transgressions. These included 17 collective farm chairmen, 12 rural store keepers, one collective farm bookkeeper, 19 collective farm brigade leaders, and four members of collective farm boards. WKP 313, p. 88.

[48]See, for example, *Pravda*, 11 March 1937, p. 6, and 15 June 1937, p. 6.

[49]Between the fall of 1936 and the fall of 1937, only one collective farm chairman was successfully prosecuted in Belyi raion, despite the shortfall in procurements. WKP 111, pp. 6, 28, 37, 74, 86, 96-97, 122-123, 155-156, 178-179, 181-182, 184, 195, 215; WKP 362, p. 1; WKP 203, p. 1; and WKP 321, pp. 50 and 258.

[50]Vyltsan, *Zavershaiushchii etap* , 260, and *Pravda*, 10-13 March 1937 and 15-16 June 1937.

[51]Vyltsan, *Zavershaiushchii etap*, p. 247, and WKP 321, pp. 91 and 196.

[52]Vyltsan, *Zavershaiushchii etap*, pp. 247-255; WKP 238, pp. 156-157; WKP 111, p. 9; and WKP 290, pp. 327-350.

[53]WKP 237, p. 174.

[54]One of the main charges against Belyi raikom secretary Kovalev and raion executive committee chairman Stogov during the Great Purges was the administrative pressures that they placed on rural officials. WKP 111, pp. 3-66, and WKP 321, p. 196.

[55]*Pravda*, 10 March 1937 p. 6; 11 March 1937 p. 6; 13 March 1937 p. 6; 15 June 1937 p. 4; 16 June 1937, p. 6; 2 July 1937, p. 6; 15 July 1937 p. 6; 18 July 1937, p. 1; 30 July 1937 p. 6; and 31 July 1937, p. 6.

[56]Earlier attempts to accommodate government policy to peasant desires include the sanctioning of the private plot and collective farm market. See Lewin, *The Making of the Soviet System*, pp. 156-157 and 179; Jerzy Karcz, "From Stalin to Brezhnev," in James R. Miller (ed.), *The Soviet Rural Community*, Urbana: The University of Illinois

Press, 1971, p. 54; and Vyltsan, *Zavershaiushchii etap*, pp. 169-170.

[57]*Pravda*, 23 March 1937 p. 1; 3 April 1937 p. 1; 24 August 1937, p. 3; WKP 238, pp. 89, 132, 254, 262, 298, 301, 360-361, and 368-369; Arina, Kotov and Loseva, *Sotsial'no-ekonomicheskie izmeneniia v derevnia*, p. 330. Nonetheless, prices on the collective farm market remained far higher than procurement prices. Vyltsan, *Zavershaiushchii etap*, p. 174.

[58]WKP 111, pp. 78-79, 204; WKP 238, pp. 132 and 361; WKP 321, p. 224; *Pravda*, 10 June 1937 p. 2; Vyltsan, *Zavershaiushchii etap*, pp. 158-165; Selenev and Gutarov, *Sovetskaia derevnia*, p. 48.

[59]WKP 176, p. 9; WKP 238, pp. 21, 43, 56-57, 66, 71, 79, 82, 96, 215-216; and WKP 321 p. 127.

[60]Peasants resented the expansion of flax growing because flax intruded on the amount of arable land devoted to pastures and fodder production thereby contributing to the decline of livestock herds. Flax also was an extremely labor intensive crop. Although only a fourth or fifth of the arable land in Belyi raion was devoted to the production of flax, half of the labor days (*trudoden*) earned on collective farms here in the mid-thirties were earned from work on the flax crop! WKP 313, p. 80; WKP 237, pp. 240 and 280; WKP 176, p. 53; and WKP 175, p. 17.

[61]*Pravda* 6 July 1937 p. 2, and Jerzy Karcz, "From Stalin to Brezhnev," pp. 47-48 and 59.

[62]The Smolensk Archive is by no means complete. It consists of files apparently saved at random by the Germans from fires set by the retreating Soviets at the time that Smolensk fell to the Nazi invaders in 1941. Fainsod, *Smolensk Under Soviet Rule*, p. 3.

[63]WKP 203, pp. 1-463; and WKP 362, pp. 1-571.

[64]WKP 321, pp. 138-139.

[65]Nineteen of the soldiers came from collective farm families. Two came from individual peasant families and the remaining soldier-complainant was a collective farmer whose family were individual peasants.

[66]Complaints, however, were made against the raion leadership to higher authorities. See, for example, WKP 239, p. 152.

[67]For relations between peasants and pre-revolutionary officialdom, see Daniel Field, *Rebels in the Name of the Tsar*. Boston: Houghton-Mifflin, 1977; and Roberta T. Manning, *The Crisis of the Old Order in Russia: Gentry and Government*. Princeton: Princeton University Press, 1982, pp. 146-149 and 169-175.

[68]In 1937, only 17 of the 239 local party members in Belyi raion possessed more than three years of schooling. WKP 321, p. 140.

[69]See, for example, WKP 362, p. 140.

[70]The ways in which collective farm democracy were violated include the existence of family circles or local patronage networks (13 cases), suppression of the right of criticism by ordinary collective farmers (12 cases), refusal to hold new elections (6 cases), physical abuse of collective farmers (3 cases), verbal abuse of collective farmers (3 cases), and refusal to consult the general assembly of the collective farm on policy matters. Such charges were filed against 27 collective farm chairmen and 10 rural

soviet chairmen in Belyi raion in 1937. In only two cases, however, were authorities above the rural soviet level cited in such complaints.

[71]Manning, *Carl Beck Papers*, pp. 4-5.

[72]See for example, WKP 203, pp. 17-18.

[73]Individual peasants, however, fared significantly worse than other categories of rural citizens.

[74]Nonetheless, the amount of time required to process complaints varied significantly throughout the year. The average complaint, which took between 100 and 200 days to process in January and February 1937, took only 16 to 23 days to process by November and December, as the post-Purge leadership of the raion and oblast appeared far more concerned with citizens' complaints. WKP 238, p. 183; WKP 321, pp. 166, and 282-283; WKP 362, pp. 126, 389, and 514.

[75]WKP 203, pp. 2, 58, 73, 100, 126-128, 152, 165, 169-171; and WKP 362, pp. 19-21, 24, 26, 28, 61, 63, 177, 191-198, 233-245, 351, 385, 394, 407-408 and 524. The collective farm officials were removed by the general assembly of the collective farm which was convened in the presence of a raikom representative.

[76]WKP 203, pp. 32, 58, 73, 114, 148-149; and WKP 362, pp. 80, 126, 128, 190, 476, and 516.

[77]WKP 362, pp. 142, 351, 388, and 467.

[78]WKP 362, p. 97; and WKP 321, pp. 191 and 220.

[79]This image dates back to the Harvard Project on the Soviet Social System, popularly known as the Harvard Emigre Interview Project, of 1950-1951. See Inkeles and Bauer, *The Soviet Citizen*, pp. 244-245, 251-252, 254 and 293, and Raymond A. Bauer, Alex Inkeles, and Clyde Kluckhohm, *How the Soviet System Works: Cultural, Psychological, and Social Themes*. Cambridge, Mass.: Harvard University Press, 1956, pp. 181-185. Since "hatred of the collective farm system" was widespread among the sample utilized in this study, Inkeles, Bauer and Kluckhohm concluded that the soviet peasant population at large must share such sentiments. However, the peasants interviewed by the project came heavily from dekulakized families who presumably tended to lose the most economically from collectivization. For the structure of Harvard sample, see Bauer, Inkeles, and Kluckhohm, *How the Soviet System Works*, pp. 12-13, and the forthcoming UCLA dissertation on the Harvard Interview Project by Charles T. O'Connell as well as the transcripts of the actual interviews. *Project on the Soviet Social System Interview Records*, 61 vols., transcript available in the library of the Russian Research Center, Harvard University.

[80]*Project on the Soviet Social System. Schedule A Interviews.* vol. 25, interview no. 483, p. 4. Despite interviews like this one, the scholarly works based on the Harvard Project persist in maintaining the myth that the Nazis failed to try to break-up the collective farms. Bauer, Inkeles, and Kluckhohm, *How the Soviet System Works*, p. 183.

[81]More support for collective farms existed among the younger peasants interviewed. Inkeles and Bauer, *The Soviet Citizen*, pp. 245 and 254.

[82]WKP 313, pp. 88.

[83]Vyltsan, *Zavershaiushchii etap*, pp. 210-212; and WKP 439, p. 4-5. The incomes

of collective farm families and their standard of living cannot be gauged from the size of *trudoden* payments alone. A study of collective farmers in the Western and Gorkii Oblasts in 1937 revealed that only 29 percent of collective farm income came from "the socialized sector," i.e., *trudoden* payments. The remainder came from the sale of produce from their private plots and household livestock and from work outside their collective farms. In 1936, as many as 89 percent of collective farmers earned income from part-time or seasonal employment outside their collective farms. Vyltsan, *V nachale bol'shogo puti: Memuarnyi sbornik*. Minsk, 1975, pp. 158-159; Vyltsan, *Zavershaiushchii etap*, pp. 180 and 204.

[84]See, for example, the memoirs of one such official of peasant origins, Iosif Mihailovich Borisevich, "V te trudnye gody."

Publications of the Third World Congress for Soviet and East European Studies

I.   *Social Sciences*: Published by Cambridge University Press

Planned Economies: Confronting the Challenges of the 1980s: Selected Papers from the III World Congress for Soviet and East European Studies, edited by John P. Hardt (Library of Congress) and Carl H. McMillan (Carleton University)

The Soviet Union, Eastern Europe and the Developing States: Selected Papers from the III World Congress for Soviet and East European Studies, edited by Roger E. Kanet (University of Illinois at Urbana-Champaign)

USSR: Party and Society: Selected Papers from the III World Congress for Soviet and East European Studies, edited by Peter J. Potichny (McMaster University)

II. *Social Sciences*: Published by Lynne Rienner Publishers, 948 North Street, No. 8, Boulder, Colorado, 80302

Environmental Problems in the USSR and Eastern Europe: Do the Greens Threaten the Reds?, edited by Fred Singleton (University of Bradford)

Religion and Nationalism in Eastern Europe and the Soviet Union, edited by Dennis J. Dunn (Southwest Texas State University)

III. *Literature and History*: Published by Slavica Publishers, P.O. Box 14388, Columbus, Ohio, 43214

Issues in Russian Literature before 1917: Selected Papers from the III World Congress for Soviet and East European Studies, edited by J. Douglas Clayton (University of Ottawa)

Aspects of Modern Russian and Czech Literature, edited by Arnold McMillin (University of London)

Imperial Power and Development: Papers on Pre-Revolutionary Russian History, edited by Don Karl Rowney (Bowling Green State University)

Essays on Revolutionary Culture and Stalinism, edited by John W. Strong (Carleton University)

East European History, edited by Stanislav J. Kirschbaum (York University)

PUBLICATIONS

IV. *Special Volumes*

Books, Libraries and Information on Slavic and East European Studies: Proceedings of the Second International Conference of Slavic Librarians and Information Specialists, edited by Marianna Tax Choldin (University of Illinois at Urbana-Champaign). Available from Russica Publishers, 799 Broadway, New York, N.Y. 10003

Soviet Education under Scrutiny, edited by N. J. Dunstan (University of Birmingham). Available from Jordanhill College Publications, Southbrae Drive, Glasgow, Scotland, G13 1PP

The Distinctiveness of Socialist Law, vol. 34 in the series *Law in Eastern Europe*, edited by F. J. M. Feldbrugge (Rijksuniversiteit te Leiden). Available from Martinus Nijhoff Publishers, P.O. Box 163, 3300 AD Dordrecht, The Netherlands

Problems of European Minorities: The Slovene Case, special issue of *Slovene Studies*, vol. VIII, No. 1 (1986), edited by Tom M. S. Priestly (University of Alberta). Available from W. W. Derbyshire, Slavic Department, 324 Scott Hall, Rutgers University, New Brunswick, New Jersey, 08903

Special issue on Linguistics in *Folia Slavica*, vol. VIII, edited by Benjamin A. Stolz (University of Michigan). Available from Slavica Publishers, P.O. Box 14388, Columbus, Ohio, 43214.

OTHER BOOKS FROM SLAVICA

Carolina De Maegd-Soëp: *Chekhov and Women: Women in the Life and Work of Chekhov*, 373 p., 1987.

Bruce L. Derwing and Tom M. S. Priestly: *Reading Rules for Russian: A Systematic Approach to Russian Spelling and Pronunciation, with Notes on Dialectal and Stylistic Variation*, vi + 247 p., 1980.

Dorothy Disterheft: *The Syntactic Development of the Infinitive in Indo-European*, 220 p., 1980.

Thomas Eekman and Dean S. Worth, eds.: *Russian Poetics* Proceedings of the International Colloquium at UCLA, September 22-26, 1975, 544 p., 1983.

Mark J. Elson: *Macedonian Verbal Morphology A Structural Analysis*, 147 p., 1989.

Michael S. Flier and Richard D. Brecht, eds.: *Issues in Russian Morphosyntax*, 208 p., 1985.

Michael S. Flier and Alan Timberlake, eds: *The Scope of Slavic Aspect*, 295 p., 1985.

John Miles Foley, ed.: *Comparative Research on Oral Traditions: A Memorial for Milman Parry*, 597 p., 1987.

John M. Foley, ed.: *Oral Traditional Literature A Festschrift for Albert Bates Lord*, 461 p., 1981.

Diana Greene: *Insidious Intent: An Interpretation of Fedor Sologub's The Petty Demon*, 140 p., 1986.

Charles E. Gribble, ed.: *Medieval Slavic Texts, Vol. 1, Old and Middle Russian Texts*, 320 p., 1973.

Charles E. Gribble: *Reading Bulgarian Through Russian*, 182 p., 1987.

Charles E. Gribble: *Russian Root List with a Sketch of Word Formation, Second Edition*, 62 p., 1982.

Charles E. Gribble: *A Short Dictionary of 18th-Century Russian*/Словарик Русского Языка 18-го Века, 103 p., 1976.

Charles E. Gribble, ed.: *Studies Presented to Professor Roman Jakobson by His Students*, 333 p., 1968.

George J. Gutsche and Lauren G. Leighton, eds.: *New Perspectives on Nineteenth-Century Russian Prose*, 146 p., 1982.

Morris Halle, ed.: *Roman Jakobson: What He Taught Us*, 94 p., 1983.

Morris Halle, Krystyna Pomorska, Elena Semeka-Pankratov, and Boris Uspenskij, eds.: *Semiotics and the History of Culture In Honor of Jurij Lotman Studies in Russian*, 437 p., 1989.

Charles J. Halperin: *The Tatar Yoke*, 231 p., 1986.

William S. Hamilton: *Introduction to Russian Phonology and Word Structure*, 187 p., 1980.

Pierre R. Hart: *G. R. Derzhavin: A Poet's Progress*, iv + 164 p., 1978.

OTHER BOOKS FROM SLAVICA

Michael Heim: *Contemporary Czech,* 271 p., 1982.

Michael Heim, Zlata Meyerstein, and Dean Worth: *Readings in Czech,* 147 p., 1985.

Warren H. Held, Jr., William R. Schmalstieg, and Janet E. Gertz: *Beginning Hittite,* ix + 218 p., 1988.

M. Hubenova & others: *A Course in Modern Bulgarian, Part 1,* viii + 303 p., 1983; *Part 2,* ix + 303 p., 1983.

Martin E. Huld: *Basic Albanian Etymologies,* x + 213 p., 1984.

Charles Isenberg: *Substantial Proofs of Being: Osip Mandelstam's Literary Prose,* 179 p., 1987.

Roman Jakobson, with the assistance of Kathy Santilli: *Brain and Language Cerebral Hemispheres and Linguistic Structure in Mutual Light,* 48 p., 1980.

Donald K. Jarvis and Elena D. Lifshitz: *Viewpoints: A Listening and Conversation Course in Russian, Third Edition,* iv + 66 p., 1985; *Instructor's Manual,* v + 37 p.

Leslie A. Johnson: *The Experience of Time in Crime and Punishment,* 146 p., 1985.

Stanislav J. Kirschbaum, ed.: *East European History: Selected Papers of the Third World Congress for Soviet and East European Studies,* 183 p., 1989.

Emily R. Klenin: *Animacy in Russian: A New Interpretation,* 139 p., 1983.

Andrej Kodjak, Krystyna Pomorska, and Kiril Taranovsky, eds.: *Alexander Puškin Symposium II,* 131 p., 1980.

Andrej Kodjak, Krystyna Pomorska, Stephen Rudy, eds.: *Myth in Literature,* 207 p., 1985.

Andrej Kodjak: *Pushkin's I. P. Belkin,* 112 p., 1979.

Andrej Kodjak, Michael J. Connolly, Krystyna Pomorska, eds.: *Structural Analysis of Narrative Texts (Conference Papers),* 203 p., 1980.

Demetrius J. Koubourlis, ed.: *Topics in Slavic Phonology,* vii + 270 p., 1974.

Ronald D. LeBlanc: *The Russianization of Gil Blas: A Study in Literary Appropriation,* 292 p. 1986.

Richard L. Leed, Alexander D. Nakhimovsky, and Alice S. Nakhimovsky: *Beginning Russian, Vol. 1,* xiv + 426 p., 1981; *Vol. 2,* viii + 339 p., 1982.

Richard L. Leed and Slava Paperno: *5000 Russian Words With All Their Inflected Forms: A Russian-English Dictionary,* xiv + 322 p., 1987.

Edgar H. Lehrman: *A Handbook to Eighty-Six of Chekhov's Stories in Russian,* 327 p., 1985.

Lauren Leighton, ed.: *Studies in Honor of Xenia Gąsiorowska,* 191 p.

OTHER BOOKS FROM SLAVICA

R. L. Lencek: *The Structure and History of the Slovene Language*, 365 p.

Jules F. Levin and Peter D. Haikalis, with Anatole A. Forostenko: *Reading Modern Russian*, vi + 321 p., 1979.

Maurice I. Levin: *Russian Declension and Conjugation:* A Structural Description with Exercises, x + 159 p., 1978.

Alexander Lipson: *A Russian Course. Part 1*, ix + 338 p., 1981; *Part 2*, 343 p., 1981; *Part 3*, iv + 105 p., 1981; *Teacher's Manual* by Stephen J. Molinsky (who also assisted in the writing of Parts 1 and 2), 222 p.

Yvonne R. Lockwood: *Text and Context Folksong in a Bosnian Muslim Village*, 220 p., 1983.

Sophia Lubensky & Donald K. Jarvis, eds.: *Teaching, Learning, Acquiring Russian*, viii + 415 p., 1984.

Horace G. Lunt: *Fundamentals of Russian*, xiv + 402 p., reprint, 1982.

Paul Macura: *Russian-English Botanical Dictionary*, 678 p., 1982.

Thomas G. Magner, ed.: *Slavic Linguistics and Language Teaching*, x + 309 p., 1976.

Amy Mandelker and Roberta Reeder, eds.: *The Supernatural in Slavic and Baltic Literature: Essays in Honor of Victor Terras*, Introduction by J. Thomas Shaw, xxi + 402 p., 1989.

Vladimir Markov and Dean S. Worth, eds.: *From Los Angeles to Kiev Papers on the Occasion of the Ninth International Congress of Slavists*, 250 p., 1983.

Mateja Matejić and Dragan Milivojević: *An Anthology of Medieval Serbian Literature in English*, 205 p., 1978.

Peter J. Mayo: *The Morphology of Aspect in Seventeenth-Century Russian (Based on Texts of the Smutnoe Vremja)*, xi + 234 p., 1985.

Arnold McMillin, ed.: *Aspects of Modern Russian and Czech Literature Selected Papers of the Third World Congress for Soviet and East European Studies*, 239 p., 1989.

Gordon M. Messing: *A Glossary of Greek Romany As Spoken in Agia Varvara (Athens)*, 175 p., 1988.

Vasa D. Mihailovich and Mateja Matejic: *A Comprehensive Bibliography of Yugoslav Literature in English, 1593-1980*, xii + 586 p., 1984.

Vasa D. Mihailovich: *First Supplement to A Comprehensive Bibliography of Yugoslav Literature in English 1981-1985*, 338 p., 1989.

Edward Mozejko, ed.: *Vasiliy Pavlovich Aksenov: A Writer in Quest of Himself*, 272 p., 1986.

Edward Możejko: *Yordan Yovkov*, 117 p., 1984.

Alexander D. Nakhimovsky and Richard L. Leed: *Advanced Russian, Second Edition, Revised*, vii + 262 p., 1987.

Felix J. Oinas: *Essays on Russian Folklore and Mythology*, 183 p., 1985.

Hongor Oulanoff: *The Prose Fiction of Veniamin Kaverin*, v + 203 p.

Temira Pachmuss: *Russian Literature in the Baltic between the World Wars*, 448 p., 1988.

Lora Paperno: *Getting Around Town in Russian: Situational Dialogs*, English translation and photographs by Richard D. Sylvester, 123 p.

Slava Paperno, Alexander D. Nakhimovsky, Alice S. Nakhimovsky, and Richard L. Leed: *Intermediate Russian: The Twelve Chairs*, 326 p.

Ruth L. Pearce: *Russian For Expository Prose, Vol. 1 Introductory Course*, 413 p., 1983; *Vol. 2 Advanced Course*, 255 p., 1983.

Jan L. Perkowski: *The Darkling A Treatise on Slavic Vampirism*, 169 p.

Gerald Pirog: *Aleksandr Blok's Итальянские Стихи Confrontation and Disillusionment*, 219 p., 1983.

Stanley J. Rabinowitz: *Sologub's Literary Children: Keys to a Symbolist's Prose*, 176 p., 1980.

Gilbert C. Rappaport: *Grammatical Function and Syntactic Structure: The Adverbial Participle of Russian*, 218 p., 1984.

David F. Robinson: *Lithuanian Reverse Dictionary*, ix + 209 p., 1976.

Don K. Rowney & G. Edward Orchard, eds.: *Russian and Slavic History*, viii + 303 p., 1977.

Catherine Rudin: *Aspects of Bulgarian Syntax: Complementizers and WH Constructions*, iv + 232 p., 1986.

Gerald J. Sabo, S.J., ed.: *Valaská Škola, by Hugolin Gavlovič, with a linguistic sketch by Ľ. Ďurovič, 730 p., 1988.*

Ernest A. Scatton: *Bulgarian Phonology*, xii + 224 p., 1975 (reprint: 1983).

Ernest A. Scatton: *A Reference Grammar of Modern Bulgarian*, 448 p.

Barry P. Scherr and Dean S. Worth, eds.: *Russian Verse Theory Proceedings of the 1987 Conference at UCLA*, 514 p., 1989.

William R. Schmalstieg: *Introduction to Old Church Slavic, second edition*, 314 p., 1983.

William R. Schmalstieg: *A Lithuanian Historical Syntax*, xi + 412 p., 1988.

R. D. Schupbach: *Lexical Specialization in Russian*, 102 p., 1984.

Peter Seyffert: *Soviet Literary Structuralism: Background Debate Issues*, 378 p., 1985.

Kot K. Shangriladze and Erica W. Townsend, eds.: *Papers for the V. Congress of Southeast European Studies (Belgrade, September 1984)*, 382 p., 1984.

J. Thomas Shaw: *Pushkin A Concordance to the Poetry*, 2 volumes, 1310 pages total, 1985.

Efraim Sicher: *Style and Structure in the Prose of Isaak Babel'*, 169 p., 1986.

Mark S. Simpson: *The Russian Gothic Novel and its British Antecedents*, 112 p., 1986.

OTHER BOOKS FROM SLAVICA

David A. Sloane: *Aleksandr Blok and the Dynamics of the Lyric Cycle*, 384 p., 1988.

Greta N. Slobin, ed.: *Aleksej Remizov: Approaches to a Protean Writer*, 286 p., 1987.

Theofanis G. Stavrou and Peter R. Weisensel: *Russian Travelers to the Christian East from the Twelfth to the Twentieth Century*, L + 925 p.

Gerald Stone and Dean S. Worth, eds.: *The Formation of the Slavonic Literary Languages, Proceedings of a Conference Held in Memory of Robert Auty and Anne Pennington at Oxford 6-11 July 1981*, 269 p.

Roland Sussex and J. C. Eade, eds.: *Culture and Nationalism in Nineteenth-Century Eastern Europe*, 158 p., 1985.

Oscar E. Swan: *First Year Polish, second edition, revised and expanded*, 354 p., 1983.

Oscar E. Swan: *Intermediate Polish*, 370 p., 1986.

Jane A. Taubman: *A Life Through Verse Marina Tsvetaeva's Lyric Diary*, 296 p., 1989.

Charles E. Townsend: *Continuing With Russian*, xxi + 426 p., 1981.

Charles E. Townsend and Veronica N. Dolenko: *Instructor's Manual to Accompany Continuing With Russian*, 39 p., 1987.

Charles E. Townsend: *Czech Through Russian*, viii + 263 p., 1981.

Charles E. Townsend: *The Memoirs of Princess Natal'ja Borisovna Dolgorukaja*, viii + 146 p., 1977.

Charles E. Townsend: *Russian Word Formation, corrected reprint*, viii + 272 p., 1975.

Janet G. Tucker: *Innokentij Annenskij and the Acmeist Doctrine*, 154 p.

Boryana Velcheva: *Proto-Slavic and Old Bulgarian Sound Changes*, Translation of the original by Ernest A. Scatton, 187 p., 1988.

Walter N. Vickery, ed.: *Aleksandr Blok Centennial Conference*, 403 p.

Essays in Honor of A. A. Zimin, ed. D. C. Waugh, xiv + 416 p., 1985.

Daniel C. Waugh: *The Great Turkes Defiance On the History of the Apocryphal Correspondence of the Ottoman Sultan in its Muscovite and Russian Variants*, ix + 354 p., 1978.

Susan Wobst: *Russian Readings and Grammatical Terminology*, 88 p.

James B. Woodward: *The Symbolic Art of Gogol: Essays on His Short Fiction*, 131 p., 1982.

Dean S. Worth: *Origins of Russian Grammar Notes on the state of Russian philology before the advent of printed grammars*, 176 p., 1983.

Что я видел *What I Saw* by Boris Zhitkov, Annotated and Edited by Richard L. Leed and Lora Paperno, 128 p. (8.5 x 11" format), 1988.